Interdisciplinary Architecture

Interdisciplinary Architecture

Nicoletta Trasi

WILEY-ACADEMY

Acknowledgement

Special thanks are due to Giovanni Narici of Editrice Libreria Dedalo,
Rome, Italy, for the idea that inspired these compilations.

Page 2: James Carpenter Design Associates, Dichroic Light Field

First published in Great Britain in 2001 by
WILEY-ACADEMY

a division of
JOHN WILEY & SONS LTD
Baffins Lane
Chichester
West Sussex PO19 1UD

ISBN 0-471-49807-6

Other Wiley Editorial Offices
New York • Weinheim • Brisbane • Singapore • Toronto

Cover design: Mario Bettella, Klára Smith

Layout and Prepress: ARTMEDIA PRESS Ltd, London

Printed and bound in Italy

Contents

Anamorphosis Architects, 'Spatial Cast' – spatial multitude of the New Acropolis Museum project

INTERDISCIPLINARY ARCHITECTURE
Art/Architecture/Landscape: Intersections

Nicoletta Trasi

The relationship between art and architecture has left far behind what was once a simple confrontation between the wall and the canvas. The way these creative fields have evolved has given a new significance to their relationship, one that cannot be limited to that of 'place'. For art, considered as work without function, and architecture, which has more contingent necessities, follow parallel developments and laws.

On the one hand, in addition to respecting place and function, architecture justifies the autonomy of aesthetic decision. On the other, art becomes ever more sensitive to its hosting buildings, cities and territories. It intermingles with these by integrating with, or transforming, how they are perceived and identified, which may be interpreted as either subtle merging or radical provocation. Contemporary art, therefore, in its most vital, demonstrative and extreme aspects explores new relationships with 'place' that follow design processes similar to those of architecture. Art and architecture evolve within the same field of enquiry: the essential issue of space. When Richard Serra digs an octagon *en face* a church in Burgundy, he is on the arbitrary limit between art and architecture.

This volume explores the collaboration between these two domains through articles from recent issues of *Architectural Design*: articles that explore the cooperative dynamic relations between art and architecture; articles on the formal definition of elements that are common to the vocabularies of both artists and architects, such as the use of colour and the conception of sculptural forms; and articles on the creative act in art and architecture.

An historical overview introduces leading *AD* pages, and thus discusses once again the recurring issue of the integration of the arts, from Art Nouveau to De Stijl and Bauhaus, highlighting the treacherous and uneven ground on which the art–architecture relationship has evolved.

> In architecture there are two essential conditions of truth: the truth with respect to the 'programme', and that with respect to 'construction methods'. Truth with respect to the programme means fulfilling exactly and with simplicity the conditions imposed by needs; truth with respect to construction methods implies usage of materials enhancing original qualities and properties . . . purely artistic questions tied to symmetry and apparent form are only secondary conditions when confronted with our dominant principles.
>
> *E Viollet-le-Duc*, Entretiens sur l'Architecture (*1863–72*)

For Viollet-le-Duc, one of architecture's most important French theorists, the dominant principles he refers to above excluded the classicist French rationalist tradition, as he explained in his École des Beaux-Arts lectures of 1853. The illustrations for the *Entretiens*, which in certain aspects anticipated Art Nouveau, clearly indicated architecture's future direction.

With the architectural birth of Art Nouveau, ratified by Horta with his 1893 house in the Rue Turin in Brussels, new materials came into evidence; materials that suggested light structures, emptiness, transparencies, sinuous floor plans, etc. The stimulating quality designs by Horta and Van de Velde meant that Art Nouveau was immediately and broadly diffused, and the first chapter of international renewal was written. Though it was heir to the spirit of the Arts and Crafts Movement, with its cult of craftsmanship and well-detailed design, Art Nouveau abused its principles by reducing its content, through a Manneristic interpretation, in response to what was a quest for the essentially ornamental. As evidenced by Bruno Zevi, it can be summed up as implying the use of highly trained craftsmen, well-educated skilled workers and an army of minor artists, and therefore postulated a difficult and costly design that furthermore necessitated spending time to create accord amongst painters, sculptors and architects. 'Imitators instead worked quickly and at lower costs; that is why some of the works presented at the Paris Exhibition of 1900, with their gratuitous linearisms, were provoking nausea.'[1] Art Nouveau was beginning to nurture from within the germs of its own decadence.

> . . .founders of a new culture call upon all those who believe in the reform of art and culture, to destroy obstacles that hinder development, in the same way as in figurative art – by suppressing natural forms – they have eliminated what hinders pure artistic expression, the exterior coherence underlying every artistic concept.
>
> *From the first manifesto of De Stijl (1918)*

In its short life (only 14 years), De Stijl was centred around three personalities: the painters Mondrian and Van Doesburg; and the architect Rietveld. Its first manifesto proclaimed a new equilibrium between the individual and the universal, and the liberation of art from the constraints imposed by both tradition and the cult of personality. The last neo-Plastic architectural work of some importance was the Café de l'Aubette in Strasbourg, completed in 1929 by van Doesburg with Hans and Sophie Arp: while van Doesburg controlled the general theme of its design, each of the artists was free to design their own space. After this, those artists who still belonged to De Stijl, including Rietveld and van Doesburg, became increasingly influenced by the Neue Sachlichkeit and, as a consequence, adhered to the new values of international socialism. Nevertheless, Van Doesburg's interest in universal order remained alive, as he explained in his last writing, *Manifest sur l'art concret* (1930): 'If the instruments of expression are freed of every particularism, they are in harmony with the ultimate aim of art, which is to generate universal language.'[2] But he never made clear how these instruments could be freed in the case of applied arts such as interior design.

> We therefore constitute a new corporation of craftsmen, but without the arrogance determined by class, which wants a wall of haughtiness to be built to divide artisans and artists! Let us join our willingness, our inventiveness, our creativity, in the new construction activity of the future, which will take only one form through architecture and sculpture and painting. It will rise

*Irena Bauman, Bridlington Promenade, chaise longue
designed in terrazzo to match artist's material*

*Tania Kovats, Ledge, 1995, paper, resin,
steel frame, 250 x 200 x 150 cm*

toward the sky from the hands of millions of artisans as a crystalline symbol of a growing new faith.

Bauhaus of Weimar programme (1919)

The principles on which the 1919 Bauhaus programme was based had been anticipated by Bruno Taut's programme on architecture for the Arbeitstat für Kunst, published at the end of 1918. Taut believed that a new cultural unity could be obtained only through a new art of building, in which every single discipline would contribute positively to the definition of final form. 'At this point,' he writes, 'there will be no more boundaries between craftsmanship, sculpting and painting; all these aspects will constitute just one: Architecture.'[3] An anarchic reformulation of the *Gesamtkunstwerk* was elaborated by Gropius in his programmes for the Bauhaus, in which he recommended the creation of a 'new community of artificers, without those class distinctions that form barriers of arrogance between craftsman and artist'.[4]

In 1919 Gropius founded in Weimar the most important architectural education centre in Europe. His programme was synchretic. It was about synthesising and equilibrating artistic contributions from 1850 to 1914, uniting the best artists. The heritage of the Arts and Crafts Movement, of 18th-century engineering, of Art Nouveau and of the Werkbund – but also of the abstract-figurative research in painting in about 1910 – was globally accepted because of the Bauhaus intervention in reconsidering craftsmanship by recognising and sustaining the productivity of manual labour. It exalted new structures and was involved in cooperation between architecture and industry. The men who met through the Bauhaus were such disparate personalities as Itten and Kandinsky, Klee and Moholy-Nagy, Breuer and Mies. Expressionism prevailed at first, then van Doesburg's neo-Plasticism.

The present-day scenario shows art moving towards architecture and architecture towards art, an interesting perspective on the evolving relationship between the two disciplines. Let us consider the first. Art moves towards architecture not when it copies or represents it (which would be exceedingly banal), but rather when it imitates it structurally – when it integrates the principles that underlie construction. From this point of view it is obvious that the art form that is most closely related to architecture is sculpture and not painting – which is intended to be on canvas – since the latter reproduces a fictitious tridimensionality and static illusion. Painting is not traditionally based on the principles of calculus, but on those of visual perception. In this interpretation it could be said that statics in painting is more complex than it is in architecture. The goal is visually to build not one building but the entire represented environment – a more subtle statics, at the same time both scientific and fictitious (the representation of gravity mixed with that of perception).

Sculpture, on the other hand, apes architecture. It follows its laws, with reduced proportions and less responsibility. In sculpture statics is almost always intuitive, and this is generally all that is necessary. Artists look up to architecture as they would to an elder brother, but without any feeling of inferiority. On the contrary, they often draw advantage from the fact that the greater MOBILITY of their project favours their affirmation. Painters and sculptors are foolish creators, regardless provokers of conscience and sensibility; they are universalists who aspire to represent macrocosm through microcosm.

Architects think deductively. From a general vision of life in all its facets they deduce a unique event, an absolute identity, a multidimensional experience of space, 'here and now'. This is not only because they have a commitment to functionality, but also because they generally have a scientific approach to design. The prejudice that arises from an eminently romantic system of education has for a long time divided architect-designers from artists, who are considered to be the real creators, protagonists in pure fantasy thinking. Today the question of boundaries between art and architecture is posed in different terms, on a definitely more elastic premise.

'*Il faut être de son temps*,' said Manet. I believe our time is characterised by constant research into how new forms of equilibrium can be defined in unstable conditions, research that gives a new meaning to design – a more docile concept that not only goes beyond the strong and inflexible modern approach, but also beyond post-modern anarchy. In relation to this semiotic picture, architects undoubtedly represent the natural manifestation of today's expressiveness.

Engineer, architect, artist. With respect to the first two there is the question of their fields of competence. Engineers are generally interested in the technical, normative and structural aspects of construction, while architects are more concerned with aesthetics and function, in addition to structure. Therefore the tendency, in the more creative sphere of design, is to leave the race to the architects and artists. Avant-garde tradition has imposed the artist-creator, inventor of forms, as the predominant figure. Over various decades architecture has followed whatever tendency has been inspired by formalistic research in art. And maybe Van de Velde, while lamenting the predominance of eclecticism, was also influenced by the infinite multifaceted forging of forms that characterised artistic production in his times.

From this point of view, art today has nothing more to say: diachronically eclectic in the avant-garde (historical and otherwise), and synchronically eclectic nowadays (the difference is obviously deep-set), art's present-day destiny is to be without substantial unity.

It is clear that this applies to architecture. But the prospect is that new signals will come from the macrocosm (architecture) and not from the microcosm (art). (The reason for this is to be found in the final collapse of ideology. Art has always been – for good and bad – the most expressive vehicle for this, an idealistic form of reference that determined a shift from idealistic to concrete, from symbolic to real). In the end, the macro wins and architecture becomes the protagonist, with or without crisis. It can be said, then, that the decades-long influence of art on architecture has been overturned; not as a surrogate, the utopian architectural design fills the present ideological void. The conclusion is that art is moving towards architecture. This new condition has been prepared for, and facilitated by, organic architecture and sculpture (from Gaudí to Asplund, perhaps including Le Corbusier, Saarinen, Wright, etc).

But new experiences have been involved in this process. I am referring to: 1) artists (almost always sculptors) who, while continuing in their artistic specialisation, design and build buildings; 2) artists who, as a consequence of a crisis in art or for other reasons, imitate architecture – essentially artists who produce 'scapes' (a new concept of artistic intervention that links habitat to landscape).

Except for the irreversible destruction of nature, things die every day and are born again, perhaps with some structural difference. And this is so with art. It is sufficient to reflect on Argan's renowned notes about the death of art, his perception of the impossibility of further cultivating the now-arid grounds on which every experience – the object – had taken place. Another step in this direction has been taken by Land Artists, whose inspiration is the death not of art, but of the object; they go beyond the 'impasse' in art by working on the connections between natural habitat and artistic operativity (an approach that is obviously dependent on an eminently subjective sensibility). And, following in their footsteps, more than one contemporary artist and architect has worked, and continues working, in this way.

Antonio Gaudí, Church of the Sagrada Familia, Barcelona

It is a way of working that: 1) takes into consideration sculpture, painting, multimedia, etc; 2) is halfway between sculpture and architecture and therefore reopens the debate on design; 3) brings back the pleasure of narrating, in different words, an elliptical communication field which is definable but not defined; 4) is a 'living object' and therefore habitable and walkable; 5) goes beyond minimalist geometry, and is essentially installative; 6) is characterised by structural, visual and conceptual self-sufficiency. In other words, art and architecture are micro- and macroplastics that communicate at a point beyond any established operative and symbolic boundary.

The recent history of art is rich in examples of artists who have occupied themselves with questions about linguistic relations to physical space. However, the interest in this kind of visual research, let alone the artist's attempt to reconstruct an autonomous analytic language and relationship with physical space, originates in the early 1960s. In those years it was English and American Land Art. Artists, searching for the antithesis to 'urbanity', seek to establish significant relationships with the uncontaminated environment of the desert. English artists Richard Long and Hamish Fulton, and the Americans Robert Smithson, Walter de Maria, Michael Heizer and Dennis Oppenheim, along with the Dutch Jean Dibbets, relate in interesting and significant ways to the natural environment or to the desert, or to the urban environment as 'data' (like the desert).

We must anyway draw distinctions between Long's delicate operation of subtracting or accumulating, Fulton's project of covering a distance using only his own footsteps, and the desert-engravings by Heizer. Dibbets and Fulton, in their environment- and urban-engravings certainly relate to the environment in the least traumatic fashion. Fulton walks the desert; Dibbets performs perspective modifications, analysing physical space by recording the sound of the sea or the sun's shadow on a wall. Oppenheim and de Maria measure the desert and produce symbolic signals where the modification of the natural environment is tempered by temporal components or meteorology: the territory is changed only temporarily and even the simple action of the wind enables the environment to regain its natural state.

Even Heizer, Christo and Smithson propose a new language which is rendered physical through poetical gestures, both titanic and minimal: an architecture which claims, in the way it is articulated, the right of eternal events and the symbolism that is always present in the traces of man to re-emerge, and which defines mental territories by giving them a physical dimension. When Smithson performed the eternal act of contextual definition that is the *Spiral Jetty* he was recalling the great lines of the Nazca desert, and the Indian tumuli.

The recent history of the autonomous reconstruction of the universe of language and of conceptualisation is also a fundamental instrument of integration and inspiration for architecture, which is imprisoned in the functionalist heritage of the first half of the 20th century. The phenomenological richness of art dedicated to redefining strategies for a new comprehension of physical and theoretical territories, represents a determined and almost inevitable evolution of the instruments for understanding and *materialising* every possible spatial or territorial modification. This is because the emergence of intimate emotional worlds that are directly in touch with one's own destiny, and the restoration of language and symbols, permits and ratifies the reconquering of the right to *materialise* secret spaces and transcribe them in the real world.

Research in architecture has always played with the other creative disciplines, but all too often the habit – in this case we may say 'the bad habit' – of rationalisation has repeatedly subordinated languages borrowed from the visual arts, so much so that referring to earlier experiences often expresses an excessive dependence.

From what is now an historical perspective, it can be seen that breaking away from conceptual and linguistic dependence on the visual arts emerged from the experimental and theoretical assumptions of the 1960s. Much can be said of the initial involutions and contradictions, of the certain and unmistakable role played by Archigram, for example, with their fantastic urban utopias, or by English and North American Pop formulations. In any case, what appeared to be particularly innovative was the conscious transformation of architecture in image, the desired mystification of design as an operational instrument. In Italy and Austria at that time there was an experimental approach that not only refused any functionalist or rationalist diktats, but went way beyond this. It attributed to architecture a centrality that theoretically could have brought about the bypassing of any barrier, in space and time. By affirming that 'everything is architecture', in both a positive and a negative sense, all boundaries between disciplines were removed; at this point, experimentation could draw on means of expression that were apparently far from those of design but which were intended to transmit reflections on the human condition, on life, on the environment and the city.

The way in which the pure form reaches *ready-made*, from monolith to totem, from 'territorial' outscaling to that which assimilates everyday objects to the architectural dimension, is more immediate than it may seem. It is obviously shaped by the significant passing from the world of rational abstraction to that of emblematic figuration and the representation of reality. Although these are contrasting opposites the connecting rod, in a peculiar specular overturning of themes, is the idea of unity.

And it is a way that, through the artistic baptism of the object[5] – an object which represents or is taken from reality, depending on circumstances – reveals the other side of the idea of unity, one we could define as real and tangible. This special unity is not referenced to the structural and spatial plane of a work – which may, on the contrary, appear more rich and multiform. Rather it refers to the iconic-semantic plane. It coincides with the recovery of representative figures, of evocative images, of visual archetypes which could evolve, in the chaotic multiplicity of symbols, to become familiar and recognisable places, universal landmarks. To accept reality as a source of inspiration and comparison, and the city as a vehicle of communication – a system of symbols – the architectural object is permeated with symbolic and allusive values instead of referring to an abstracted, distant, contemplative image. Far from the order and synthesis of abstraction, a building reveals the nature of its components, its sepa-

Frank O Gehry, Vitra International Headquarters, Basel, Switzerland

Frank O Gehry with Claes Oldenburg and Coosje van Bruggen, Chiat/Day Building, Venice, California

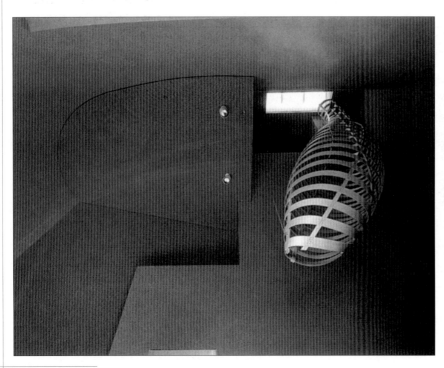

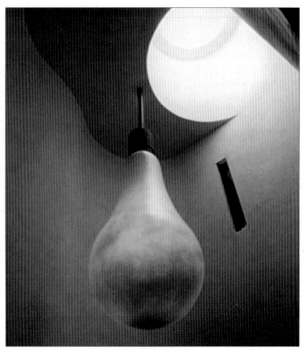

rate parts; in this way it tends to renounce tectonics and gains a scenographic impulse, thus becoming a place of happening. An *event* may therefore be defined by the appearance, amongst the variety of expressive materials of architecture, of a binocular, a fish or an enormous apple, as in designs by Gehry and Venturi.[6]

The Duchampian irony of the *ready-made* is Dadaism's deconsecrating provocation: never to be thought of as convertible to architectural form, this anti-art reappeared in 1960s Pop. There is no obscure allusion, no subtle symbology: the object is introduced straightforwardly. Following a linear sequence, it moves from its original function and is transformed into a mainly aesthetic object, only to acquire a new, unexpected function (architectural), through a change in scale and place, and through the presence of interior space.

Can architecture communicate? The debate has lasted throughout the century-long history of aesthetic ideas and art criticism and seems to be an essential one today. Architecture *must* communicate in order to survive as a product of human expression. Therefore, if architectural design was originally structured as a vehicle to transmit ideas, as speech does, informational theory teaches us that what assumes major importance is neither of the two main subjects – author and user – nor the contents of a building. It is instead the communication apparatus set up by the design – the ways in which the structure's contents are expressed.

Charles Jencks described the resemanticisation of architecture 20 years ago, in 1981.[7] Today, however, with Post-Modernism's loss of its initial impetus, the meaning of resemanticisation has greatly changed, freed from its earlier limits. The term now refers to a much wider and more variegated process which, by contemplating a possible enhancement of the architectural and artistic object's power to attract, considers richness, variety and linguistic renewal to be primary necessities for constituting new and significant 'texts'.

As a result, many architects think that closer cohabitation and transcultural/translinguistic collaboration are essential. In this continuing

Frank O Gehry with Claes Oldenburg and Coosje van Bruggen, Chiat/Day Building, Venice, California

shuffle, art, the everyday and technology intersect by using and nurturing each other. Everything is consumed and everything is immediately returned to a *reproductive* cycle, an 'eternal present' that renovates and regenerates values even when they are fragmented and deconstructed.

One of the most explicit architectural resemanticisation instruments is, naturally, ornament (pattern and colour). But we must remember that there are substantial differences between ornamental types. On the one hand there is the simple polychromy of Botta, Stirling or Valle, who put the building in a privileged relationship with context: 'Colour for me,' says Stirling 'is not a trend, but a sign.' On the other there is the introduction of graphic pattern, both abstract (Nouvel, Herzog and de Meuron, Ciriani) and figurative, naturalistic or historicist (Venturi and Graves).

Polychromy as an architectural design technique is linked to the belief that colour can intervene not only as wall decoration, but also as a means of enhancing space. Classical architecture has always relied on the capacity of colour to perfect optical corrections: in Greek temples polychromy played a major role in how perspective was perceived from a distance, and in singling out and accentuating details in the whole. Colour revealed both contrasts and reciprocal affinities between single elements by superimposing a kind of second nature, brilliant and artificial, on the apparent homogeneity of construction materials in order to stabilise and emphasise the hierarchic order between different parts. The subtle fascination of architectural polychromy is in this superimposition of illusion on reality: in the classic temple it created a harmonious rhythm over the statics of walls, interweaving new and surprising links between surface and volume. It almost imperceptibly altered the appreciation of distance and depth, reinforcing the rhythmic succession of the columns that projected towards the Mediterranean landscape, the intense colours of which they took up and transfigured.

Robert Venturi, Times Square Plaza, project

Robert Venturi, Allen Memorial Art Museum, Oberlin, Ohio

For a more precise idea of the surprising effect of a Greek temple's polychrome peristyle it is sufficient to transpose our image of this to a modern building like the Unité d'Habitation in Marseille. Walking below this we see colour combining rhythmically with the concrete walls of the facades in a way that is in many aspects similar to the way it is likely to have been used in the temple of Poseidon in Paestum or the Acropolis in Athens. What enables colour to become an architectural design theme (and not an artistic one) is this capacity to stress and accelerate spatial perception.

The 1960s' research into space and its structural and theoretical definition is ever more present today, and has not been made obsolete by false contemporary experiments. But ideological tension, research, the eagerness to renovate instruments and disciplines, and the impartial application of experimental disciplinary research have disappeared. Even if the ideological tension and conceptual rigour that structured, and gave meaning to, not only radical architectural thought but also to 'land' are now absent in architectural research, they will certainly not be reproposed in connection with the newborn freedom sought through contemporary experimental eclecticism.

Instead they will be revisited in terms of criticism, study, information.

It is only by resolving the confrontation between architecture and the visual arts, not by ignoring the debate and the historical relationships of the two disciplines, that we can hope for a new development, achieved through research that should no longer be divided into two categories: architecture and art. On the one hand, architecture has discovered that it has the capacity and total freedom to experiment through design, and that it can even rediscover, without historicising, areas of enquiry that have already been studied and solved by more recent research in the visual arts. On the other, artistic research has for many years, and on different planes, been concerned with finding the instruments it needs to deepen its enquiry into the domain of space and environment.

Critical analysis of these experimentations reveals that at the time they were being carried out there was the necessity to describe, in new terms, the structure of both the urban and its 'outside'. This has resulted in a new vocabulary for the understanding of context and of an environment that was ignored considerably; and in the reappropriation of territory through symbolic instruments that define and fill

Anamorphosis Architects, 'I am not the man you think I am', spatial multitude

urban or metropolitan spaces with meanings that are 'other' alongside the spontaneous instruments of use, connection and transport. A new experimental and critical discourse has been introduced, oriented towards reading the global environment as a place of yearning and expectation, an instrument for contemporary symbologies where yesterday's past is compacted. If the working of the contemporary environment is mainly about infrastructures or agricultural and mining developments over vast areas (where architects and planners are concerned principally with the application of norms and regulations) and rarely about the environmental consequences of these initiatives, we can understand why the artist's relationship with the environment is less bureaucratic than the architect's.

From the urban context to the desert, the environmental artist derives a relationship with the infinity of space which is 'other' by observing even the most mysterious of human interventions. The implicit symbology of every sign of man is interpreted to see what it may mean today, regardless of why it was generated. The result of this interpretative action is itself both metaphoric and symbolic.

The aspect of environmental art with which Land Art is most con-cerned is the architectural dimension or, better, the para-architectural dimension as defined by art critics: the artificial sign in the natural landscape evokes the act of construction, therefore architecture. We must notice that the reference to architecture is often ironic or nega-tive. Land Art is, in fact, about forms whose main figurative essence is in the dissolution of architectural terms into the landscape. Even where typological schemes are found they recall morphologic sym-bologies like the labyrinth or the spiral, or an elementary geometrisa-tion made of simple actions: a series of straight lines or semicircumferences.

But the most peculiar tendency, and one that is somehow common to many artists, is a hypogeal – or, better, the tendency towards a structural interaction with the ground, which assumes a hypogeal character. What is evident in this attitude is the will to manifest a mes-sage that the natural, symbolised by the ground, has been betrayed by the artificial, represented by the work which symbolises the installing principle. Therefore, a reference to architecture in the poetics of Land Art will be found in the annihilating of the material and dimensional characteristics of the natural landscape.

François Roche, Villa Malraux Artists' Residence, Maïdo Road, Reunion Island

Tower of Babel

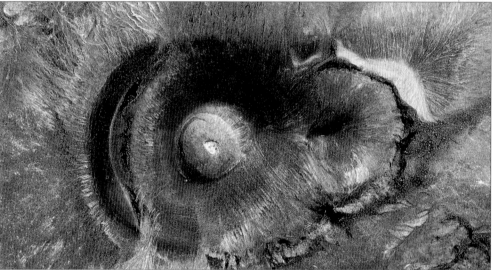

James Turrell, Roden Crater, Arizona

Because the architectural object is a symbol of compromised values it has lost credibility, and the way to transcend its essence is to dissolve its technological and structural order in the natural landscape. What art hypothesises for architecture is therefore a radical integration with landscape, where the most extreme expression is obtained through a hypogeal experimental figurativity.

There are many compositions based on hypogeal schemes in Land Art. The excavation, like the trace, symbolically represents human modification of the natural environment: the first act of any installing action. This is why it is charged with a planning value in Land Art. But excavation is extremely compatible with the natural environment, provided it is not followed by any architectural intervention; is not the premise for a vertical volumetric construction. It is the only act of environmental modification that does not imply visual impact.

The movement of soil, the excavation, the refilling of soil, *traces* of moved earth surfacing from the horizon. The artistic aesthetic has discovered a new material for art: earth. It seems ideal for embracing the ideological and figurative stances of *arte povera* – art inspired by the everyday. It is a primitive material that recalls the origin of the act of construction, and is therefore the perfect vehicle for an aesthetic

quest to find a beginning for the creative act. Moreover, on a conceptual level it represents the deepest synthesis of nature; it is the element from which the natural world develops, and contributes structurally to the morphological determination of territory.

Earth represents an elementary technology or, better, the absence of technology, and in this way it corresponds directly to the objectives of Land Art. At the same time it is an extremely ductile material that can be used creatively in the plastic modelling of form: elementary morphologies and modifications of superficial soil strata, which underline the relationship with a creative object that is clearly *topographic* and *archaeological*, are obtained through manipulation. This simple technology for producing simple forms linked to the concept of 'ground' is the connection and analogy with architecture – a discipline where the modification of ground is the atavistic and structural sustaining logic.

To return to the present day, if human activity can be found in all kinds of territories, the environment in its wholeness constitutes . . . an inseparable unity of cultural and natural elements[8] and landscape is identified by deposits that are the result of the way man has transformed nature. It then becomes necessary to consider archaeology which, according to a new epistemological concept, can determine the design process.

Landscape archaeology developed in England. It is based on interpreting surface traces on the ground and was systematically approached for the first time by C Taylor.[9] Taylor considers landscape as a tridimensional palimpsest whose stratifications can be interpreted not only horizontally, as in representative systems of traditional geography, but also vertically. In architectural culture themes of stratification and interpretative representation are examined from different perspectives: on the one hand, they are based on topographic and geographic research[10] and, on the other, on research into the city and territory as a dynamic aggregate.[11]

The latest developments in landscape archaeology formulate an important distinction between *panorama*, which gives rise to purely aesthetic reactions, and *landscape*, 'a panorama examined with an expert eye'.[12] Because this distinction requires an interpretative process, it brings about the romantic conception of ruins, which allows a new orientation in the dialogue between perception and constructed form. The expert eye then interprets the true secrets of traces and, through combinatory mechanisms, builds a relationship between different 'scapes' opening up different methodological horizons for design.

Notes

1 Bruno Zevi, *Architettura della Modernità*, Newton Compton (Rome), 1994, p 26.
2 JH van der Broek, C van Esteren *et al*, *De Stijl* (Amsterdam), 1951.
3 M Taut, OM Ungers, *Die Gläserne Kette. Visionare Architektur aus Kries um Bruno Taut 1919—1920* (Berlin), 1963.
4 H Wingler, *Il Bauhaus. Weimar Dessau Berlino 1919—1933* (Milan), 1972.
5 cf P Restany, *L'altra faccia dell'arte*, Edizioni Domus (Milano), 1979.
6 In the case of Frank O Gehry's office building in Venice, California, it is important to recall his active collaboration with artist Claes Oldenburg, friend and collaborator in other projects, and author of the binocular set at the entrance.
7 Charles Jencks, *The Language of Post-Modern Architecture*, Academy Editions (London), 1987.
8 V Hoesle, *Philosophie der Okologischen Krise*, Oscar Beck (Munich) 1991.
9 C Taylor, *Medieval Archaeology* (London), 1974.
10 C Olmo, 'Dalla tassonomia alla traccia' and M Quaini, 'Per un'archeologia dello sguardo topografico', *Casabella*, 575/ 576, 1991, pp 22, 13.
11 A Corboz, 'Il territorio come palinsesto, 1983', *Casabella*, 575/576, 1991.
12 BK Roberts, 'Landscape Archaeology' in *Landscape and Culture: Geographical and Archaeological Perspectives*, Basil Blackwell (Oxford and New York), 1987.

Neil Spiller, Bioscape Vertigo

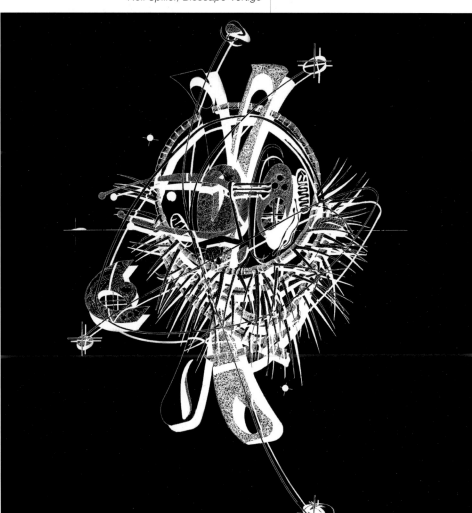

ROBERT MAXWELL

TRANSGRESSIONS

Crossing the Lines at The Royal Academy

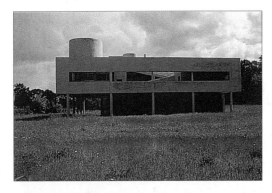

A
rchitecture as Expression:
Can it Approach the Condition of Art?

Le Corbusier, Villa Savoye, Poissy, 1929-31
Giuseppe Terragni, Casa del Fascio, Como, 1932-36

The Modern Movement in architecture was a continuation of rationalist aspirations that first took shape in the 18th century, and the hard-edged white prisms of Le Corbusier and Terragni have roots in the pure geometrical forms of Boullée and Ledoux. The difference is that, largely through the impact of abstraction, architectural forms have been liberated from the duty to represent propriety through convention, and hence from the domination of the classical orders. But they are still temperamentally in favour of strong light and high definition – what we might call the light side of art – and consistent with the idea that art produces a radiance .

Giambattista Piranesi, Tomb of the Metelli (Antichità Romane)
Giambattista Piranesi, A prison (Carceri – Pl. VII)

However, the light side is only apparent because there is a dark side. There is another tradition that also has its roots in the 18th century but which develops in a different direction, by way of probing the limits of lightness and the edge of the dark. It may seem paradoxical that the 18th century, the Age of Enlightenment, should produce Piranesi, who was fascinated by the disappearance of the past, by ruins and by prisons but he is as much part of the Enlightenment as was the Marquis de Sade. In both we see a search for the limits of the darkness. In the succeeding Romantic Movement, this search gains in confidence and in power of expression and gives a new value to darkness, as, for example, in qualities attributed by Baudelaire to cats:

> *Amis de la science, et de la volupté*
> *ils cherchent le silence et l'horreur des ténèbres*

16

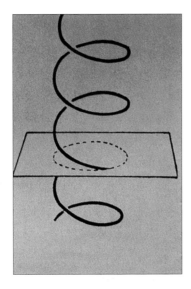 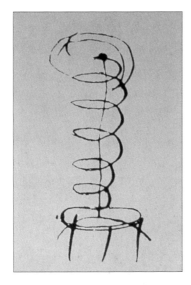  

Charles Howard Hinton, Spiral Intersecting a Plane, *1904*
Marcel Duchamp, Handler of Gravity*, 1934*

Hans Scharoun, Drawing for a Glass House, 1920
Wenzal Hablick, Cubic Exhibition Building, 1921

There is a sense in which this side of human nature has been reinforced by the development of science, with its trust in rational procedures, because it seems to attach to all those things that remain mysterious *in spite of* the discoveries of science, that is, to the unknown. The unknown is the dark edge of the known. But the rational only covers a very small domain and most of life remains outside of it. Duchamp's response to Hinton's *Spiral Intersecting a Plane was called Handler of Gravity.* In the early years of this century, scientific ideas based on N-dimensional geometry produced among artists a fever about the Fourth Dimension, analogous to our fever about Virtual Reality.[1] The unknown has always exerted a deep fascination for us, and is, in a sense, the source of all art, since art is as much concerned with disturbing order that is too complete, as with making a fresh, an as yet unknown, order. Good art of course does both.

Around the year 1907, with the development of Cubism, Abstraction began to produce forms that were no longer imitated from nature but reflected the artist's feelings in front of nature. It was Cézanne who prepared the way for this transformation. He still interrogated his motif, the evidence of his eyes, but he took certain freedoms to produce an equivalent, not a copy. He freed himself to determine the outcome by reference to his composition on the canvas, not to the raw facts. The Cubists went further in this direction. After Cubism and De Stijl, the artist's gesture was completely liberated. Art became gestural and with this new flexibility, shapes on the canvas could become the direct expression of the artist's feelings.

By the 1950s, when art began to centre on New York instead of Paris, the liberation of the gesture reached another stage. Now we see the actual marks of the paint, the gesture itself makes the final form, a form which rises through the actual movement of the artist's arm. We have reached the era of Abstract Expressionism. In fine art, the artist was entirely liberated to express feeling. In architecture, however, by what now seems a questionable development, a similar freedom from convention led to a new tyranny – the tyranny of function. The new, the unexpected, which the artist could seek inside his own subjectivity, had entered architecture from outside, from the science side; it had to be justified from a world of facts.

Moreover, what the artist may do gesturally on a sheet of paper has to go through a social and technical process if it is to emerge as a built work. The emphasis on expression, as opposed to a rational emphasis on the building process, has the effect of privileging the gesture over the construction; the building task may bring a certain loss of expression. It is interesting to compare Wenzal Hablick's Cubic Exhibition Building of 1921 with Hans Scharoun's Drawing for a Glass House, of the previous year. In both cases we have a glass tower, diminishing as they ascend and crowned by diagonals. Scharoun's free gesture in pen and ink has to be transposed into a set of forms suitable for building in stages. It regains its freedom by dislocation of the expected geometry.

It is a question of great interest how the impact of abstraction, which had such a strong effect in 20th-century painting, was not matched within architecture. Between the free gesture and the constructed reality lay a space: the space of functionality. Buildings had to be responsive to the uses and activities they were to shelter and had to be constructed more or less economically according to the technological resources of the times, so they tended to come out as rectangular boxes. To get round these constraints and still present the result as artistic, required an idealisation of the programme and the act of construction, and this is what gave rise to what I have called the Myths of Space and Function in the theory of modernist architecture. Both these aspects were distorted far from reality.

However, there was a brief moment in the early 20s, when architects of the Russian Revolution could claim to be both avant-garde artists and constructors of the new reality. Abstraction, which liberated the artist, began to liberate the architect.

Note

1 Hinton, Charles Howard, *The Fourth Dimension*, 1904

Bruno Taut, Alpine Architecture, *1919*
Zaha Hadid, Project: Club for Peak, Hong Kong, 1982

Today, we see a remarkable change, in which an attempt finally seems to have been made to free architectural forms from rectangular constraints, with a return to the early 20s in spirit. Zaha Hadid's drawing of 1982 for her project for a club on the Peak at Hong Kong, seems to hark back to Bruno Taut's fantasy *Alpine Architecture* of 1919. In both cases, in order to make the link between natural and artificial forms, the mountains and the buildings are merged together in the drawing. Nature is idealised in the same direction as the architecture.

In her drawings for *Planetary Architecture*, 1987, Hadid seems to be referring to Malevich's drawings for Suprematist Architecture. The drawings express an architecture that is so free it escapes gravity. It is clearly in the realm of art – abstract, weightless. The forms are light but well-defined, taken from the vocabulary of the Modern Movement. Her boldness lies precisely in the fact that she does not compromise with conventions but behaves as an artist, following her gesture. The fire station at Weil am Rhein showed that the gesture could be built, although not without somewhat changing its effect.

Konstantin Melnikov, Project – Palace of the Soviets, 1932
Daniel Libeskind, Jewish Museum, Berlin: site model, 1993-95

Le Corbusier relates how he refused a commission to design a church in the 20s because he did not see how the sort of abstract forms he was exploring could be used in a symbolic role. By 1951, when he designed Ronchamp, he had revised this view. However, the Russians embraced symbolism. In his design of 1932 for a Palace of the Soviets, Melnikov designed from the abstract to the symbolic. The building expands upwards, it consists of a pyramid accompanied by an inverted pyramid. The meaning was to cancel out the conventional pyramid with the ruler at the top and the mass of people suppressed at the base; now, the people were to be at the top; a liberation. Built form does not readily lend itself to this kind of symbolisation as in this case, the building resembles rocket launcher.

More successful is Daniel Libeskind's Jewish Museum in Berlin, a piece of modern symbolism that works through the juxtaposition of spaces. The main gallery is laid out in a zig-zag, based on part of the Jewish six-pointed star, crossing and re-crossing a mausoleum space below, into which one cannot enter but can only sense it as a forbidden world. This is potentially a very powerful way of expressing empathy.

 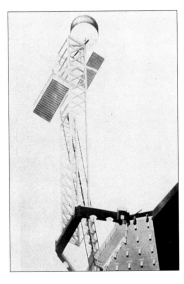  

El Lissitzky, Workshop (UNOVIS) – Speaker's Platform, 1920
Rem Koolhaas, Observation Tower – Rotterdam Project, 1982
Hadid began her career with OMA – the Office of Metropolitan Architecture – with Rem Koolhaas and Elia Zenghelis. Koolhaas is another architect who has used architectural drawing to liberate himself from convention. Here, we can compare his Observation Tower in a Rotterdam project with El Lissitzky's Speaker's Platform of 1920. So Koolhaas too takes a leaf from the Russian Constructivists, although with a preference for the purer forms of the early Leonidov. In his case, he has not abandoned the desire to build.

Rem Koolhaas, House near Paris, 1990
Rem Koolhaas, another view
In his subsequent work Koolhaas has kept quite close to the prismatic forms made canonic by their association with the Modern Movement. However, at the same time he has subjected these prismatic forms to a peculiar kind of subversion, so that instead of looking rational, they look arbitrary, the result of unconscious irony or subconscious machination. In this way, by frustrating our, by now, normal expectations of functionalist architecture, Koolhaas restores us to a world of feeling.

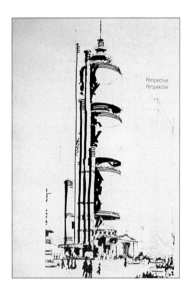

Richard Rogers, Project for Seattle, Washington, 1984
Chernikov, A Call for Industrialisation, *1929*

However, perhaps on closer examination Rogers yearns for the mantle of the avant-garde artist as well. Compare his Project for Seattle of 1984 with Chernikov's *A Call for Industrialisation* of 1919, and the connection becomes clearer. Where Koolhaas returns to the heroic period in a spirit of irony, Rogers returns with his enthusiasm intact.

Coop Himmelblau, Residential Complex, Vienna, 1983
Norman Foster, Interior, Hongkong and Shanghai Bank

In Norman Foster's Hongkong and Shanghai Bank everything is apparently rational and technical, except that a good deal of accident is allowed to enter, perhaps so as to stand in for the idea of freedom, or stimulus. The space in which the escalators rise into the atrium provides us with a rich variety of juxtapositions, producing an effect which is not so far removed from the accidental look that Coop Himmelblau, the Viennese architects, deliberately cultivate as a form of expression. So the High-Tech school is slipping into the current re-valuation of expressionism.

In the modern architecture of the 20s, the attempt to bring science and technology to bear went along with rational procedures and standardisation. Today, computer technology allows all the parts of a building to be individually different. Frank Gehry pioneered computerised control of fabrication with his design for the Guggenheim Museum in Bilbao. Similarly, Nicholas Grimshaw was able to create varied parts of his Chunnel Terminal at Waterloo so that the overall form could conform to the sweep of the curves determined accidentally by the site plan. At the same time, by adopting a three-pinned arch structure, he could make the structure disappear halfway across, so that the space seems to be a result of a structural miracle instead of structural rationality. Hence, the rectangular boxes once thought to be part of rational control have given way to more sophisticated methods, and architecture is now free to follow the expressive gesture in a way it never has done before.

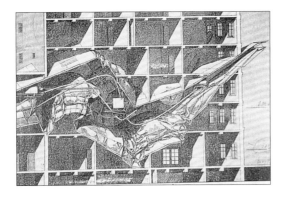

Lebbeus Woods, Berlin Free-Zone: Free-Space Section, 1990
Northern Ireland: a bomb explodes

Lebbeus Woods, an American architect of German extraction, wants to express impatience with the excessive rationality of the German State, and its tendency to impose a too rigid order, as many would see in the planning controls exercised by the city authorities in Berlin. His Berlin Free Zone – Free-Space Section makes a sharp contrast between order and disorder, and here the expression of disorder is equated with violence. What looks like disorder becomes freedom, what looks like order becomes servitude. His Zone of Freedom rips through the frame of a conventional building like a bomb exploding. On the right we have an actual bomb blast in Northern Ireland.

Lebbeus Woods, Underground Berlin, Alexander-Platz, Projection Tower, 1988
Lebbeus Woods, Lima, Peru, an improvised shanty

The image of dissolution which opposes itself to the excessive order of our presumably oppressive governments is matched by the unwanted dissolution of our cities. There is a world of difference between the forms employed by the artist to *express* dissolution and the experience of the dissolute life of a city slum, as here in Lima, Peru. To be subjected to this life where crime has become normal must be an ordeal; for the artist, to represent the forms of a dissolving order is a search for freedom. As always with fugitive meanings, we have to recognise that the state of freedom is subjective, and that the adoption of conventions so as to be able to communicate at all, while it involves a loss of subjective freedom, represents a gain in commonality and so in liberty. Architecture may approach the condition of art but so long as it is inhabited, it has other duties as well.

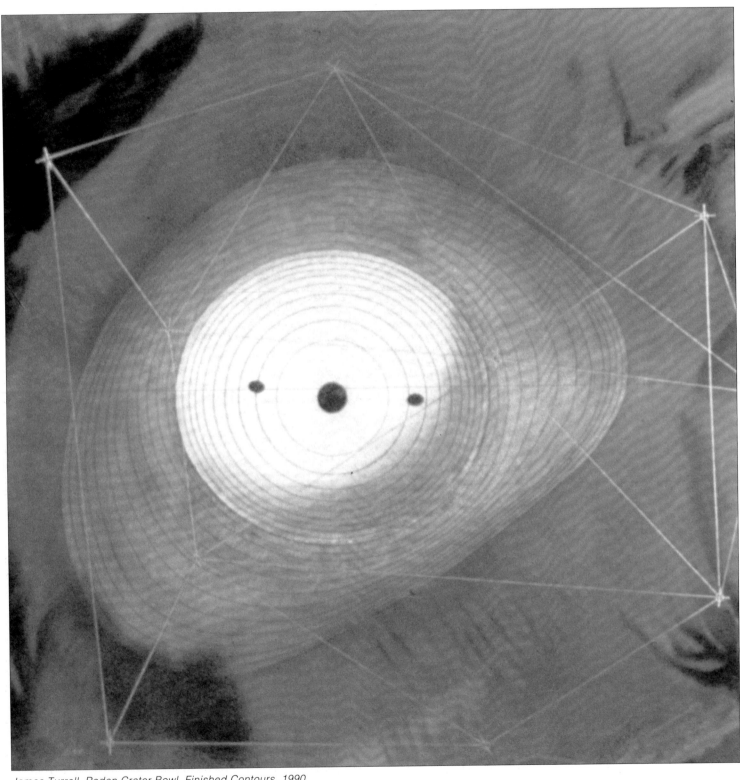

James Turrell, Roden Crater Bowl, Finished Contours, 1990

CLARE MELHUISH
ART AND ARCHITECTURE
The Dynamics of Collaboration

'Come on mates, we're artists too, we have to deal with those people outside that don't even care a damn what any of us are about', appealed Peter Cook at the International Public Art Symposium organised by the Public Art Commissions Agency in 1990. His *cri de coeur* was uttered in the face of much apparent disunity among artists and architects; the symposium organised specifically to address the problems of collaboration shortly before the Arts Council's Percent for Art scheme was instituted. It was this scheme which capitalised on the burgeoning public art movement in this country, bringing it decisively into the domain of buildings and architecture with the recommendation that one per cent of the total construction budget should be spent on art. The idea came from the United States, along with the movement itself, motivated by the desire of artists to liberate themselves from the economic and ideological constraints of the gallery system, and bring their work to a wider audience. The result was a diffusion of art practice which aimed at reintegrating art with everyday life and the city.

One of the prime instigators of what she now calls the 'ghastly public art movement' in this country during the 1980s was Isabel Vasseur, who joined the Arts Council in 1980, soon after the launch of its Works of Art in Public Places scheme (1978). The main aim was to create a better economic environment for artists, at a time when only ten per cent of art in galleries was selling to British buyers and, through a level of economic liberation, to give them a greater degree of autonomy in their work. The establishment of Percent for Art a decade later was primarily intended to extend the opportunities for artists: it was not necessarily suggesting that buildings would benefit from embellishment by works of art, or, as is now the case, that artists should be more involved in the conception of building projects from the beginning of the process, working in collaboration with architects.

However, the immediate results of Percent for Art, along with the increasing amount of public art initiated by the new public art agencies and the regional development corporations, were not very satisfactory. Many buildings and public spaces were adorned with quite inappropriate art works that were not 'site-specific' in any way except by virtue of their location. 'Some northern cities are littered with ephemeral or irrelevant pieces', says Vasseur. Furthermore, the operation of the public art agencies, she suggests, led to a polarisation of public art into a world of its own. The answer to the problem was seen to be a greater level of collaboration between artists and those, including architects and planners, responsible for the environment.

The result has been a huge proliferation of collaborative projects for buildings, public spaces and even gallery installations, which has in the last two years been fuelled by Lottery funding. The Arts Council Lottery fund, covering all forms of art including architecture, explicitly encourages collaboration by underlining the desirability of artists and craftspeople contributing to a project. Further funding for the involvement of artists in building and environmental projects has become available through schemes such as the RSA's Art for Architecture awards, or the Arts Challenge Grants for regeneration administered by the regional arts boards.

It would seem to be true to say that these initiatives have been largely motivated by the desire to improve conditions for artists and bring their work to a wider audience, rather than by a specific interest in improving the quality of the built environment, or a belief that architects and their work can fundamentally benefit by working with artists. Jess Furnie of the RSA says 'we're just offering a different dimension'. Nevertheless the agenda is present by implication and this can and has been a source of conflict. Some architects have been offended by the suggestion that they somehow have an inadequate aesthetic sense. After seven years training they may not take kindly to Vasseur's suggestion that they could benefit from artists' ability to 'think laterally'. And for the huge number of practising architects who view architecture itself as an art, and who long for the freedom from planning regulations, building regulations, briefs drawn up by often ill-informed clients, desperately tight budgets, little public respect, and even aesthetic planning control, to produce architecture they feel worthy of the name, it is all too easy to imagine that artists are stealing that ground from them – leaving architects, in the worst case scenario, with little more than the administrative and technical side of the job. When the American artist Jack Mackie announced at the PACA symposium that 'We're in it for a level of integrity that's been stolen from the profession and science of architecture – there is a gift coming back', it was not entirely clear what he meant. Likewise, architects do not welcome the idea that, as a result of the postwar emphasis on functional determinism, survey analysis, and the plan as generator, they have lost to artists their right to exercise intuitive judgement and give reign to their creative sensibilities.

On the other hand, it is precisely this sense of deprivation on the part of many architects which has predisposed them to the idea of working with artists – 'we can slip into being more creative', says Julian Feary of Feary and Heron. At one level, of course, it is simply an opportunity – just as it has been for artists. Working on a piece of public art or a gallery installation can be a stimulating break from normal design commissions, and a chance to present architectural ideas in a different forum. Incorporating some art content into a building project can open the door not only to additional funding but also to a relaxation of planning requirements: art, it seems can break the rules in a way that architecture is simply not allowed to. Architecture is expected to underpin the establishment, while art is expected to be subversive. Above all, however, most architects believe that closer integration between architecture and art is fundamentally beneficial to the whole – and always has been in some way or another.

Art and architecture, and indeed landscape, automatically went hand-in-hand until relatively recently. The Renaissance villa was a masterpiece of integration; the great architectural theorist Alberti wrote on painting and sculpture (*Della pittura e della statua*) as importantly as on architecture (*De re aedificatoria*); while the great Baroque architects, sculptors and painters frequently interchanged roles and mediums, as Anthony Blunt demonstrates:

> Architectural members are sometimes replaced by sculpture or are so contorted and decorated that they seem more like sculpture than supporting elements. Sculptors introduce colour – almost like painters – in the form of illusionist marble inlay, by imitating the texture of velvet or silk, or by creating effects of false perspective. Painters use this last device on a vast scale and set up complete buildings on the ceilings of their churches or the saloni in their palaces. Architects execute similar effects of *leger-de-main* in three dimensions, producing, for instance, arcades which appear twice their actual length.

Baroque and Rococo, ed Anthony Blunt, Granada, 1978
The Industrial Revolution had a profound effect on the role of both architects and artists. The discovery of new manufacturing processes threatened to undermine craftsmanship and the production of art, and to open the way for the standardised production of buildings – which indeed it did. The Arts and Crafts Movement developed out of the concerns which emerged: it manifested, for the first time, a feeling that there was a need to nurture the continuing vitality and integration of the arts, crafts and architecture against the depredations of the modern world.

It is often forgotten that the entire Modern Movement, a few decades later, was founded on a vision of 'the new building of the future, which will embrace architecture and sculpture and painting in one unity . . .' (proclamation of the Weimar Bauhaus, 1919). The Bauhaus taught fine art, applied art and architecture and promoted a teaching system based on stimulating individual creativity through making collages of different materials and textures. It is paradoxical that this sort of approach has been favoured in some of the more experimental architecture schools in this country recently, while rejecting the conventional architectural drawing, or the 'plan as generator' as a modernist anachronism. The emphatic equation of modernism with functionalist dogma since the 60s has obscured the fact that modernism in architecture was powerfully influenced by Cubism in painting and its radical rethinking of two-dimensional space and form.

Modernism was built on a long historical relationship between art and architecture, but at the same time they were growing apart, asserting a somewhat resentful autonomy of each other. The professionalisation of architecture was designed to safeguard standards but it was also, in effect, a defensive mechanism designed to keep others out of the building process, which has now been consolidated by the increase of regulations and liability. Simultaneously, the rapid technological developments in the construction industry, and the standardisation of building systems, led to a heightened emphasis on the 'scientific' and technical side, as opposed to the 'art' of architecture. Meanwhile, art had long rejected its scientific basis in geometry, as it was understood in the Gothic period, and the symbolic representational role which it played throughout the pre-modern era. As a result, its traditional patrons were replaced by the commercial gallery system, and its traditional audience by dedicated 'experts' who visited galleries. What remained of public art was reduced to the level of propaganda, often in conjunction with architecture, in the hands of powerful, repressive political agencies during a turbulent period of world history. Outside this highly controlled domain, the overlap between art and architecture was gradually reduced to the physical structure of the gallery itself. Eventually that too became a source of conflict, as artists accused architects of dominating art with design.

The public art movement of the 70s was born out of the recognition that the gallery system represented a cul-de-sac, and out of the desire for free political engagement in the public realm. At the same time, modernism was failing in architecture, while socialist idealism was stifled by Thatcherite free-market capitalism, and architects found themselves in a political and economic vacuum. For two decades, the major developments in architecture were based on theoretical ideas drawn from other disciplines, notably literature, or a fetishisation of construction itself. The reaction has been a re-politicisation of architecture as an engagement with social and cultural conditions. This, combined with the instinctive desire of architects to be more creative, the collapse of the construction industry during the recession, and the result loss of normal building opportunities, has prompted a new interest in art practice as a paradigm for architecture.

According to Tony Fretton, an architect who has designed several galleries and studios for artists, art has 'an intelligence about the way objects exist politically', while 'architecture is much less willing to understand it is representing the values of society and the people it is built for'. Although he admits architecture is constrained by use, he maintains that 'art has produced much more interesting thought and form than architecture . . . said bigger things . . . in the last 30 years'. He suggests architecture has much to learn from art, but fears architects will misinterpret art practice as yet another style: 'eventually architecture will commodify and use up art', as it did with poetry and literature.

Fretton's view is very uncritical of art, a common tendency among certain architects. It overlooks the fact that much art has little or no political content (even if it does, it is not necessarily good), and it disregards much of the best architecture produced during this period; but if his pessimism is justifiable then there seems to be every reason to encourage the formation of true collaborative relationships and a more fruitful interchange of ideas between architects and artists. There has certainly been an element of faddishness in the embrace of art-derived practices in some of the schools of architecture, which one suspects has been inspired as much by the success and glamour of the young British art scene – especially by contrast with the grim outlook facing architectural students – as by a desire to express a more politicised view of architecture. But while there has been a plethora of what the cynics have described as 'third rate art', there has also been an invigoration of the architectural culture with some provocative work.

Kevin Rhowbotham was behind much of the more interesting work that came out of the Bartlett, for instance, in the late 80s and early 90s, and some of his students have gone on to operate as FAT – Fashion Architecture Taste, a young art-orientated architectural practice. Rhowbotham's concerns focused on what FAT partner Sean Griffiths describes as an intense investigation of the 'role of the drawn product in relation to architectural ideas', with a political intent. The discussion about the representation of space and the adequacy of the conventional architectural drawing to describe its occupation, generated a debate about power relations and gender politics which, Griffiths maintains, was 'the staple diet of art'. The debate stimulated an investigation of alternative means of representation, such as video and photography; computer technology – Photoshop, not CAD – had a dramatic impact, opening up a field of surfaces and iconographic elements that offered a completely different approach to architectural design from the plan-generated method.

Griffiths suggests similarities between FAT's work, using familiar elements to build up new situations and the idea of 'theming', and that of artists such as Julian Opie, Dan Graham and James Turrell, contrasting it with what he describes as the 'essentially modernist aesthetic' and legitimising values of most other architects. This tendency to relate to contemporary art as a source of inspiration representing opposing values to those of modernism is echoed by other young practices such as Caruso St John, architects of Walsall Art Gallery working in collaboration with artists Richard Wentworth and Catherine Yass. Adam Caruso states that the way contemporary art is 'installed' in a space, rather than hung formally, should be the model for contemporary architecture; he condemns modernism's aspiration to idealise and order the world, contrasting that with art's concern to 'interpret' the world, the principle of their own work. These sentiments are paradoxical in view of the parallels with modernist architects' fascination with art, manifested particularly in the influence of Cubism on the configuration of architectural mass and space. The difference seems to lie in a shift away from the fundamentally spatial concerns, aimed at physically reconfiguring the world, inspired by Cubism, towards an interest in more ephemeral forms of representation, designed to alter one's perception of the world, inspired by contemporary art.

'Most people see art as a representation', comments architect and artist Mark Pimlott, 'whereas architecture aspires to be the reality – but it often isn't; it's another form of representation'. He says it was art which opened his eyes to this. In an installation at the Todd Gallery, Pimlott aimed to reveal that 'as a place [it] conforms to certain stereotypes of what a gallery should be. It is involved not only in housing the fictional occupant of art, but is a fictional housing itself'. At the same time it is part of the city: city, gallery and art are all part of a mental construct. Pimlott's concern is to break down the understanding of architecture as a collection of facts and reveal the creation of architecture, like art, as a process of making visible the conditions in which it is made at a poetic level.

However, there is clearly a fundamental difference between art and architecture at the level of use. It is reiterated by Liza Fior of Muf, who recounts that as she and her partners – Juliet Bidgood, an architect, and Katherine Clarke, an artist – tried to work out their relationship, the question of 'use' quickly emerged as a concern shared by the architects but not by Clarke: 'Katherine said it could just be what it was'. Clarke defines her interest, as an artist, as 'the way that ideas take up existence in the world as objects or spaces'. This is the basis of the critical discussion that has come out of art practice and provides the yardstick for a definition of public art: 'if art is to exist in the public realm it has to exist critically'. But once an artist's ideas are embodied in a work of art, the process is finished: there is no further level of transmutation into a reality of space and matter defined by use and determined to a very large extent by the outside agencies of client and various authorities.

This is a complex issue which, on the whole, only a few artists seem to have addressed. For Clarke, the significant aspects of working with architects initially were the extremely precise notation of ideas through the drawing 'in a way that is completely foreign to art education', and the re-evaluation of space, in opposition to the object, as something that was not neutral but highly charged – a development that was already beginning to take place in art practice. Tania Kovats, currently working in collaboration with Levitt Bernstein on the design of the Ikon Gallery in Birmingham, funded by an RSA Art for Architecture award, was already interested in the manipulation and conventions of space, in buildings and big objects, and their effect on people, and how cities are shaped – but in a 'mainly recreational' way. She appreciated the introduction to another language and scale, while the concept of permanence implied in the proposition was both stimulating and alarming, the scope for change and substitution drastically reduced by comparison with the laboratory of the studio: 'you don't know if you've made the right decision until it's all in place'.

For artist Ron Haselden, currently working with architect Robert Barnes on a public art project funded by the London Arts Board, the appeal of architecture lies less in the opportunities it may offer to explore spatial concepts in physical terms, than in the rich field it provides for exploring human response to the built object. He actively dislikes the idea of being drawn into a collaboration with an architect from day one, preferring to be given a situation, 'like a found object', where he can 'just lay something which can change your perception of it'. Another artist again, Tess Jaray, who worked on Birmingham Centenary Square in collaboration with the city architects, describes her interest in, and engagement with architecture as being essentially visual and to do with ideas of place: 'For 30 years, architecture was one of my main sources of inspiration as a painter. The shapes, the colours, the sense of light, all came from my responses to architecture and to a feeling for place.'

Despite the apparent extent of common ground between some contemporary artists and architects, it has proved not particularly easy to forge collaborations, even in cases where there seems to be a shared outlook and goal. Part of the problem lies in the primitive preconceptions that artists and architects may have not only about what collaboration has to offer but also about each other. Architects resent being viewed by artists as technical, or 'jobbing' people (as one artist put it), lacking in creativity or intellectual ideas, and the fact that, as Ted Cullinan has put it, architecture, unlike art, is not understood as 'a central issue in the culture of the nation'. On the other hand, architects often speak with disdain of artists' lack of professionalism, naivety and inability to make decisions and keep deadlines – except for the new 'entrepreneurial' breed epitomised by Damien Hirst. Both sides seem to regard each other in equal proportion as egocentric, precious and lacking in generosity. According to one architect, there is an active dislike of architects among artists and even art administrators, and a general climate of suspicion.

Such accusations suggest there are serious obstacles to be negotiated by those interested in nurturing a collaborative relationship between the two parties. The misconceptions are reinforced by significant differences in working practice. At the PACA symposium, artist Andrew Darke stated: 'An art work has integrity because the artist is in total control, he works on every aspect in the studio.' Architects, by contrast, have to work in close collaboration with each other in teams, with their consultants, their clients and, increasingly, the general public through public consultation. They are accustomed to instructing subcontractors who will fabricate or supply the products which the architect has designed or specified. The suggestion may be that this automatically results in a loss of control and forces compromise. Many artists are not totally studio-based, and routinely employ assistants to undertake much of the hard physical labour – Ron Haselden, for example, rejects the studio approach and often designs things which are fabricated by others, preferring to 'use the outside world' – but there are many others for whom the haven of the studio and the principal of 'getting your hands dirty', maintaining the purity of the work by executing every bit personally in a relationship of close physical involvement, is religiously observed. This attitude may also be compounded by a level of possessiveness and secrecy about certain techniques regarded as highly personal which creates a resistance to the involvement of others in the making of objects.

For artists who have made the passage from the studio into the public domain, the exchange of solitude and 'total control' for the collaborative relationship and compromise, assailed on all sides by the demands of third parties, is often a shock and a challenge, but also very stimulating. It seems clear that one of the reasons Bruce McLean has undertaken so many successful collaborative ventures with architects – notably Will Alsop, John Lyall and now Irena Bauman of Bauman Lyons – is that he naturally enjoys working with other people; no doubt the fact that his father was an architect, as is his son, has created an additional level of empathy with the architect's mind. Originally a performance artist, McLean has never sought the confines of the studio, and particularly enjoys working in communities: for instance, a major part of the project for the public space in front of Tottenham Hale Station which he is working on with John Lyall is a 'Path of Knowledge' which is to be made up of work produced by children in workshops directed by the artist. However, Bauman observes that even McLean is protective of his own creativity, showing a reluctance to let assistants from her office help him in the making process at Bridlington Promenade, and refusing to deal with letters or have a fax machine – options that simply are not open to architects.

The most difficult part of any architect-artist collaboration seems to be the transition from the conceptual or design stage to implementation. This seems to be the point at which there is most likely to be conflict over definition of roles, authorship and responsibility. Landscape architect Kathryn Gustafson stressed at the P... conference that 'It is very important to talk about the contract ... before in the beginning – whether it's moral, verbal, define it well. Where's the money going? Who puts ... down on ...' Among artists, there is a greater freedom ... notation of ideas in different media than ... s customary in architecture, and there may be little ... of a brief as such: according to artist Richard Wentworth, who also teaches at the Architectural Association: 'you let the work happen, you're not looking for a solution.' While the sort of architects who are attracted by the idea of working with artists are likely to be more experimental and flexible in the way they approach a brief and notate ideas, a common understanding of the role of the brief and the shared language of the architectural drawing is the basis of the architectural education system. The development stage of a collaborative project seems to provide both parties with an opportunity to explore other approaches which is generally found to be stimulating and enjoyable, rather than to engender conflict – even when, as Julian Feary says of his collaboration with Patrick Heron on a public art work in Stag Place, London, for example, 'Patrick's idea of space is completely different from ours [as architects]'. In the case of Bridlington Promenade, Irena

Bauman describes the process of developing the idea with the artist as a very 'exciting and experimental' stage; alternatively, architect Axel Burrough reports that the main medium for collaboration between Levitt Bernstein and Tania Kovats at the Ikon Gallery was discussion, avoiding the problem of notation. While this process, in whatever form, may work very well, the presentation of ideas is likely to reveal the differences in the way that architects and artists are accustomed to work. For instance, in John Lyall and Bruce McLean's scheme for the regeneration of Barnsley through public art, McLean's vividly-coloured abstract collages seem to bear almost no relation to Lyall's apparently 'fixed' architectural drawings. Underlying tensions are likely to emerge once realisation of a project gets under way. Tania Kovats – who describes herself as generally 'very pleasantly surprised by the whole experience' – observes that at the Ikon Gallery the additional pressures of construction and the need to make firm decisions led to a focus on issues of authorship which had not been evident before. This can easily undermine the basis of a collaboration, since, as she says, 'one of the attractive things about collaboration is that shared responsibility'.

For Irena Bauman at Bridlington, it made no sense that, having developed the whole concept for the scheme jointly, she and McLean were then obliged to separate certain isolated collaborative elements' in order to make an Arts Council Lottery funding application. ... the early stages of collaboration ... the 'sense of freedom' ... ed from working with an artist ... because ... the fact ... architect, she was contractually obliged to take responsibility for the realisation of the project and for the artist, with power to penalise him financially if need be. She hopes that in future collaboration with the ... artist Jonny Savale, they will be able to have completely equal contracts. At Bridlington, McLean himself had to take out sufficient liability insurance ... Bauman fears that the sheer weight of contractual obligations generated by health and safety regulations could become a serious impediment to collaborative ventures in the arts in the future, since most artists are simply not in a position to take on the sort of responsibilities that architects are subject to. At some point, she warns, 'someone will take someone else to court' and 'it will change the whole nature of collaboration'. Bauman suggests that if the gallery could expand its traditional remit as the artist's agent to encompass a new role in this sphere it would be a significant step forward in safeguarding the continuing viability of collaborative ventures.

This year, art and architecture collaborations have reached their apogee, celebrated in a whole series of different events at the main London arts institutions. In the glare of publicity, however, an important reality has been obscured, and that is that art and architecture are merely generic terms, each covering a great multiplicity of manifestations inspired by an enormous variety of intellectual and artistic interests. There is a danger in elevating the desirability of collaboration between architects and artists to the level of an ideal per se, independent of any interest in, or proper understanding of the motivation that lies behind the production of art and architecture by individuals. Although there are people who would support the idea of collaboration for its own sake, this seems to suggest an investment which has little relation to the real basis of collaborative relationships: a coming-together of minds, with a desire to pursue common interests for the sake of the work and the role it might take up in society.

Irena Bauman, Bridlington Promenade, chaise longue designed in terrazzo to match artist's material

Tania Kovats, Ledge, 1995, paper, resin, steel frame, 250 x 200 x 150 cm

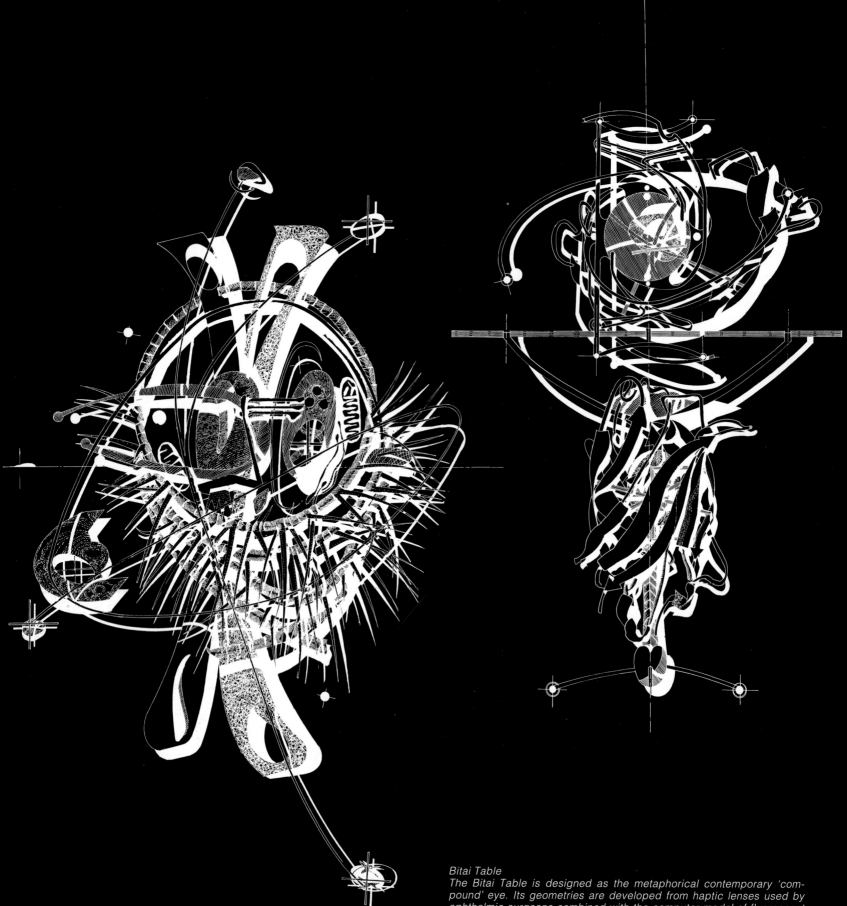

Bioscape Vertigo
This is an attempt to transcribe some aspects of the new landscape and the geometries of the new conic 'un' sections of vision. It is without scale and without navigatable order. The traveller in its nested dynamics teeters on the edge of Bioscape Vertigo. The relationship between parts is not snapped to any Platonic conspiracy. The architecture of the cell is held and supported by the 'Extended Phenotype'. DNA is the new crucifix and a religious reading is possible; the thorns are not an accident . . .

Bitai Table
The Bitai Table is designed as the metaphorical contemporary 'compound' eye. Its geometries are developed from haptic lenses used by ophthalmic surgeons combined with the computer model of fluorescent protein. As well as the word play of 'BIT' and 'AI', bitai is Japanese for 'sexual allure'. The changing eye is still a useful symbol for the effects of digital and soft technologies but this new eye like the new flesh will be hardly recognisable. This new eye is the synthesised amalgam of organic and mechanic, wet yet dry, binary yet analogue and focused everywhere simultaneously. Its cone of vision is no longer conic; the conic sections of perception are bent out of shape and of a higher order topology. It is simultaneously fluorescent and luminates all it scans with hyperreal exactitude.

'Form follows Function', 'Truth to Materials' and other such calls for architectural censorship still echo around my head attempting to curb the architectural sinner in me. The worry starts every time I set out to design, paint or make something, 'What is it and why is it useful, will it be expensive?' This rationalist modernist sensibility was burned into my soul by a provincial architectural education which sought to teach me how to feed the system with unquestioning mundanities. Even now the guilt and excitement of flagrant nonconformism sends shocks of shrill pleasure through me as I throw out deformed shapes and summon the ghosts of symbolism. I wage constant battles against the warrior monks of whiteness, those crusaders against dust, rust and the slant, whose habits are beautifully sewn but which only mask total nakedness. These disciples of the orthogonal are willing supplicants to their clients/Masters of the Universe as they burn in their bonfire of vanities.

I am an architect; this gives me great pride but also great pain. Conventional wisdom dictates that architects are the servants to their clients, providing the necessary professional expertise with which to realise their wishes. I am afraid I am not that kind of architect. This begs the question of what type of architect I am, or indeed if I am an architect at all? All my documents say I am: none tell me I am an artist or a writer. In the early 90s I wrote about my work in terms of a blurred boundary: 'An Interstitial is a drawing that is neither art nor architecture: it is a graphic means of exploring an idea and allowing randomness to influence the conception . . . the poetic drawing teaches us the notion of "betweenness": between architecture and art, between reality and fiction, between black and white. In a continually changing world, this seems an advantage.' It is this idea of change that is forever throwing up new areas of research. The arena of my work is always shifting as I hang onto the coat tails of the technological imperative, leading me into strange worlds, which at first seem much removed from the world of the professional architect. Architecture is the yardstick with which I measure and learn about the world. My trajectory has made me familiar with Fractal geometry, virtual worlds, machine ecologies, the arguments for and against Dolly the sheep and the joy of 'sketching' in steel. These lessons and thoughts provoke and enable my architec-

ture both to form and be expressed. It is in these obsessions that the elusive thing, 'the personal architectural lexicon', becomes developed and debated. I encourage my students not to follow the vagaries of fashion or the sycophancies of style but to create a language of architecture that is personal to them, an architecture that operates and is composed with reference to their individual way of seeing and being in the world. The first few steps in this new and, at first, bare world are full of fear. The call to renounce sophist dogma and the traditional architectural brief with its retarded view of the world and humanity is greeted with a sickening reaching out for hackneyed abstraction and fruitless analogy. Paradoxically, it appears that technology holds the key to the students' intellectual paralyses. This technology is not the technology of Le Corbusier or of the Baroque Master of Hi-Tech. It has little to do with the machine aesthetic and even less to do with the sparsity of mass production and economies of scale. Students can easily accept the idea of the progress of science yet become incredulous once its full pace is revealed to them. They are happy with a concept that can guarantee faster Game Boys but are shocked by the ontological changes that such a pace of innovation brings. Nonetheless, I believe architects' and architecture's central purpose is to create environments that exploit these continually new found technological opportunities in ways that satisfy the demands of human comfort or titillation the sublime harnessed to the ridiculous one might say. Whilst my work is consistently referred to as art, I prefer to believe its guiding force is that of technology. But then again, how would I know? I am only the author.

Obviously technology is but one aspect of the complexities within art and architecture. The idea of the architect/artist as not fully in control over his work/design is not a new one. This issue of the author's ambivalence as to the exact status of his own work is crucial in creating a dynamic and symbiotic relationship between product and designer. Something weird happens when one creates without forethought. Conventional architectural wisdom does not trust the playful making of marks or the joyful juggling of shapes unless it is to satisfy some initial concept to which every subsequent move must adhere to. It does not believe that totally unpredictable product could have the same status as a predictable one. There is a critical and creative mind in the artist, and the exceptional one balances the needs of both.

The making of work that is not controlled by the conscious mind frightens architects, who are trained to be the ultimate control freaks. It seems that as technology grinds on, architectural control becomes a thing of the past. The materials of the future will not always remain in the dogmatic configurations but will readjust to liberate users from the crippling inertness of today's architectural form. My work, I hope, is about the art of architecture in an accelerating technologically mediated future. But then I am also of the opinion that the artist/architect usually invents an explanation for the work after it has been created.

MICHAEL SPENS
ART CONCEPT, ARCHITECTURAL PROCESS

The difficulties with the purely conceptual have always been those of verification, consummation and ultimate fulfilment. The necessary exchange between concept and process has to be formalised within precepts of continuity. Colin Rowe drew our attention to the essential copulation of ideas as long ago as 1975, by quoting Samuel Johnson:

> Wit, you know, is the unexpected copulation of ideas, the discovery of some occult relation between imagines in appearance remote from each other. And an effusion of wit therefore presupposes an accumulation of knowledge stored with notions which the imagination may cull out to compose new assemblages.[1]

Within this continuum of opposites, we have learnt to recognise the Sublime, even if reminded of it to excess in the past five years. In the context of a simulated attempt to correlate the initiatives of artists with the hesitant embrace of architects today, a field is available where synergies can be readily conjured together – that of the Sublime. As Burke recognised, concepts of the sublime infuse beauty with a codicil, a propensity with foreboding, where a hinterland of catastrophe is normative. That mood occurs in the best type of detective novel; Raymond Chandler crafted such a scenario in *The Long Goodbye*:

> I went out and left the door open. I walked across the big living room and out to the patio, and pulled one of the chaises into the shadow of the overhang and stretched out on it. Across the lake there was a blue haze against the hills. The ocean breeze had begun to filter through the low mountains to the west. It wiped the air clean and it wiped away just enough of the hear. Idle Valley was having a perfect summer. Somebody had planned it that way. Paradise incorporated, and also Highly Restricted. Only the nicest people . . .

Chandler has prepared a scenario of doom. Beauty and perfection are the veil. Even Capability Brown could not have composed things better – the lake, the hills, the haze, an Arcadian breeze – or Claude, or Poussin. The figures in the landscape are likewise incidental, in the middle ground:

> It was quite a long time before the speedboat came tearing down the lake again . . . it was almost four o'clock when I heard its distant roar swell into an ear-splitting howl of noise . . . I walked down to the edge of the lake. He made it this time. The driver slowed just enough on the turn, and the brown lad on the surfboard leaned far out against the centrifugal pull . . .

The sound, in fact, concealed the gunshot noise when Marlow's host was shot by his wife inside the house at that precise moment. The Sublime is never far from shock-horror, as Chandler's hero already knows.

In film in the 1990s, the Sublime has proliferated; whether as repeatedly orchestrated in Anthony Minghella's production *The English Patient*, or parodied in Bertolucci's *Stealing Beauty* and in contemporary art, through the work of Damien Hirst, for example, it has firmly consolidated a reflex-generating hold on

Salzburg Art Museum, Hans Hollein

Life and Death, installation at 1972 Venice Biennale, Hans Hollein

Le Grand Bleu, Will Alsop

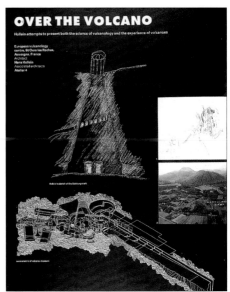

Museum of Vulcanology, Hans Hollein

current *zeitgeist*: as characteristic of the decade as the 'Picturesque' was of the cultural 'mish-mash' of the 1980s.

In architecture, a growing aspiration to acclimatise within the cognitive field of the sublime, to tolerate the symptoms of 'vertigo' that it cultivates, can be traced back to the 1970s. Such architects as Stirling, Behnisch, Piano, Hollein, Gullichsen, Pallasmaa, Coop Himmelblau and Bernard Tschumi, have been followed more recently in this direction by Bolles-Wilson, Hadid, Koolhaas, Holl and Will Alsop.

The common ground of the Sublime had, of course, been tested early on by land artists in the 1970s, including Richard Serra and Robert Smithson; both made stringent efforts to adhere, and to avoid the constant threat through critical misrepresentation, of affiliation to the 'Picturesque'. Richard Serra would claim emphatically that his sculpture *Clara-Clara* is concerned with the effect of parallax, the progress around the work of the spectator, and of formal disjunction. And Robert Smithson, similarly, would abhor the depiction of his work 'Spiral Jetty' by aerial photography as utter distortion of an experience essentially derived at ground level. The Picturesque, as such, is always lurking around, it seems, ready to appropriate artistic visions, defuse them, and render them harmlessly void of creative impulse, eliminating disjunction, disarticulation, dismay.

It is revealing to examine the work of two architects in particular, whose work is wholly different and yet in both cases ranges freely and productively across the common ground of the Sublime – a symbolic territory inhabited predominantly by visual artists, film-makers, and novelists, and mostly avoided by architects. It is by joining this common ground that both Hans Hollein (b.1934) and Will Alsop (b.1947) have developed their quite unrelated work. What they display in common is a creative attitude that refuses to acknowledge that their architecture is other than the leading edge of art.

Hollein has achieved and sustained a continual presence in this area, aided by a close correlation with installation art concepts. Other commentators have drawn attention to Hollein's concern for iconographic substitutions or inversions, and their pre-eminence in his work. There was a strong strain of ambiguity, coupled with uneasiness over the persistent appetite for monumentality amongst corporate clients. This was the time when Hollein first began to sink his architecture into the landscape. The famous Aircraft Carrier collage (1964) and Wippel House (1966) indicate this urge. The church project for Turach (1974), on a lake site surrounded by mountains emphasises identity with a horizontal 'jetty' *qua campanile*, jutting along into the lake, instead of probing the sky.

The Mönchengladbach Museum of Art (1984) has been described as a surrealistic earthwork, swelling up out of the sloping site. Today, more than ten years later, the site has greened over effectively so that a disjunctive, reactive topography is revealed with the fluid responsiveness to extraneous pressure of a bed of volcanic lava. The institution, too, appears deliberately as an institution *manqué*, but highly accessible nonetheless.

Hollein's most successful venture into a purely symbolic installation art came in 1972, at the Venice Biennale. The construction entitled *Work and Behaviour – Life and Death* was constructed at the Austrian Pavilion beside a small canal. The placement of every enclosed or open scenario was contrived with precision of thought to establish a mood of foreboding, of infinity, and of the oppositions of life and death in the human predicament. What was increasingly evident from early on was that Hollein is fundamentally a part of the continuing tradition of the contemporary sublime.

A special characteristic in Hollein's work has always come from the urge to exploit unusual site conditions, even to confound what might appear as immutable circumstances – whether of scale, or elevation, or conjunction, or typology. At Mönchengladbach, for instance, the museum appeared as several buildings. At Frankfurt, the isosceles triangle-shaped site of the Museum of Modern Art is reconciled consummately with the existing urban grain, with the entrance made at the base rather than the apex of the triangle (as convention might have prescribed) so giving the 'prow' a dramatic precedence. At Salzburg the idea of establishing an art gallery in a sunken, rock-hewn cavern has inevitable atavistic references. To expand this concept to a series of deep caves and recesses lit spasmodically by shafts of sunlight or daylight involves delving, which has profound implications for human sensibility. Hollein has offered a schema so fundamental that its seemingly atectonic condition simply re-endorses basic timeless experiential codes in a way that utterly confounds the trivialities of the Neopicturesque faction. Hollein characteristically invoked first principles here; a resolutely purifying immersion in space is prescribed, or rather a sequence of subterranean spaces to be experienced yet which cannot, a priori, be imagined.

Hollein's negation here of conventional tectonic criteria, while still deploying fundamental (albeit catacombic) means of enclosure to satisfy human requirements in the literal sense, harnesses subconscious human reflexes to being underground to advantage in optimising focus on objects, and their timeless meaning. The whole is achieved reductively, through a minimisation of the formal system of the museum as institution, hence encouraging fuller concentration on the exhibits displayed.

Hollein's more recent work, the Museum of Vulcanology currently under construction at St Ours-les-Roches, Auvergne, France is central to his importance in the progression of the contemporary sublime. Located in an area of high former volcanic activity (which has bestowed clear regional characteristics in geology and building), this museum building unites a number of Hollein's earlier formal preoccupations, and develops further the idea of the rotunda. The Museum at St Ours-les-Roches is inserted to merge with the surrounding undulations of the landscape. The complex is signalled by a great truncated cone, the *cone doré*, which is an abstraction of the extinct volcanoes outside. The remaining series of volumes are either wholly, or at least partially, submerged.

The design brief was complicated, with exhortations to remind visitors of Jules Verne, of Dante's *Purgatory*, of Plato's protective cave. 'Fire was to be present in an atmosphere both sinister and threatening, but also exuberant and joyful.' Nothing less than a 're-definition of sublimity' seemed to be demanded. Hollein has accepted this.

Visitors will penetrate an earth womb to embark on a journey of discovery to a depth of some 9 metres (30 feet). A ramp winds down round the top of a 29-metre-deep crater which belches smoke and vapour. A series of routes provides a revelation under ground, a kind of initiation into the underworld, cut through basalt. Hollein has rendered the built complex indistinguishable from the experiential totality of the site: both are one. Hollein has specified local materials such as basalt (used in the immediate vernacular building), grass and water and deploys them wherever appropriate. Many of Hollein's preoccupations of the past decade are incorporated: a ritualistic processional route; a void carved out of solid geology; conical space as core element covered by translucent or transparent rooflight or shallow dome; movement by visitors or occupants peripherally up or down a conical space (via circulation elements adjacent to the surface edge of the cone or cylinder); and external concealment of the new building by not disturbing its pre-existent surface, whether in the case of a palazzo or a fragile landscape.

Will Alsop commits himself to architecture through painting his concepts out. His best known work has always been made abroad, primarily in Germany and France, rather than at home, which is perhaps still significant in 1997. However, here I intend to address in detail only one building, where, as with Hollein, further and deliberate 'transgressions' occur between architecture and art in the contemporary sublime. This building is generally known as 'Le Grand Bleu'. It was completed in 1994, in Marseilles, France, as the regional centre of Government for Les Bouches-du-Rhône (Region No 13). The design was the result of an open competition in which Alsop beat Norman Foster into second place. The building is essentially tectonic in character, and so displays its emblematic roof apparatus boldly, eschewing any idea of weightlessness, yet embracing the play of light.

The technology transfer of lightweight panel elements with their necessary ribs, spars, skins, and incorporated hydraulic systems for the operation and control of moveable components within and without (roofs, wings and flaps) represented an aspect of sublimity which, as Burke would say, 'arouses the initial passion of "astonishment", with some degree of horror . . .', as Colin Rowe quoted Burke:[2] 'hence arises the great power of the sublime . . . it anticipates our reasonings and hurries them on by an irresistible force.' Then, noticing this:

the inferior effects are admiration, reverence and respect, and sensations of the sublime will further be induced by terror, obscurity, power, privation, vastness, infinity, succession and uniformity [which Burke designates as the artificial sublime] magnitude, light, and very importantly pain.

So we do not need the morphine, rather the valium in our contemporary dilemma.

A deliberate uneasiness becomes apparent at Marseilles after the initial Burkean tremor of 'astonishment' in the visitor's reaction on arrival at the site. The Alsop building divides very logically into the '*administratif*' blocks, two in parallel, which house the staff of civil servants: and the '*déliberatif*' which as its name implies, is the chamber of government, where decisions are debated and ratified. The two are linked by bridges, and escalators, housing the council chamber and its ancillary functions. The architectural denomination of the '*administratif*' and the '*déliberatif*' is utterly different. The space between the two parallel blocks of the '*administratif*' is an enclosed atrium.

More characteristically, and of special significance here, is the looseness of parts – and of their connections. This reflects the clear 'enabling' policy pursued as idiomatic throughout the building, by Alsop and indeed the clients. Such a positive philosophy inherited by the political institutions of France was, of course, propounded by Edmund Burke in his 'other' major text, *Reflections on the Revolution in France* (1790). Burke, even then, recognised that society was an 'organic' construct rather than a mechanistic phenomenon.

Le Grand Bleu exhibits the antithesis of articulation: Alsop 'disarticulates' the *parti* of his building. It is relevant to say that the transitive verb, '*désarticuler*' (to dislocate) has no English equivalent as such. This looseness in the architecture is fine-tuned here. Such operational necessities as the wind lip at the base of the slabs, the fire flaps proposed within the stack itself, the screens and the essential walkways contribute to this idiom of adaptiveness. Just as a painter is unequivocal in choosing colour, Alsop made Le Grand Bleu a blue to match, in exact tonal and spectral colour composition, that prescribed by Yves Klein in defining what he dubbed 'International Klein Blue'. The clear suggestion of infinity was implicit in the choice.

A member of Alsop's design team described the evolution of the atrium thus:

> the imagining of the double glass walls was precise in scope and detail. All the circulation in the *administratif* blocks was contained within these. The narrow spaces would have been threaded with walkways – moving along between two apparently endless glass planes, lateral sunlight streaming through, filtered and dappled, fresh air moving freely upwards and along. He might have felt obliged to commission music in such a compelling experiential mechanism, to be played within those spaces, to complete the enchantment.[3]

At Le Grand Bleu, a concept of political, hence physical accessibility is fostered by the arrangement of elements: by clear differentiation of functional spaces and structure in a wholly tectonic apparatus; and, overall, by the idea of infinity, symbolically inferred also by colour schemata, especially on the exterior of the whole. It is, too, a curious coincidence, noted only by the politicians of Region No 13, that each '*administratif*' block stands on two parallel rows of thirteen columns each. At night this apparent symbolism glows effusively in the starlight of the *Midi* sky.

The '*délibératif*', by contrast is separate, yet linked in, equipped with a massive sun-shielding canopy on the eastern side, removing the maximum effects of the morning sun as it burns down on the chamber of government, itself a separate identity, disarticulated from the remainder of the complex.

In the early 1990s a new realism has been evident, a search for something more appropriate to this time, more profound than the games of the 1980s. The novels of Martin Amis convey this changed mood, portraying a society in the throes of disintegration and the dispersal rather than the dissemination of wealth.

If today, looking back, it appears that the bland prescriptions of Francis Fukuyama are the logical conclusion to *Complexity and Contradiction*[4] (or indeed its corollary) compounded further perhaps in this cuisine by the elaborate metamorphoses of Lyotard, one can envisage all three suppositions as mutually supportive rather than as ultimately conclusive; supportive of, a *tendenzia*. If we rely upon CNN to validate the contemporary *zeitgeist*, we are all reminded that historical precedent supposes, to quote Fukuyama, 'the re-emergence of illiberal doctrine out of economic failure'.[5] New fundamentalisms are set to distort pluralisms now recognised as commonplace, while the homogenisation of mankind seems the inevitable result of a contemporary technology driven fast by modern economics, and enhanced by rationality; simultaneously, in debt to both Kenneth Frampton and Hal Foster, we can acknowledge the survival of a 'resistance', not only geographically-based but underpinning a culture reliant upon the issue-based assertion of political and cultural identities. As Damien Hirst said in an interview: 'you worry about your complexion but you'll be a skull in less than a hundred years.'

In the vanguard of contemporary art, the leaders such as Hollein and Alsop reach a common ground – the hazardous territories of the Sublime – today more than ever. It is here, within the context of the Sublime rather than in the cloying orchards of the Picturesque, that truly innovative creation develops, equally potently for architects, artists, writers or film makers.

This is an abbreviated version of a lecture given by the author in honour of Professor Colin Rowe at the College of Architecture and Planning, Cornell University, on 27 April 1996.

Notes
1 Dr Samuel Johnson in *The Rambler*, 25 January 1752.
2 Colin Rowe, *The Architecture of Good Intentions*, 1994, Academy Editions (London), p111, quoted from *The Works of The Right Honourable Edmund Burke*, London, 1845.
3 Michael Spens, *Le Grand Bleu – William Alsop*, 1994, Academy Editions (London), p48, J Adams.
4 Robert Venturi, *Complexity and Contradiction*, 1966, Museum of Modern Art (New York)
5 Francis Fukuyama, *The End of History and The Last Man*, 1992, The Free Press (USA).

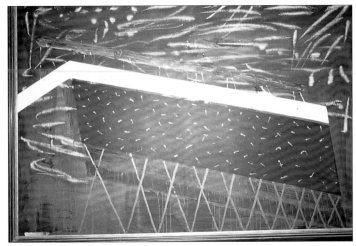

Development painting for Le Grand Bleu, Will Alsop

Le Grand Bleu, Will Alsop

Cardiff Bay Visitors' Centre

WILL ALSOP
FRAMES OF MIND

I was born in 1947. To date I am what my culture has made me, combined and mixed with a sense of my self. What culture has formed this life and this person? Post War – Baby Boom (even though my father was 64 when my twin sister and I were born) – rationing – uncertainty – a separation from Europe (from the former threat). The radio (Home Service, World Service) presented Red Skeleton and Fats Waller and the TV (bought by my parents to allow access to the Coronation) gave me *Children's Hour*. Waller to Dominoe. Haley to Elvis. (Somewhere was big Boy Cruddup). Vera Lynn lingered on but to an 11-year-old Little Richard was better. Dave Brubeck was more interesting than Chris Barber but neither were as good as Miles Davis. Culture came from America and as I became more familiar with the subject of architecture (I had wanted to be an architect from the age of six), I realised that with the exception of Le Corbusier, this too came from the States. When in 1968 I arrived at the AA in London, all eyes were on the USA: they had Mies Van de Rohe, Wright, Soleri and the Whole Earth Catalogue. Buckminster Fuller prodded the conscience and expanded the perception of architecture to an awareness of environmental responsibility; Philip Johnson never retired and we were sent Charles Jencks to tell us what was going on. Our very own P Reyner Banham even went to live there – such was the attraction of the West. This was the age of the Brain Drain and this was fed by money. My culture up to and beyond the age of 21 was in fact the culture (modified) of another country. The majority of art emerged from the county somewhere over the western horizon, the people of which started their evening when we were all in bed. My world was formed by their art, their films, their comics and their music. Life was already a collaboration. Even sex was American. The boundaries between all these activities was broken down into a soup – I was at one with this soup. Cross disciplinarianism was natural – it was the status quo. Today the problem in America is that there are no boundaries; there is no courage to accept that one discipline is different to another. There would appear to be a democratic right to allow any person to announce that they can do anything yet very few have the courage to challenge this. As a result of this the collaboration has often become more significant than the work; the means rather than the end; the process, not the result; the sensation not the responsibility. The filling in of meaningful time, not a mission.

There is, of course, a point to cross-disciplinary work. This point is dependant on a number of issues:

• mutual respect – the architect and collaborator must know each other. The work of each collaborator must in itself present an attractive possibility to each of the parties.

• the terms of the collaboration are clearly there for the sole benefit of the collaborators. No intermediary agency must be allowed to promote collaboration. They must come from the individual disciplines themselves. In this way 'art and architecture' cannot exist without the agreement of the participants. All 'arrangers' of collaborators are leeches who take money out of the system – for nothing.

• where the will exists the opportunity exists for collaborators to discover what they do not know.

The first collaboration for the architect and the artist is with their own history. The background to ones' life feeds the work. It is only in architecture, however, that a culture has developed which denies architects the use of their experience. A code of behaviour, or manners, has evolved within architecture that has resulted in its criticism becoming self-referential. Often the code (resulting in named styles and movements) becomes very simplistic and highly accessible to the general public. This accessibility results in architecture being hoisted on its own petard. The other arts – painting, sculpture, dance, music, etc, do not suffer the rigours of public debate at the point of creation. Often artworks are rejected by the public, usually through a fear of the unknown. The architect is an artist and must be allowed to develop and test concepts and projects beyond the limits imposed by public debate. The function of a building is not a constraint. I am an architect who believes in working with the same openness as an artist. In this way I do not need to collaborate with anyone.

Curiously, because of this attitude, I collaborate with artists as a matter of course. I also collaborate with engineers, clients, acousticians, traffic engineers and so on.

The architect is free to collaborate.

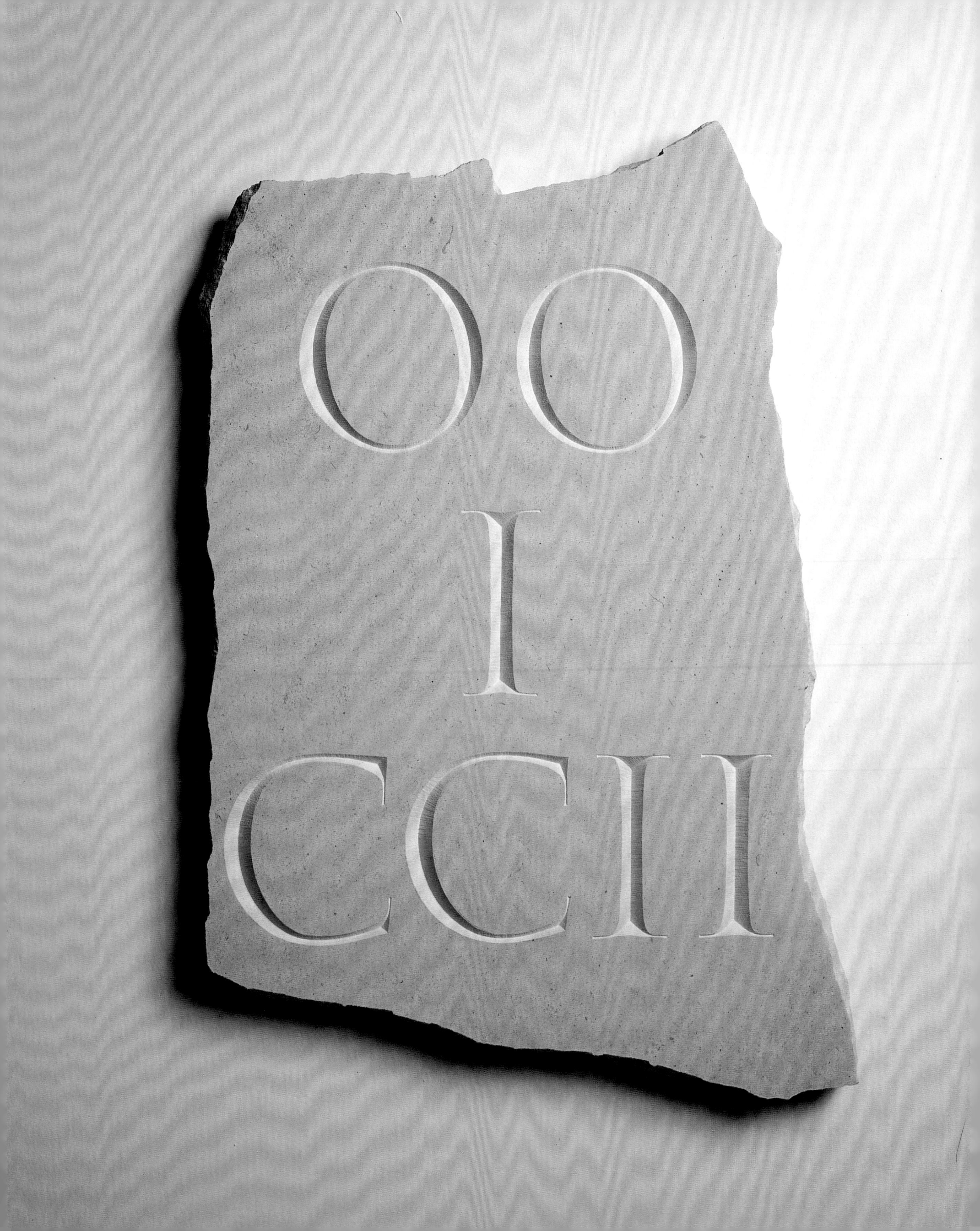
OO
I
CCII

OM UNGERS AND IAN HAMILTON FINLAY

BUILDINGS WHICH DEPICT A BETTER WORLD

A Critique by Harry Gilonis

. . . all great buildings [are] put sui generis *into the utopia, the anticipation of a space adequate to man.*   Bloch

How might architecture (which Bloch saw hovering, havering, between the Extreme Box and kitsch) depict, or enact, a better world? In a text published in English in 1987, Oswald Mathias Ungers (b1926) had this to say about the 'New Abstraction':

the formal language . . . is a rational and intellectual one, not based on accidents or sudden and fanciful inspiration. Emotion is controlled by rational thinking, and this is stimulated through intuition. The dialectical process between the two polarities is almost essential in a creative process aimed towards a gradual improvement of ideas, concepts, spaces, elements and forms. It involves the process of abstraction until the object in its fundamental structure, the concept in its clearest geometry and the theme in its most impressive image appear.

(He went on to acclaim 'basic concepts of space . . . for instance . . . the four column space . . . the courtyard block . . . the perfect cube . . . ') Turning from the page to the work, we see what he means. His 1989 private library, built next to his own house in Cologne (1958-9), is a cube – known, indeed, as 'the Cube House'. The exterior skin of the building is light-absorbent dark basalt, helping to highlight the object, the concept, the structure: a pure platonic form, the simultaneous appearance of idea and building, of an idea embodied in a building.

In the light of this ethos, this practice, Ungers' collaborations with the Scots poet, artist and landscape gardener Ian Hamilton Finlay (b. 1925) can be simplistically explained: Finlay is well-known for his commitment to Neo-classicism, and that school produced, of course, powerful and revolutionary architecture obsessed with the pursuit of pure platonic forms. (Claude Ledoux is said to have built in nothing but cubes, spheres, pyramids and ellipses). But 'Revolutionary' appears above with a lower-case 'r'. Finlay is equally famous for his commitment to the French Revolution, which, far from realising any of these monumental projects actually went so far as to imprison Ledoux and guillotine his client – not for a lapse in taste, but for building (1784-87) the 46 *barrières*, tollhouses in the customs-wall around Paris. (Its breach in the night of 12-13 July 1789 was far more Revolutionary, and far more important, than the taking of the Bastille a day or so later.) Ledoux, then, was revolutionary, not Revolutionary; and for the majority of his contemporaries his tax-houses were far from being emblems of a better world. Was that implicit in his architecture? On the contrary. Bloch, an admirer of Ledoux, wrote of the *opposite* stance, Functionalism, that it 'reflects and doubles the ice-cold automatic world of the commercial society . . . its alienation . . . its human beings subject to the

division of labour . . . its abstract technology'.

Ungers, a vehement opponent of the Functionalist ethos, would doubtless agree, having said that it is 'by means of formal language that function and construction are translated into art'. Of course, this is not to say that *bad* Neo-classicism cannot be inhuman, amounting as it does to the sterile incarceration of history, implicit in its conclusion (*pace* Semper) that – since style results from the harmony between a building and its historical origins – everything has already been done, and done properly. Even if the variations of form might be nearly endless (and it is perhaps impossible to conceive of them all), this still leaves the architect as the actor, if not the puppet, of history. Hardly Revolutionary *or* revolutionary. Construction in a tradition has to be more than cloning, more than the refined conclusion of sequence leaving the onlooker no part but silence. Some of what occurs in historical sequence is anticipated and continues to be relevant, and this constitutes a surplus, a continuation of the implications, open or hidden, of the cultural 'constellations' of the past. This is vitality, utopian possibility, not repetition, closure and the 'End of History'. The architect, referring to history and tradition, transforms and modifies. As Ungers has said, this is not imitation, 'for that would mean . . . that one considered history not as an existential problem, but as a series of episodes'.

We are here a long way from PoMo Heritage Architecture; as, too, is Finlay's stone sculpture *Vitruvius/Augustus – Vitruvius/ Robespierre* (1986, with John Sellman). It consists of four stone blocks, to be read in sequence; these recapitulate the origin-myth of the Corinthian capital. As they grow, acanthus leaves curling form volutes; as these 'freeze' into architecture, a Revolutionary rosette appears between them. Robespierre is implicit in *pierre*; and he appears again in Finlay's work (with Nicholas Sloan) for Ungers' library. Within the four-columed space (one of Ungers' 'basic concepts'), a series of railings frame a two-storey central well, the heart of the cube. Each railing is divided by a plinth and each plinth supports a white plaster bust. Each of these represents one of (in the historian Robert Palmer's words) the 'Twelve Who Ruled'. These, the members of the Comité du Salut Public, made up the *de facto* government of Revolutionary France. Barère, Billaud-Varenne, Carnot, Collot d'Herbois, Couthon, Hérault de Sechelles, Jeanbon Saint-André, Lindet, the two Prieurs, Robespierre and Saint-Just appear and re-appear in Finlay's work; not a pantheon – they were human – but exemplars. Neo-classicists often placed statues of sages and worthies in their libraries, preferring them to licentious and foolish classical divinities, Finlay concurs; the Twelve are key figures in his programme of 'Neo-classical rearmament'. Saint-Just observed that 'authority belongs not to the individual but to the law whose agent he is', so it is entirely apposite that the busts – based on an original in the British Museum – should be identical save for the

Library fragment, *Karlsruhe, 1987-92*

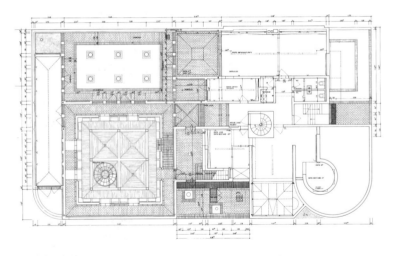

names. As similar as platonic forms, as different as individuals, they stand as a reminder that true Neo-classicism has both a history and a human face.

. . . if number, measure and weighing be taken away from any art, what remains will not be much.
Plato, as quoted by Zukofsky

Ungers is adamant that the architect's chief responsibility is for *form*; 'functional principles contain no form-giving elements', which is to say, they cannot be *a priori* bases for aesthetic decisions. This flies in the face of Functionalism that finds beauty in the way technical requirements can *necessitate* form. For Ungers, as for classical architects since Vitruvius, function is subordinate – or, as Finlay put it once, 'Technology – Epic Convenience'. *Firmitas*, *utilitas*, *venustas*; structurally stable, useful (spatially appropriate) – and beautiful. Functionalism, by negating memory, risks the loss of cultural and historical values which – for Finlay equally as for Ungers – are implicit in form. Our concern, then, is not with pattern, the appearance of regularity found when any sufficiently rich structure or system is examined closely (a paradoxical lesson of chaos theory); it is, rather, with order. (The architectural pun is unintentional, but apposite; both Ungers' garden in Cologne and Finlay's in Scotland contain freestanding – that is, non-structural, non-functional – classical columns.) Such an interest in order – in *coherent* pattern – is clearly evident in the second collaboration to be considered here, the 1980-84 Baden regional library in Karlsruhe. Built from scratch as a new regional capital in 1715, much of Karlsruhe is itself ordered; much of it was laid out, in a fan shape – a Neo-classical city, radiating, if not *radieuse* – by a local architect, Friedrich Weinbrenner (1766-1826). Ungers too has spent time thinking about how to relate, to correlate, elements in a landscape, built or natural; how to transform what he sees in order to derive the components of a vocabulary from it. As he has said, 'architecture means an analytical discussion with the environment which is developed and stamped by time'. The *Landesbibliothek* in Karlsruhe is very much a homage to the classical heritage of the city, which means in effect Weinbrenner; and much of the building is shaped by a thinking consideration of his Stephanskirche (1808-14), which faces the new library from across a road. The Stephanskirche is derived in part from Roman baths fenestration and gable – and the Pantheon – the high dome. All these elements reappear, transformed, in the library. To a naive onlooker Ungers' response might seem anachronistic, over-simplified or stark; but Neo-classical architects also preferred unbroken contours, clear lines, sharp angles, wall-openings unsoftened by surrounds, and limited articulation of facades. Weinbrenner himself on occasion used 'Tuscan', that is *unfluted*, Doric columns, in order to give a clearer, more formalised outline, adapting strict classicism to contemporary needs; he was no pedant. His first design was a rotunda rising from a cube; the church is actually cruciform with a rotunda. Ungers' building is a cube, mixing Weinbrenner's *pronaos* with the entries to two long wings to give something of the same spatial effects. The church interior has columns of the ornate Corinthian order, whereas the library's are simplified into unornamented piers, neither protruding nor recessed, smooth white plaster between openings. Ungers' interior is also referential to other libraries, including the Bibliothèque Ste-Geneviève and Smirke's round reading room in the British Museum. The interior piers bear stone sculptured reliefs (by Finlay with Brenda Berman and Annet Sterling), irregularly-shaped, regularly lettered. (There is not space here to go into the Neo-classical interest in the irregular and rough-edged, a 'natural' signifier to set against 'cultured' forms.) Each 'plaque' carries Roman numerals, with – perhaps unexpectedly – zeros. These too are not anachronisms; Hellenistic mathematicians used a symbol similar to the zero to indicate empty spaces, and the concept was carried to India, to re-enter Europe via the Islamic world. Here it hints at spans of time, extents of space, other cultures. Appositely; for the figures, translated into 'arabic' numerals, give the dialling codes for cities with major libraries – 00 30 1 Athens, 00 39 6 Rome, etc. (One might remark that these works are not as easy to decode as Ungers' building but it can be fairly said that the finer points of both emerge only with intelligent scrutiny. If neither is entirely open and giving, Finlay's remark is pertinent: 'Neo-classicism emulates the Classical while at the same time withholding itself'.) Just as fragments of classical stone inscriptions have ended up in museums, so their successors, books or scraps of parchment, are now stored in libraries; here a number-system millennia-old meets the zero, potent signifier of the computer age. In the hush of this four-storey reading room machine talks silently to machine, library to library, around the world. The ordered satisfaction of the interior is paralleled by the calm regularity of the world of numbers – 'sensual logic', in Schlegel's phrase. Yet the presence of 00 20 3 Alexandria – a library, the storehouse of a culture, burnt as fuel by the caliph Omar – might remind us of the fragility of learning, of libraries, so easily reduced, with their contents, to fragments.

> . . . architecture's task lies in so manipulating external inorganic nature that it becomes cognate to mind as an artistic outer world. Hegel

Ungers' work was shown at the Hamburg Künsthalle in 1984; his exhibition, *OM Ungers Architect*, combined schematic drawings on the walls with, in front of these, to scale and thus presenting an overall abstracted and sculptural effect, white plaster models. It is thus apt that he should employ the abstract, unornamented cube here too, in this, the second extension to the Künsthalle. All

Fragments of the library, Karlsruhe, 1987-92

New Künsthalle, Hamburg

three buildings occupy a raised space between two lakes, the so-called 'Museum Island'. The earlier buildings (1868/86, by von der Hude and Schirrmacher, red-brick Neo-classical; extended in 1907 by Albert Erbe, grey travertine turn-of-the-century modern) face the new building across the low truncated pyramid that makes up the courtyard. The first Kunsthalle was, in a quite revolutionary manner, lit by lantern rather than natural light on the upper floor; Ungers' building likewise has reduced upper fenestration, giving carefully-aligned views, particularly across the Innenalster and Aussenalster lakes to either side. As with the Karlsruhe project, thought about the history of the site is evident at a glance (in sharp contradistinction to projects Ungers has condemned as offering 'the anonymity of an environment based upon functional organization [where] evolved places and distinctive historical characteristics were sacrificed on the altar of the utilitarian constraints of functionalism'). Again, this is *Neo-classical* revolution; Lodoli wrote that 'ornament is not essential but accessory to proper function and form', and Perret put it more bluntly: 'ornamentation always conceals a structural defect'. The pure form has its own strengths. Pertinent here is Finlay's sculpture (one of the 1984 *Talismans and Signifiers* set, with Richard Grasby) which cites Vitruvius on the cube as a form – 'it stands firm and steady so long as it is untouched'. The new Kunsthalle again combines two of Ungers' basic spatial concepts, the cube and the courtyard, and it is in the latter, outside the building, that Finlay's contribution can be seen. Ungers has linked his design and the French revolutionary architecture of pure geometry, and it is to French Revolutionaries that we return, specifically Saint-Just. (There is a series of plaster busts of him inside the main entrance to the new Künsthalle, modelled on that made by David d'Angers, each bust bearing a quotation from his writings: these are by Finlay, with Annet Sterling again.) Guillotined after the *coup* of Thermidor, Saint-Just left behind him an incomplete manuscript, the *Republican Institutions*. In the second chapter, 'De la Société', we can read this phrase: 'La patrie n'est point le sol, elle est la communaute des affections'. Mindful of the unprecedented and committed internationalism of the French Revolution (as international in its way as the Neo-classical style it helped spread), Finlay has chosen to permute this phrase in four languages. (His 'correction' of Saint-Just's idiosyncratic *point* to *pas* only helps universalise the text.) These words, in laser-cut grey granite letters (with Berman and Sterling again), are set around the periphery of the red granite of the courtyard:

LA PATRIE N'EST PAS LE SOL SIE IST DIE GEMEINSCHAFT DER GEFVEHLE [THE NATIVE LAND IS NOT THE LAND] *ELLE EST LA COMMUNAUTE DES AFFECTIONS LA PATRIA NO ES LA TIERRA* [IT IS THE COMMUNITY OF FEELINGS] *DIE HEIMAT IST NICHT DAS LAND ES LA COMUNIDAD DE LOS AFECTOS*

'The native land is not the land, it is the community of feelings'.

This is absolute idealism, the idealism that reshaped a continent – 'Happiness is a new idea in Europe'. And, like all public inscriptions, it must perforce address *any* potential passer-by; not an arcane communication coded in Latin but a plain message which has, built into its form, a statement about its nature. Were the languages unmixed, or were there but one, the statement could be naive, or prescriptive; but here it has become performative, enacting however temporarily for any single reader – what it wishes to see happen. How apt this work is for an artist and an architect who both operate internationally, speaking international artistic/architectural 'languages'; as too for this site, an internationally renowned museum housing art from all over the world. Ungers has said in an interview that 'social architecture is a degree of quality (not quantity) in the design of public places . . . experienced and lived in by the community, the most important basis of identity for people in the town'. Architecture, as built environment, is unavoidable, unlike any other art; and thus must have a public ethical content – or, by denying this, implicitly negate such.

To close, Bloch again, on Hegel's definition of architecture (given above):

> architecture sees as its task to work inorganic nature into such a shape that it becomes allied to the mind as an artistically valid outside world . . . The architectural utopia is thus the beginning and end of a geographical utopia itself, of . . . the dreams of an earthly paradise. Great architecture ought to stand as a whole like a constructed Arcadia.

For Ungers, the metaphysical content of architecture lies in each individual's fulfilment and enrichment; for Finlay 'Classicism aims at Beauty, Neo-classicism aims at Virtue'. In these projects – and in others which are in process – these two attributes are inextricably melded. For, as Bloch further said – noting that architecture must 'retain man as a question' – 'hope is as old as architecture'.

Further Reading (covering the first two projects only):

Martin Kieren, *Oswald Mathias Ungers*, Artemis Verlags, Zurich, 1994

P Simig (ed), *Ian Hamilton Finlay: Works in Europe 1972-1995*, Editions Cantz, Ostfildern, Germany, 1995. Includes text by Harry Gilonis and photography by Werner J Hannappel

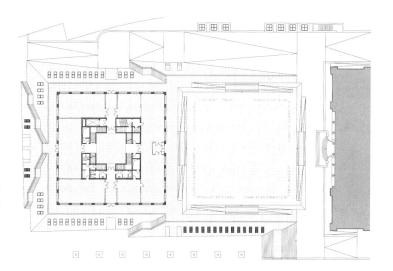

New Kunsthalle, Hamburg, FROM ABOVE: Courtyard; plan of the ground floor

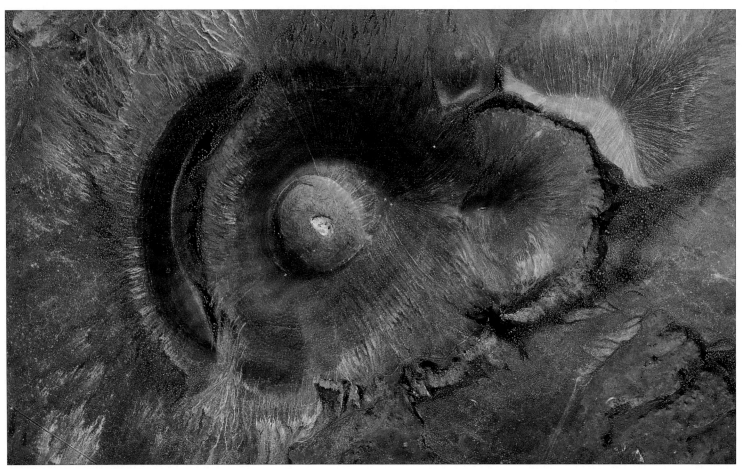

Roden Crater, Arizona

JAMES TURRELL
INTERVIEW BY ESA LAAKSONEN

Esa Laaksonen: I would like to discuss your views on light which is the main issue within your work, and the sensitivities of the human body to light and colour, and also your thoughts about perception. I understand that you have spent a long time in solitude, in prison and in darkness – therefore, it seems to me that the power of force in your work lies within the experiences that you had in asylum. Is that correct?

James Turrell: It was certainly formative in a sense that these experiences formed the will to work with light. In terms of being an artist I can't say that I took that experience well, because it was forced upon me – nor did I systematically explore what it is to have that aloneness, that solitary quality, without being forced into it. Now, with will and with free choice, I enjoy it.

The question about light. First of all, I would like to say that there is never no light – the same way you can go into an anechoic chamber that takes away all sound and you find that there never really is silence because you hear yourself. With light it is much the same way – we have that contact to the light within, a contact that we often forget about until we have a lucid dream. Asking ourselves where the light in the lucid dream comes from gets us near to these thoughts about the power of light. This power has, first of all, power in its physical presence. I like to bring light to the place that is much like that in the dream – where you feel it to be something itself, not something with which you illuminate other things, but a celebration of the thingness of light, the material presence, the revelation of light itself. This is something that allows light to live more than the forming of it. A lot of the learning to work with light, since it doesn't form by working with the hands as clay does, is this working with light through thought. There is an architecture of thought, the structuring of logic, of thinking, of the space of thought, and that is the province of architecture as much as building these buildings that we work in and use in a very pragmatic sense. Music structures this as well, as do certain things in art.

At this moment, I'm working very primitively with light, because I don't have many instruments with which to work it, but I work it in the way I can, and that is mainly to bring to the conscious awake-state, the light that inhabits these spaces that we know in the dream. So it's not a surprise for anyone to see the light like this, but it is a mild surprise to see it here because it seems to have this other quality, slightly other-worldly in that we know it from another place but we do not know about it. In architecture we discuss the space between form and it being positive and being filled. But rarely do we create this space. It's more rhetorical. So that when you see it, it is not a surprise.

EL: This brings us to the idea about entering a space, the entrance, airports and coming.

JT: Submission and the idea of what it takes to enter the space of a book. When we open a book and read it, often people pass through the space where we are reading and we are so in the space of the book that we don't notice people passing by and in a sense we are more in the book, in a space generated by the author, than we are in the physical space where we physically sit. This price of admission that was paid by submitting and giving over to the book, is also something that is required in terms of looking at architecture and entering a building, entering a space with that kind of quality, as well as is in looking *into* a work of art as opposed to looking *at* it. Looking at it is something that's very difficult. You see this in how people react to contemporary art, because there is some reason why they have difficulty deciding to enter it

So that's the price of admission. That we've made the price high, maybe a bit too high, is something art needs to think about, architecture as well. But we've made it high because it has taken a lot to do this and I guess that's a part of the reason. In terms of spaces, spaces before the space, spaces before the work, you have this pre-loading in the way of setting someone up for the experience to come – whether its just with dark adaptation, the time to let the eye open, or whether it is a loading with a certain colour so that when they come into another colour, this mixing of after image and colour from the image happens and enriches the experience. There's a lot of this that does go on in making these spaces.

EL: So you are also talking about concentrating and giving time and allowing time for perception when entering.

JT: Yes, this entry is very important, because, first of all, in time given there is grace. This mercy asked for is actually time. Time to change your life as in asking God for mercy, it's like asking for more time to change, to alter, whatever. But in terms of an experience, that grace is to give it time so that it does not have to be an impact piece that is seen and beheld with one glance. I want something to grow on us. So that it begins to realise itself slowly, not all at once.

EL: It is like entering an old cathedral in relative darkness and giving yourself time to adjust to the peace and the light and the interior colours.

JT: Your colour sensitivity will open up, your eyes open up to themselves. By giving it time there is discovery. It is sort of sublime and this is part of it for me, this something that doesn't happen at once: this revelation that isn't given all at once. It's a bit like the difference between sportive lovemaking and then actually making love with someone you love, its quite a different situation.

EL: At the moment you are building this huge project in Arizona in Roden Crater and I find the architecture that you are building

Skyspace I *(day), 1972*

Skyspace I *(twilight), 1972*

there really special. Actually, you are not really building space but you are building instruments for light.

JT: Generally I would say that I make these spaces to capture and hold light. So I must use form, but I'm really involved in making architectural space. For me the form must become secondary. It's nice to have a volcano because that's going to be the form and that's not something I made. But it allows me to have many curvilinear spaces that are neutral. If I have a rectilinear space, as we have in this room and most rooms for the exhibition of art, and if I can make an elliptical space in those rectilinear rooms, it's very strong because it is no longer neutral in the rectilinear building. But our vision is not rectilinear, our vision is sort of two spheres together that actually make an ellipsoidal shaping of the perceptual field.

So if you create spaces that are rectilinear and still have them neutral in this very curvilinear, voluptuous earth form of the volcano in which all the forms are actually parabolic or elliptical . . . There's one circular part, one crater that is actually within seven feet of being circular on a radius of 800 feet, 814 feet. It is within seven feet of being a perfect circle, which is amazing. This gives me a way to make curvilinear spaces neutral, whereas it is not quite as appropriate in museums and spaces that are rectilinear. The rectangle, sort of the slightly off square is much more neutral than is a circle or an ellipse in these situations. Otherwise it can become shaped canvases. When you come in you can see that there is forming of form, but what becomes very positive is this thing between the space, in the work that I do. At the crater I make an architecture of space and I use these forms to capture the light, to hold it, to, in a way, give it form, give it the space to reside. But its clear that its done so that it doesn't reside on the wall. The light seems to fill the space. I think that's something you can feel. But it needs this architecture of form as well to capture light. Because I don't want to take away from the form of the volcano, making everything underground avoids actually forming the outside of these spaces into a building. They are in fact built but they are underground so that the outside really continues to be the volcano. The reason that they are underground is partly for that fact, but more for the fact that I make light powerful by isolating it, and also that it is not very much light that I isolate. You may be looking at the light of Venus alone, if you are dark-adapted for about an hour and a half . . . We see that well!

The reason I do this is that if you take your flash into a cave or a place that excludes all other light, it becomes quite powerful. So I need to have these spaces that are protected from other ambient light. I'm just taking the light from where I want it. So that's why there is this underground architecture that in a way shares its outside form and opening with the bunker as in bunker architecture. Where the openings are made precisely, everything else is protected. In that way it also gives protection, it's cool in

the summer and actually somewhat warm in the winter. You can have places that capture and hold heat by being contained at the top and will become cold sinks by letting hot air go out and yet are shaded. This gives me a way to have a kind of a sparkling elegance in the human inhabiting of these spaces but it's made primarily for the habitation of light. That is something we can walk through, even though all these sinks are completely open. That is, there is no glass: I can make the feeling of glass or the ending of the space quite easily, visually without having to do it with material. Everything is open, but at the same time it is protected, that's why it's underground.

This architecture, in terms of its forms, shares similarity with the bunker architecture, in terms of its openings, except that we're not looking at fields of fire, we are looking up to certain portions of the sky and protecting all else, and on the interior formed out in a way that it speaks of the naked eye observatory, say at Tycho Brahe or the work of the astronomer Jai Sing in Jaipur and Delhi. So it has that kind of design from the outside-in aspect and it does have an architecture of form which I utilise to capture the light and hold it, thereby making a certain architecture of space.

I also pay attention to looking out from a space as in PSI Gallery's 'Meeting' (1980-86, Long Island City, New York) so that there is not only accepting light in maybe deeper space and out of the space. So I'm trying to pay attention to those qualities and in doing that in the outside form – where architecture normally has its sense of style – I have nothing because that's just the volcano.

EL: Is Roden Crater your lifework?

JT: Well, a little bit that way. But on the other hand I'll have to get that done so that I can get on with my lifework. It's a project that is a little bit too big for me to bite off and chew easily. We'll be finished a little bit before the year 2000. But we decided to restore the natural site and that will take time and then we also need to prepare some other things in terms of access and in other things of this sort. That's a good time for us to begin.

EL: For me the life span of the happenings at the Roden Crater projects is enchanting.

JT: To some degree I made a pre-made ruin. I have to confess that I have a great love for civic space that is emptied of use. Which would be something like Monte Albán or Chitzen Itza or Delphi or Valley of the Kings. These are things that once had use. Now these are just open to the elements and you have to just feel what goes on there by the feelings that the spaces gives to you and you surrender to that experience. In a way I wouldn't mind seeing Washington DC emptied of use. It would be very bizarre. Here is this giant man sitting in this house: Abraham Lincoln, a

Afrum-Proto, *1967*

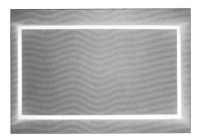

Raemar, *1968*

sort of bizarre human being in terms of his appearance. We have made huge reflecting pools and then little pavilions that almost turn into follies which is very interesting to me. I'm interested in making a space that has qualities we discover just from the space itself, not through any sort of use of other than some imagined use to them. That kind of space that you wander in and out of and through things is a space that I like very much.

I like the quality in permanence and impermanence. There are some airfields for World War II that the Americans used in the American desert to practice. Now they are being taken over by sands and by sage brush and also they are going under the ground. Ground is closing over them . . . But if you fly over you can just see the ghosting of this, even though it is completely covered with sand. Very thin at the moment, but its only 45-50 years now. The lines of Nazca form a very beautiful plan. Its like the earth is an emulsion that you are looking at. You see some things developing, coming out early in development and then some of these things can get covered by other things at later

stages of development. Also, there are some things that can be sort of blown away and then they start to come out. Old civilisations that begin to be exposed.

EL: I think somehow you are now touching the main qualities of art and architecture.

JT: Well, I hope so. I'm just one artist. You have just a view point in any work. It can't be everything to all people. You have some parts that you work on. I'm interested in those, time-sense, and that's one reason I use light. Even though light is passing through at 186 thousand miles per second, in fact there is a certain permanence to it, which is interesting . . .

This interview first appeared in ARK (Finnish Architectural Review), 5-6 1996. The conversation was held during the 'Permanence' Symposium at the Virginia Polytechnic Institute Department of Architecture, Blacksburg, Virginia, on 23 March 1996.

Hover, *1983*

ABOVE: Derby Cascade; BELOW: Primates Gallery, Natural History Museum, London

PAWSON WILLIAMS ARCHITECTS

ART AND ARCHITECTURE

Contribution and Collaboration

In finding the solution to an architectural problem, architects have frequently used the creative collaboration with the 'usual' construction team consultants, such as structural and environmental engineers and landscape architects in order to both solve problems and to generate new design approaches. However, the opportunity for a direct design liaison with an artist during the early design stage of a building is not as commonly found and may not always be on either the architects' or clients' agenda! For, whilst in some circles architecture seems increasingly to be viewed as a technical discipline, I believe there is a fundamental problem in seeing the architect as an enabler or a technician whose labours are merely to provide functional containers which are unconnected to the world of abstract creative thought. This position would deny that architecture is an art form capable of being a creative medium in its own right, or that an architect and an artist can act collaboratively.

The following four projects by Pawson Williams describe a wide range of possibilities created by the building process in relation to the artist and their work. Each of the projects has presented design challenges which have benefited from an abstract dimension and have created opportunities and new ways for exploring ideas. The proposal for the Langdon Cliffs Visitor Centre reflects the architects' creative exploration of a series of abstract issues and their relationship to the physical world. The second project, the architects' second placed entry for an invited competition for a new theatre and music college in Argenteuil, Paris, creates the potential for a major art work as a vital component of the building's composition and organisation. The final two projects, the Primates Gallery in London and the Derby Cascade, describe two occasions where the architects worked directly with artists from the inception of a project in the development of a design concept.

Langdon Cliffs Visitor Centre, Dover Harbour, Kent

The design response for this modest building was generated by a direct response to the particularly potent location and site which sits on the edge of the cliff overlooking the English Channel. With such an exposed elemental location, the building looks to address the unique sense of place by using a spatial language and sequence to create three distinct experiences, inspired by the most powerful properties of the site – the sky, the land and the sea. The building is organised as two simple timber boxes, joined and partially wrapped by a third element, a thick masonry wall. On entering the first compartment by the masonry portal, all reference to the sea and the dramatic views are obscured. This first enclosed volume becomes a place to pause and to refocus. Having cut off the views, this windowless space emphasises the relationship of the visitor to the sky and is lit from above through a fretwork of timber screens which are oriented to exclude direct sunlight whilst allowing a halo of sky to be seen as a personal window directly above the head of every visitor.

The second stage of the sequence is contained within the volume of the masonry wall and consists of a circular ramp which slips gently into the contours of the site, creating a linear exhibition space, whilst the dynamics of the landscape and site contours are felt through the gentle descent. The earth-like material of the walls and the floor, the sloping ground and the enclosed cavelike form of this space are all intended to reinforce the feeling that one is not only part of the landscape but also almost within the earth. At the bottom of the ramp the volume opens out into the final space where the solidity of the walls drops away to reveal the panorama where the sky meets the sea in a single line between two simple blocks of colour.

Centre Régional de la Musique et de la Voix, Argenteuil, Paris

The practice was invited to prepare designs for a new music college and theatre complex as part of an overall masterplan for Argenteuil on the edge of Paris. In formulating the early design strategy, the architects were convinced that the building should offer a public focus for the area by creating the required foyer space in such a way that it would relate to the whole of the new public square and the adjacent parkland. In addition to the high degree of transparency of the foyer walls, it was proposed that the main visual focus was to be a 17 metre-high projection screen on the back wall in order to draw the eye into the building in an attempt to further dissolve the barrier between inside and outside. The screen becomes an opportunity to creatively interpret and develop the internal artistic programme of the building.

The Primates Gallery, Natural History Museum, London

Inside the main hall of Alfred Waterhouse's Natural History Building, the Primates Gallery contains the work of a number of artists and is intended to work at several levels of interpretation.

Overlooking the main hall and running the full length of the existing first floor balcony, the new gallery is a formally weighted, linear deck insertion and sets up a rigorous architectural order to define the rhythm of the new work. Bronze, glass and stone are used to place the insertion in context by using materials common to the existing building but used in an entirely contemporary manner. The new architecture acts as a framework for a series of installations and new sculpture which echoes the zoological sculptural decoration of Waterhouse's existing building, whilst setting itself apart as a clearly separate insertion. The open edge of the gallery facing the main hall has been organised in a more familiar museological manner of display cases, lecterns and text, whilst by contrast, the window wall lays down threads of man's role as a creative animal with artistic reflections on other primates in sculpture, music, film and poetry. The whole composition aims to be seen as a development of two traditions: the architectural tradition set by Waterhouse's existing building and the historic museological tradition of the museum, whilst making a third reference directly to man as the 'creative primate'. By making comparisons between mankind and other primates, the normal role of the exhibition visitor as external observer is blurred, since, in part, the onlooker is engaged in self-observation, thus gaining a sense of proximity to other primates.

Derby Cascade, Derby

Whilst the previous project was fundamentally an architectural programme with the creative input of artists included as part of the developing architectural proposition, the Derby Cascade has no functional brief to resolve and was the development of an initial idea by the artist, William Pye, through joint input. This close collaboration between artist and architect developed following a competition run by Derby City Council for a new civic feature to form part of the remodelled Market Square. It is one of a number of public art projects which have been commissioned in Derby as part of a general re-landscaping of the main public areas of the city. However, this project was unusual in that due to the scale of the 'art work', it became like a small building with architectonic qualities and considerations. The initial concept of the cascade by William Pye was to produce a curtain of water running from a bronze weir which people could walk around and see from a variety of angles. The challenge was to have a water feature which invited interaction and was of sufficient scale and monumentality to address the square. Through a process of discussion and drawing, ideas were jointly developed which looked at achieving the initial artistic goals, whilst new ideas were introduced to the work by considering certain architectural and urban issues. The development of ideas about the public interaction with the water seemed to take the place of the normal fundamental architectural concerns of ordering circulation and providing enclosure and shelter: simply put, the Derby Cascade did not become a building by involving an architect and developing architectural ideas, but remained firmly a work of art.

We have found that our collaborations with artists have encouraged a continuing re-evaluation of the design process. Architecture, like art, must be an exploration of ideas and therefore strengthening the position of architecture firmly within the arts, should be firmly on our agenda.

The following essay gives a particular view of the relationship between 'Art Product' and 'Architectural Product' through the medium of drawings. Whilst the essay can be seen as separating the artist and the architect because of why they draw, the roles are transposable, with both being common bedfellows in the pursuit of the creative ideal.

Representation and Reality: The Artist and the Architect

The works of the artist and the architect have a significant and close relationship, with both being concerned with a number of common areas – the human condition, the use of light, composition, culture, ideas and the relationship of ideas to the physical world. They will also both spend much of their time drawing. The idea that the act of drawing is a common ground which lies between the artist and the architect, connecting the purpose for which the artist will draw or paint, to the architect, is a common belief. However, it is perhaps also within this same area of potential communality that the two disciplines are divided at a crucial stage of intent. For example, the apparent relationship between the painting by Corot of Santa Maria della Salute in Venice, the three dimensional object which we know as Santa Maria della Salute and the drawings from which the building was

constructed, seem to fall neatly into categories. At first, it would appear that the two drawings are different kinds of representation of a 'real' object, and that the *building* is the only reality. However, there is another interpretation that the motivations which generate drawings, with the painting of the building and the building, have more in common than the plans from which the Salute are constructed. In order to understand how the finished building, the formal plan drawing and the painting relate – which is real and which is merely a representation of reality – it is necessary to provide a clear definition of both representation and reality.

In his book *Objective Thinking*, Karl Popper set out in the essay entitled 'On the Theory of the Objective Mind', a means of understanding and interpreting reality. Popper's theory states that there are three separate and distinguishable worlds and that reality exists within all three. The three worlds are 'the physical world or the world of physical states', 'the mental world or the world of mental states' and 'the world of intelligibles, or of ideas in the objective sense'. Within the theory, the second world, the world of mental states, acts as a mediator between the other two worlds, as the first and third world cannot interact except through the intervention of the second.

The definition of representation given by the *Pocket Oxford Dictionary* is 'a calling of attention to something, a description of something', which for our purposes will therefore relate specifically to the description of a 'third world' concept or idea in terms of a 'first world' reality, the reality of the tangible object.

Other words, whose meaning may be confused in the context of this essay and which need clarification, are architecture, building and drawing. The word 'architecture' will be used when referring exclusively to the 'third world' concept embodied in a building and the word 'building' will be used when referring to the 'third world' idea and the 'first world' constructed and tangible object. The term 'drawing' which normally means 'art of representing by line in black and white or a single colour' (*Pocket Oxford Dictionary*), will be broadened to include all of the creative two-dimensional media such as painting and printing.

It is important to make the distinction clearer between the two different types of representation which are available to describe an idea or concept. Both the building and the drawing have the potential to represent, in the 'first world', ideas which originate in the 'third world'. The distinction between the two is obvious in that they express the idea in entirely different media. A building is made up of physical material to create a three-dimensional object which is occupied and used. A drawing, on the other hand, is made up of marks on a surface and is confined to two dimensions. However, this does not make any distinction between different types of drawings – for example, the painting by Corot of the Salute would appear to be of a completely different nature and intent to those drawings from which the building was constructed. The difference between the two types of drawing has obviously to be made in another context, not associated with the physical qualities of the medium. This context is concerned with the way in which a 'third world' idea can be expressed as a tangible object which the mind can interpret and therefore understand. It is also concerned with whether the medium used is intended as a final product, capable of interpretation as it stands, or as an intermediate stage on the way to the final expression of the idea. For example, it is the building Santa Maria della Salute which ultimately represents the creative ideas and objectives of the architect. The plans and sections were never intended as the final product, only diagrams depicting the physical form and arrangement to be interpreted by the master builder, from which the final form, the creative and abstract ideas will be manifest. However, Corot's drawing of the Salute and its surroundings was not essentially trying to describe the building. His concern was with exploring other ideas within the medium of painting and hence, he was using the Salute as a tool towards that end. This then appears to give us two categories of drawing which for convenience we shall call absolute-drawing and interim-drawing.

Absolute-drawing is a drawing which is used as an end in itself and is the representation in 'first world' terms of a 'third world' concept. Interim-drawing is a drawing which is an intermediate stage on the way to the final expression and as a diagram. This category includes drawings such as plans, sections, elevations and even working drawings, all of which have one thing in common: they do not directly represent the idea but describe how the idea will be represented in the building. This makes interim-drawings a second-hand description of the idea and any interpretation of the drawing needs to take this into account. Within this method of distinction, it seems to indicate that a completed building and absolute-drawings have more in common as a method of representing ideas, than do the two distinct types of drawing. Both absolute-drawings and buildings are final products (in terms of representation) and they are chosen to express a particular idea by the artist/architect, as being the most appropriate medium for the idea.

However, ideas are not mutually exclusive to the media, as it can be seen that similar abstract ideas may be explored in both absolute-drawings and completed buildings. This dual exploration is pointed out by Colin Rowe and Robert Slutzky in their essay, 'Phenomenal Transparency', where they attempt to show how the concept has been used in both building and drawing.[1] Although examples such as Robert Delaunay's *Simultaneous Windows* (1911) and Juan Gris' *Still Life* (1912) are compared in this essay, the drawings of Le Corbusier's *League of Nations Project* are compared to the constructed examples of the *Bauhaus, at Dessau* by Walter Gropius (1925-26). They are therefore comparing absolute-drawing examples in the first instance, but in the latter, they compare an interim-drawing example to a completed building. However, it is certain that when Rowe and Slutzky use the drawings of the *League of Nations Project* as examples, they are not using the drawings themselves but are interpreting them into what they think the building would be, as it is only through this interpretation that the idea of 'Phenomenal Transparency' may be perceived.

In conclusion, this interpretation of drawings, or any other creative medium, by looking more at its purpose than its form, gives a new possibility of understanding the creative output of either the artist or the architect. If we return to the three examples of the Santa Maria della Salute given at the beginning, the Corot painting is, hence, a first hand representation of ideas within the medium of drawing – an absolute-drawing; the plans of the Salute are second hand, two-dimensional representations of the ideas of the architect and therefore interim-drawings; and the completed building being a first hand representation (in three-dimensions) of those same ideas, making it an 'absolute-object'.

Notes

1 Rowe, Colin and Robert Slutzky, 'Transparency: Literal and Phenomenal', 1955-56; Colin Rowe, *The Mathematics of the Ideal Villa and Other Essays*, MIT Press, 1976.

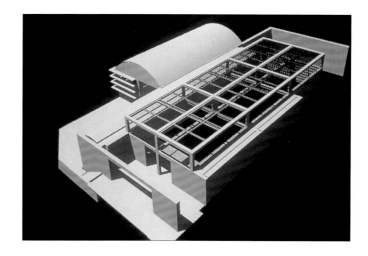

FROM ABOVE: Langdon Cliffs Visitor Centre, Dover Harbour; Centre Régional de la Musique et de la Voix, Paris; Downpour, British Embassy, Oman

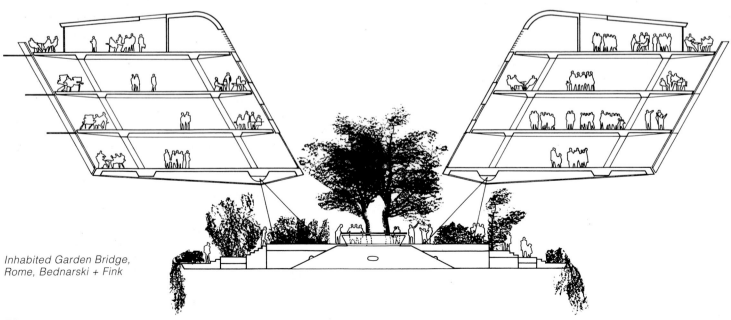

*Inhabited Garden Bridge,
Rome, Bednarski + Fink*

CEZARY M BEDNARSKI + PETER FINK
ART AND ARCHITECTURE

After two decades of active development of public arts in the UK very little progress seems to have been made in exploring the pivotal issues and rationale for collaboration between artists and others involved with the built environment. The discussion was, and is still, led by Public Art agencies and lobbies and does not seem to have developed beyond a series of general pronouncements on the desirability of such collaborations, and an advancement of mostly unsubstantiated socio-economic arguments, frequently used as a means to validate government led investment into the concept through either arts incentive awards or regeneration budgets. The emergence of lottery funding in this situation has considerably enforced the clear and strong economic self interests of the Public Art lobby and its motivation to promote artist/architect collaboration. The current understanding of the whole issue amounts to no more than restatement of the pragmatic adoption of culture since the Second World War by Western mass societies distinguished by a level of universal affluence as well as by a corresponding level of social stratification. Consequently, the discussion does not really touch on the underlying paradox of a society that feels comfortable with the idea of art and culture as an educationally instilled concept, but in practice is disinterested in the issue of critical legibility leaving culture to be dominated and driven by market forces. In turn this effectively condones the denigration of culture to a social engineering concept producing on one hand, an all pervading symbiosis of culture tourism and mass culture and on the other the extraction of 'high art' into the self validating and self serving art establishment. It is our belief that to be able to make any progress in exploring the issue of collaboration one must start from the examination of the actual personal practice and experiences of those engaged in collaboration. This is the first step towards an authentic and constructive understanding.

It is interesting to note that the discussion of the issue of collaboration seems to cause real difficulty all round, even though architecture was, and remains, a human activity highly dependent on team effort, not withstanding the individualist and lead role of the architect. Architecture is highly dependent on the active exchange of ideas, knowledge, skills and of labour. However the critical issue of who leads, when and how, and who dominantly shapes this process is not often discussed in any depth, as architects are accustomed to be nominally in charge. This notion is culturally endorsed by the emergence of the small percent of 'signature architects'. In the daily psychological reality of architecture as exemplified in the relationship between an engineer and an architect the question of who leads is never this clear.

Peter Rice in his book *Engineer Imagines* examines some of these issues by looking at what might be the difference between the engineer and the architect by saying that the architect's response is primarily creative, whereas the engineer's is essentially inventive.

The architect, like the artist, is motivated by personal considerations whereas the engineer is essentially seeking to transform the problem into one where essential properties of structure, material or some other impersonal element are being expressed. This distinction between creation and invention is the key to understanding the difference between the engineer and architect, and how they can both work on the same project but contribute in different ways. Indeed, now it is important that engineers start to educate both people within the profession and the public at large on the essential contribution that the engineer makes to even the most mundane projects.

He then concludes that the beginning of this process requires a full understanding of the problems faced by engineers as well as the examination of the position of the engineer in general.

In an interesting way this issue and some of the surrounding ambivalence can be currently detected in the relationships between architects, structural engineers and engineers specialising in large civil engineering projects such as bridge building. As bridges became the design icons of the nineties there is an intense revival of interest in exploring how architects could contribute to what was principally, until the arrival of Calatrava, the domain of a handful of niche civil engineering firms. It is interesting to note, in this context, the extent to which many engineers and architects in the UK are fundamentally critical of Calatrava's work in private, for example, frequently pointing to the extent to which its engineering clarity is, in their view, compromised by wilful architectural design. At the same time in public they pay lip service to his work as a 'positive' example of integration between engineering and architecture.

Ken Shuttleworth of Foster Associates in his talk 'Lipstick on a Gorilla' presented at the DHV conference on bridges tried to make a case for the inclusion of an architect in bridge building by saying:

On a building, even a really big building, the architect is the king. On a bridge, even a really tiny bridge the engineer is the master and the architect chooses lamp posts. Why is this? Why is there a such a colossal difference in the way projects are organised? Why is it seen that there has to be a difference?

He then proceeds to make the case for architects to be included, by pointing out that:

For me as an architect, the advantage of us working on the design of a bridge, is that we bring fresh approach. We encourage new thinking, challenge preconceptions and force engineers who have been designing bridges in the same way for years, to think again. More often than not an engineer will look at a solution for a bridge within a familiar and existing framework of ideas. Our advantage is that we don't bring any preconceptions to bridge design as we haven't done any before! This is our greatest strength.

It would be extremely interesting to see what the reaction would be if one substituted the notion of the bridge engineer for that of an architect, in an increasingly style orientated practice showing the first signs of design fatigue, and that of the architect with that of an artist. One could easily construct the dialogue around the example of the artist only being used by the architects in a patronising manner akin to specifying the lamp posts on a bridge. One could expect that this sort of argument about lack of practical experience being the greatest asset, if made by an artist, would not go down so well. Why then should bridge engineers be so enthusiastic to collaborate with architects on the basis of such an assumption?

In the light of this type of argument it is interesting to look at the engineers' reaction to the several bridges in existence or under construction in the UK where the design was architect led. In his article 'Should architects lead on bridge design?, Sydney Lenssen wrote: 'Don't be surprised to see the Department of Transport appointing an architect to design a major bridge sooner rather then later, leaving the architect to choose the engineer'. That would be taking matters too far for Ahm Povl of Ove Arup, who more fervently than most, led the crusade to improve British bridge design with the help of gifted architects. He said: 'But the danger is there and needs to be stopped.' Clearly if the engineer of his status is worried the issue at stake, i.e. of collaboration, warrants much more attention than it is receiving.

As a result of our collaboration on several bridge projects with both structural and bridge engineers we grew aware of these issues. Our experience of dealing with them became the catalyst for our exploration into the nature of the dialogue within the team and the need to deal directly and creatively with the issues of individual and mutual empowerment. As Peter Rice observed, the progress towards a concept of an expressed objective in the team design situation can be greatly influenced by the use of verbal communication and language as a key to what is happening. He observed that in his own experience in Britain sketching rather than talking is by far the more usual method of communication, a fact that he found constraining. In such an approach to architecture, the firming up of forms and the consistency of detailing assumes a value in itself. This in turn dramatically limits the opportunity to work collaboratively as it tends to exercise a deterministic control over such issues as intellectual basis, depth of meanings, external aesthetics and contextual urban design, all being project specific.

In the case of an artist and architect collaboration the key question is whether the artist is capable of making a contribution which opens a different perspective to architecture, or is this something to do with what the architects should be doing in the first place. Isamu Noguchi is one of the few artists working this century whose work made a coherent case for collaboration. In the fifties and sixties he worked with Gordon Bunschaft, the chief designer at Skidmore, Owings & Merrill and this still offers many useful pointers for today. They were introduced through Louis I Kahn, whose own thinking on architecture and art was profoundly akin to Noguchi's. As Kahn put it:

I only wish that the first really worthwhile discovery of science would be that it recognises that the unmemorable, you see, is what they are really fighting to understand, and the measurable is only a servant of the unmeasurable; that everything that man makes must be fundamentally unmeasurable . . . At the threshold, the crossing of silence

and light, lies the sanctuary of art, the only language of man. It is the treasure of shadows. Whatever is made of light casts a shadow; our work is of shadow; it belongs to light. Around the same time Noguchi wrote: 'There is a difference between the actual cubic feet of space and the additional space the imagination supplies. One is measure, the other, awareness of the void of our existence in the passing world.' Kahn's reverence for light as a shaper of all things was, of course, particularly satisfying for a sculptor. When looking at the long and productive period of collaboration between Noguchi and Bunschaft it is important to note the extent to which Bunschaft as an architect consciously empowered the artist on one hand and on the other the extent to which the artist went in his desire to understand the concerns of the architect. Bunschaft was a firm believer in initiating the artist at the beginning of the project, so that his contribution became a functional part of the overall design, and it was his idea to have a sculptor to design the total space adjacent to a building as a means of humanising the ground level areas around it. Defining the physical limits of a project, serving as an interpreter of the client's needs, and projecting his own definite views, Bunschaft constantly urged Noguchi towards inventive solutions for these spaces.

The example of Noguchi illustrates another important aspect of the interrelationship between art and architecture. Throughout most of his life Noguchi in spite of numerous large scale projects around the world, was actively ignored by the art world considering him to be only a commercial artist. He even remarked that he was 'the successful, unsuccessful sculptor'. Only when it became apparent that trying to uncritically import gallery artist into architecture could lead to disappointments, did Noguchi's work start to be seen for the achievement it represents.

In the UK we can now see the same process at work producing many local projects equivalent to Richard Serra's arc for New York, such as the now defunct Ash and Silk glass box by Vong Phaophanit in Greenwich. In this instance a Public Art Agency involved a gallery artist who produced a major work out of glass for an urban park in an industrial neighbourhood of London. This wholly inappropriate response to a site led not to a removal of the work as in the case of Serra but to its damage through vandalism. Whilst many participants in this project were doubtful about the direction it was taking, they were swept aside by arguments about aesthetics and the need not to compromise the artistic vision. The role of aesthetics is particularly interesting in relation to collaboration between architects and artist, and in relation to the public perception of the personal aesthetic iconography. The personal is of lesser interest, what matters is the shared.

Peter Brooks, the theatre director, in an interview recently touched on one of the fundamental dimensions of collaboration when he said: 'For the person who is touched by the transcendental nature of human experience, the WHY forgets the HOW. On the other hand, everyone who is acclaimed as a good craftsman and a real professional carries the danger that through their craftsmanship, their professionalism, their routine, the great WHY shrinks to the proportion of HOW'. Comparing the rhythm of a game of football with a theatre play Brook says: 'Within playing, lightness, seriousness, all fall into place as the movement of the ball which is sometimes quick and sometimes slow and sometimes stops for a moment.' There is no preconception or control behind the rhythm of a football match. Yet the natural rhythm and excitement is always there.

As can be seen from our joint work our current position has

evolved from a shared and firm belief that the times of an architect 'architecting', an engineer 'engineering' and an artist 'decorating' are over, and that the issues facing architecture and art are best tackled in 'the natural rhythm of the football match'. Undoubtedly this does require in the first instance a mutual will to play on the same team and a trust in the abilities of your fellow players. Many artists at the moment, similarly to many architects, do not seem to realise that this involves a conscious decision to prepare yourself and to make an effort to understand each others' method of working and concerns. It requires a conscious decision to leave your 'usual hat' behind and open yourself to the unknown world of a new project. It seems to us that various issues such as using information and emotions as building materials in architecture, the exploration of the cultural and contextual limits of materials, interactivity and mutability of object architecture, the sustainability beyond the environmental, to mention just a few, could benefit from a process of investigation involving a broader collaborative base, where an artist could have a valuable contribution to make.

We share in the belief that the childish fascination with our newly acquired ability to force technology to do anything we can think of, so evident in the late twentieth century, will subside in the next Millennium. It will give way to an intelligent and creative search for more reasoned, deeper felt solutions to our architectural needs. We consider that none of the well established and, indeed, already worn out, bridge design idioms and stylistics will be of interest. No 'Calatravesque' or other stylistics. In fact no style at all. As Balanchin used to say 'refining all possibilities to one that is inevitable, simple and clear' is the way forward.

> Genuine courage requires facing reality, facing accelerating change in a world that has no automatic brakes. This poses intellectual, moral and political challenges of great substance [. . .] Our machines are evolving faster than we. Unless we learn to live with them safely, our future will likely be both exciting as well as short.

This statement by Eric Drexler sets out explicitly our concerns as well as setting out a 'playing field' for our collaboration.

Albert Dock Bridge, Liverpool, Bednarski + Fink

BAUMAN LYONS ARCHITECTS
LEEDS CHINESE COMMUNITY CENTRE

If architecture is an art form then architects are by definition artists. Once this is recognised, argues Simon Warren, project architect of this warehouse redevelopment in Leeds, there should be no theoretical barrier to other types of artist collaborating on buildings when the programme requires.

When artists from disciplines other than architecture are involved, Warren believes there is no limit to the range of collaborative work that can be undertaken. Either the visual artefact is not produced by the artist, but the encompassing direction and the theory of the project is or, at the other end of the scale, a visual artist creates an artefact that is integrated into the architecture.

This small scheme by Bauman Lyons Architects started out as the latter type of collaboration, with an artist creating an artefact. However, halfway through the project, circumstances changed and the architect ultimately took on the role of 'visual artist' as well.

The Leeds Chinese Community Centre is a four-storey, turn-of-the-century warehouse on the edge of the developing Chinese quarter near the centre of Leeds. It had been out of use for a number of years and was severely dilapidated when purchased by the Leeds Chinese Community Association.

Most of the work involved essential structural repairs and weatherproofing, with only limited scope for innovation. However, the brief required that the new centre act as a visual focus to promote the activities of the Chinese community in Leeds. It was clear that the best means of achieving the required impact within a restricted budget was a new 'shop front' The facade was opened up to provide views in and out and increased daylight at ground floor level. A sculptural screen in metal designed by artist Madeleine Millar was inserted into this void at high level, with a secondary screen of etched glass to be placed behind it.

The brief for the screen was set by architect, client and artist, focusing on the narrative content of the design as well as its practical function – to protect the expanse of glazing behind it. Chinese cultural references are depicted in filigree-like metalwork which casts beautiful shadows into the building.

The sculpture combines found objects in steel with steel bars to form a Feng Shui-inspired composition of protective door gods. Bicycle chains are employed to great effect as moustaches for the figures, and for the dragons which symbolise good fortune. A specially designed structural frame holds the sculpture in place.

Unfortunately, halfway through the project funding for the etched glass screen (which was to have been commissioned from another artist) was dropped. This led to the architect himself undertaking the work, armed with a £15 roll of sticky vinyl (a signage industry standard for mimicking the effect of etched glass).

Although the architect was initially somewhat uncomfortable about 'fooling' the public with the vinyl, he set out to explore the scope of the material. The vinyl was be cut out freehand with a scalpel blade, so sketches for a design were loose and amorphous abstractions.

The function of the 'etched' panel was to create a level of privacy for the centre users without restricting natural light. The design detail was ultimately shaped by consideration of patterns cast by shadows on to the floor, walls and columns of the space.

In the end the 'negative' of the design cut out for the lower panel was repeated in the upper panel, making the fullest use of the single sheet of vinyl and creating a dialogue between solid and void.

RICHARD WENTWORTH
LITTLE DIFFERENCES
Christ Church Picture Gallery, Oxford

Richard Wentworth emerged as a new force in British art in the late 1970s. His sculpture creates unexpected alliances between familiar objects and evolves from an acute observation to the details of his surroundings. In 1996 Wentworth was commissioned by The Laboratory at the Ruskin School of Drawing and Fine Art to create a work which related specifically to the architectural surroundings of Christ Church Picture Gallery. The result was a show entitled 'Little Differences' created in collaboration with Jim Moyes.

Wentworth has said about this project: 'Christ Church Picture Gallery presented me with an overwhelming sensation of a collection in its bunker. The fact that the Powell and Moya building is indeed purpose-built is more than confirmed by the actual physics of the pictures in their container – the feeling that the buried building is filled to capacity with its pictorial contents, now retrieved from the old library home.'

'I have used the opportunity to exhibit . . . in two distinct ways. Firstly, I have separated two or three pictures and given them "pride of place", which is sufficient uninterrupted space to consider them exclusively and, by "calming" some of the walls, to point out some of the architectonic aspects of the place. Secondly, I have introduced into the space new works by myself and one by artist Jim Moyes. I have recently made various works using books, as much for their physicality as their content. By producing "kebabs" of differing lengths made of books, I have "sized up" the building, mimicking some of its details and measurements, lengths, heights and widths, much as cubits, rods and chains once did. Books are thereby used simultaneously to furnish and describe the interior . . The long shelf which accompanies the corridor is an internal datum of the ground level outdoors, a massively elongated threshold which reminds us of the spaces of cloisters and from which we view the lawn. Into this lawn, I have set a number of books cast in ferric gypsum, half-buried so that they appear to float in their host, the grass.'

FROM ABOVE: Making Do and Getting By, *1972;* Legend, *1996;* *OPPOSITE:* Little Differences, *1996*

TOM PORTER

COLOUR IN THE LOOKING GLASS

While researching colour preference at Oxford Brookes University I became aware of a similar project at Cambridge University. Whilst I was testing humans, the Cambridge University project focused on the colour preference of Rhesus monkeys – which possess a colour vision very similar to humans. The results of the two tests were very similar – in descending order: blue, red, green, purple, orange and yellow.

Our tests evolved into studies of colour preference and context. For example, one test was carried out in conjunction with Rowntree Mackintosh which produced some specially coloured Smarties and discovered the popularity of the blue Smartie. It took Rowntree Mackintosh six years to pluck up the courage to mass-produce this highly popular colour.

The preference for blue crops up in a survey by *The Pulse*, the newsletter of the American Roper Organisation, where almost 50 per cent of those tested named blue as their favourite colour, with red in second place. Blue is also America's best-selling car colour, with red cars in second place. Meanwhile, Britain's top auto manufacturers identify blue, red, and white as consistently holding the inside track for the top sales positions.

The fact that many architects seem reluctant to use colour fascinates me. I believe this is something to do with their education and is best illustrated by two ways of viewing of the Parthenon in Greece. The first is an architectural perception that sees this temple as a monochromatic essay in proportional excellence. The second perception sees it as it actually appeared on its opening day in 447BC. Then, it was completely covered in paint and gilding. Both interpretations – the architectural and the Ancient Greek, concern concepts of purity. The coloured version involves 'purity' because this is the very meaning of the work 'Parthenon'.

A dramatic influence on architectural colour came in the 1970s when artists began to use buildings as canvases. In the early 1980s, we conducted two surveys at Oxford: one compared responses of both lay people and architects to powerfully coloured buildings. This found a remarkable enthusiasm among the public for a more richly coloured built environment – much more so than the architects in our survey would allow.

A second survey investigated the incidence of colour teaching in educational design programmes in the UK. This found only two in operation at that time. However, a more recent survey of architecture and design schools finds a vast increase in colour education – an improvement that suggests colour is now being considered as an important facet of the design process. A study of how architectural colour is used by architects seems to break down into a series of functions: first, there is its symbolic use – a function that spans from the colours of the Parthenon to an ocean-linked B&I Ferry Terminal in Dublin. Another function seems to respond to those psychologists who plead for a greater environmental clarity. This uses colour coding as a 'supergraphic' to discriminate between the forms or main working part of a building. However, a third function takes us back to one of the earliest uses of colour on buildings. That is, the blending of architectural form into its setting. This is a kind of colourful camouflage. The fourth function is the complete opposite. This colour approach seeks to detach the building from its setting and uses its colour to decorate or to refer to concepts and ideas that exist beyond its setting.

However, whatever the function of colour in buildings, the choice of hues together with the intensity of their variables – value (colour plus black) and chroma (colour strength), seem to respond also to a kind of colour fashion. This in turn appears to reflect a spirit of the time. Furthermore, within this constant 'recycling' of the colour experience one can detect high points, such as in the brilliance of hues used by Owen Jones in Paxton's Crystal Palace in the 1850s and, again, on the Art Deco 'temples' of the 1930s. This continuously shifting fascination for different parts of the spectrum can be interpreted as an exploratory journey through the world of colour; an adventure that can also be documented on a decade-by-decade basis.

The 1960s

This decade opened with a fascination for black, white, and metallic neutrals. These were expressed in the fashions of the period, including those from the design houses of Cardin, Courreges, and Quant. Meanwhile, fine art was engaged in the scientific study of optical illusions – Op Art confining itself to the disturbance caused by visual fields using intense and geometric combinations of black and white. This mania for achromatics was, of course, a direct reflection of a science fiction fantasy – a recurrent theme is fashion and product design in which we become bedazzled by the glitter and gadgetry of black and silver electronic products. Indeed, the mathematical and hard-edged mood of the first part of the decade simply responded to the advent of space travel and our mental journey into outer space.

Meanwhile, the second half of the 1960s witnessed a complete change in our colour mood. This followed the birth of the package holiday in Great Britain, the possibility of cheap travel to faraway places coinciding with a thirst for the experience of other cultures. Consequently, the bright organic hues of ethnic folk cultures entered the British home. Much of this colour display centred on Indian culture, an interest that recycled an earlier focus on ancient Egyptian decoration, which in the 1930s had followed the discovery of Tutankhamen's tomb. However, this half of the decade also saw the emergence of the hippie and an hallucinogenic drug-inspired psychedelia that represented our journey into the inner space of our mind.

The 1970s

The 1970s saw our return to a science fiction fantasy but this time expressed in an exposed technology. We became deeply interested in how things worked. The need to confront the working parts of a complex technology saw visible mechanisms, such as exposed wristwatch architecture where the hitherto hidden working parts of buildings became exposed – their mechanical guts being spilled directly into the street for all to see. Perhaps the most famous example of the time was the Centre Pompidou, in Paris. However, this adventure into a high technology had to be clarified. To do so, bold primary and secondary colours were enlisted to diagram individual elements and the concept of 'colour-coding' had arrived. These 'high tech' expressions of black, white, and the bold primary colours were also found in fashion and product design, where the influence of a revival of interest in the work of De Stijl designers brought slabs of red, black, blue, and yellow to our lifestyles.

The 1980s

The early 1980s saw a new mood which, albeit short-lived, accompanied an economic boom. This triggered the beginning of the 'pastel phase' – a period when fashion hues became mixed with white to represent 'upmarket' and 'sophisticated taste'. Pastel colours spread quickly and became associated with lifestyle, a concept that involved various groups of colours aimed at different attitudes or fantasies of living, such as 'nostalgia', 'natural', 'sporty', 'classic', and 'ethnic'. Subdued colour ranges became co-ordinated across all kinds of products associated with a particular 'style of living', from clothes to cars and from interiors to luggage.

Fed by such popular television programmes as the highly influential *Miami Vice*, the pastel trend became truly international in spirit. For example, the co-ordinated hues of men's and women's clothing in New York in 1985 appeared in the same year and in the same colours for new automobile models launched at the Frankfurt, Paris, and Tokyo Motor Shows. Colours hitherto considered suitable only for baby clothes were worn by adults and were even used on Parker Pens and aggressive machines like Honda motorcycles and Fiat cars.

However, this quest for status through colour was also tinged with a nostalgia for the past. The search for 'real bread' and 'real ale' was embedded in the concept of an idealised rural life and a 'cosy country cottage' style – a need being fed by the fashion and interior designs of Laura Ashley, Conran's Habitat, and Next. The 'natural' theme also saw the success of ICI's Natural Whites, a range of white paint tinted with a hint of colour. There was also the rise of 'Muffin,' a soft beige pastel that became Britain's best-selling paint colour (after white) of the decade.

An international expression of pastel colours was stimulated by the painted facades and interiors of the Post-Modernist reaction to the drabness of a Modernist creed. Highly influential were the more figurative designs of Michael Graves, whose Mediterranean palette became transposed to product and electronic goods. This colour mood was quickly adopted in the Japanese electronic industry, which launched pastel-pink televisions, powder-blue telephone handsets, soft grey and yellow transistor radios, as

FROM ABOVE: Smarties, Rowntree Mackintosh; Parthenon, Greece, drawing detail. As it would have looked when first built in 447BC.

well as steam irons highlighted in pale yellow, blue, and pink.

The 1990s

News of the discovery by British scientists in 1987 of a hole in the earth's ozone layer had sunk into the public conscience by the end of the 1980s. Issues such as deforestation, global warming, and chemical pollution caused a deep concern for the future of the planet. By functioning as the watchdog of this deterioration, the hue of the green movement became the target of high fashion. While this colour association found 'responsible' yet gullible reactions to environmental awareness – green representing lead-free gasoline and the previously mentioned ascendancy of the green-coloured automobile – green had become adopted again as the symbol of survival. This was simply an updating of the fertility hue found in antiquity from the green-painted floors of ancient Egyptian temples to symbolise the fertile meadows of the Nile, to the myth of the Green Man and the Lincoln Green of Robin Hood.

The age of 'greenness' has also started to modify traditional colour meanings. It was predicted in 1990 that white, traditionally associated with the packaging of such refined white foodstuffs as salt, flour, and sugar, would be replaced by earth brown, in reaction to the disturbing environmental effect of chlorine bleaching. However, by 1991 the 'back to nature' fashion saw earthy browns, terracottas, golds, and silvers accompanying moss greens, grass greens, and leaf greens widely used in interior and product design.

However, by looking back in order to peer into the future, this approach is necessarily broad in scope. Obviously, there are countless sub-plots (smaller eddies and currents of colour trend, which are detected on a season-to-season basis within the larger waves of predilection). For instance, in focusing on colour trends in interior design with particular reference to paint, my work has involved the monitoring of seasonal paint colour sales as one means of plotting the rise and decline of individual hues, but this has always been conducted within the broader approach. However, within each branch of the manufacturing industries, each process of colour prediction aims for the same result. Indeed, as these industries rely upon accuracy of forecast for their survival so do forecasters rely on accuracy for theirs.

As we move on through the 1990s, our quest for survival has demanded environmentally safe pigments and dyes for the more variegated and chromatically adventurous colour ranges that have followed the green phase. However, several forecasters predict a return to the science fiction dream in the years immediately preceding the year 2000. In other words, a renewed interest in the subdued hues of blacks, greys, grey-blues, and grey red-blues will hallmark the dying years of the present decade. This seems to point to nothing more than a pause in neutral before the onset of the next century – a lull before the storm of exuberance and innovation that is bound to accompany the thrust into the new millennium. After all, we still live today in the wake of the shock waves triggered by the exhilaration in design at the beginning of the twentieth century.

Tom Porter is a colour specialist and senior lecturer at Oxford Brookes University School of Architecture. He is the author of numerous books on colour and design including The Colour Eye.

Traynor O'Toole Partnership, B&I Ferry Terminal, Dublin

GALEN MINAH
READING FORM AND SPACE: THE ROLE OF COLOUR IN THE CITY

Colour in architecture, in architectural drawings and in the facades and interior spaces of built projects, has been a characteristic focus in work from the early 70s at the birth of Post-Modernism through the current late Modernist and Deconstructivist phases which dominate the architectural media. The most published architects in the last fifteen years have been highly skilled in graphic abilities; some being accomplished painters and graphic artists, whose most memorable work is not their buildings but their splendid presentations. Michael Graves, Zoe Zenghelis, Zaha Hadid, the models of Frank O Gehry, and the bright red follies for Parc de la Villette in Paris by Bernard Tschumi are familiar to every architecture student. The current wave of interest in colour began when Robert Venturi sanctioned American subculture, ignored the restraints on colour from early Modernism and used colour in architecture as imagery in much the same way as roadside advertising.[1]

Much of the work of the 90s, particularly the recent work of Peter Eisenman and Bernard Tschumi – architects associated with the Deconstruction movement in architecture – has used theories of language and meaning as arguments for their conceptual design in which ambiguities, contradictions, and multiple meanings are translated through their interpretation into architectural form. Colour is strongly integral as a component of this form-language, but its rationale is often part of the designer's own subjective language of colour.[2]

In academic circles there are personalities who are noted colourists, such as Robert Slutsky at the Department of Fine Arts, University of Pennsylvania, and John Hejduk at Cooper-Union in New York City, who have been influential in stimulating an interest in colour among architecture students, but their teaching is often very esoteric, and related strongly to their own ideas developed through their painting.

Although colour has been used in architecture for the last 20 years, colour theory as part of an objective methodology for design in which colour becomes part of a conceptual understanding of architectural form in the design process, or is used as a critical tool for evaluation, seldom enters architectural design education.

It is important to look closely at the formative period of the early Modern movement, particularly at the attitudes toward colour and architecture, and examine the ways in which colour was incorporated in the theory, teaching, and production of those times.[3]

A schism in approach to design education known as the 'Norm vs Form debate' took place during the Deutsche Werkbund Exhibition of 1914. 'Norm' represented the belief in the development and refinement of prototypes in architecture and industrial design; and 'Form' represented the creative sovereignty of the individual artist.

This controversy carried into the early years of the Dessau Bauhaus. Johannes Itten was an artist and colour theorist who sided with the artistic, anti-authoritarian 'Form' side of the argument. Itten established a very important teaching document in his book *Art of Colour*, which is still used in teaching colour theory to artists and architects. Itten taught the basic design course at the Bauhaus, in which his teaching methods were subjective, very inner-directed and focused on individual creativity. Itten was interested in how personality could be revealed through colour exercises, and had a somewhat mystical approach to colour and design. His anti-authoritarian beliefs often clashed with the strongly rational approach of Bauhaus director and architect Walter Gropius. When Gropius proclaimed his support for professors in the industrial production and craft design faction of the Bauhaus, Itten resigned. He was replaced by László Moholy-Nagy, a Hungarian artist with constructivist leanings who took over the basic design course. Moholy-Nagy practised 'programmed art', and was well known for his 'telephone pictures' which were executed by calling colour specifications to a factory supervisor who then produced the work of art in enamelled steel.[4] Moholy-Nagy fitted in very well with Gropius's rational objectives, and he became a powerful influence in the Bauhaus.

At the same time, *Neue Sachlichkeit*, or 'New Objectivity', emerged as the intellectual basis for design theory in the late 1920s. New Objectivity practitioners sought to make the design process a highly rational one, stressing materiality, economy, and function, and divesting designed artefacts of any ideal implications. New Objectivity was the foundation for many early twentieth-century movements in design such as Suprematism and Neo-Plasticism or De Stijl .

The Dutch De Stijl movement was an important accomplishment in the use of colour as a tool in theoretical approaches to architectural form. The best known members of this movement were the artists Piet Mondrian and Theo van Doesburg, who became the prime spokesman for the movement, and Gerrit Rietveld, an architect who produced some of the only built objects of this period. Their lofty goal was, 'to work through the arts to achieve an ideal future when all walls that separate men would be broken down, society integrated and capable of constructing an urban environment of abstract forms.'[5] These artist architects saw the three-dimensional properties of mass and volume as antithetical to their movement, and they attempted to counteract and destroy these formal characteristics through the use of colour. Their methodology was to use primary colours, white and green planes of colour defined by black borders, displacing corners and the boundaries of floors and ceilings with these colour planes, thus changing the volumetric characteristics of architectural space. In its place, one experienced floating planes of colour, some advancing, some receding, dissolving all the references to cubic volume and becoming an assemblage of spatial effects created by colour juxtapositions.[6]

De Stijl was a dramatic development in the use of colour as both an integral part of the design process and as a tool for the creation of a new spatial experience. No other movement had employed colour as a conceptually spatial idea to this extent and

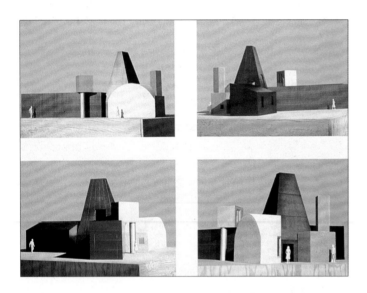

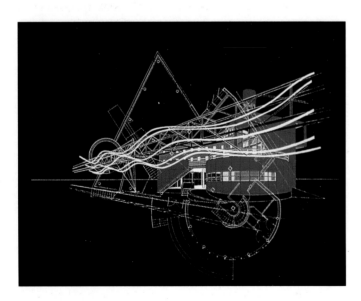

FROM ABOVE: Peter Eisenman, University of Frankfurt Bio-centrum; Frank O Gehry, Winton House, Wayzata, Minnesota; Bernard Tschumi, Parc de la Villette, Paris

none had recognised and used in practice the destructuring capability of colour.

Other movements employing colour as a basis for their conceptual design were Constructivism, in which colour played a symbolic role,[7] and Expressionism. The Expressionists were artists and architects who saw their creative role as a calling to save society through their inspired artistic achievements. Colour for the Expressionists was powerfully emotive and highly individual and subjective, as seen in the architecture of Hans Poelzig and Hans Scharoun.[8]

Le Corbusier was influenced by De Stijl, particularly in his use of colour in Pessac Housing of 1929. With the artist Ozenfant, Le Corbusier established Purism, which among other influences, brought machine aesthetics to the attention of contemporary architects. The colour white was a dominant theme in the architecture influenced by Purism particularly in the 1930s; later, white surfaces and structural members became a characteristic of the International Style. Mies van der Rohe and Walter Gropius were influenced by Le Corbusian theories, but their work was characteristically restrained in the use of colour except for the qualities of colour and texture in unadorned materials such as steel, glass, concrete, masonry and stone. Colour was considered ornamental and thus superficial when applied purposely.

Gropius and Mies went to the United States as teachers in the late 1930s, and their influence in architectural education is still felt in the design studios of professors today, who were students of these two men. This accounts in part for the continuation of their attitudes about colour in US architectural education today.

Except for the teaching of the early Bauhaus and the brief emergence of colour in the movements described above, colour theory and teaching has been considered supplemental to the mainstream of architectural education. Architecture students in the United States have few courses in colour theory or studios which focus on colour in architectural design. Rarely is a course offered in which colour in design and the relationship of form and colour to architecture is the focus of the instruction.

An exception to this is a course offered by Christopher Alexander at the University of California at Berkeley, in which Alexander's pattern language is expanded to employ the use of colour by studying cultural precedents for the use of colour in various spaces based on functional similarities.[9]

Colour in student work, for the most part, remains a matter of individual expression most often influenced by journal graphics and high quality photographs of built projects in which the colouration is often exaggerated. A student's involvement with colour at the University of Washington Department of Architecture is entirely elective. Occasionally students from fine arts who matriculate for a professional degree in architecture have some knowledge of colour theory, but for the most part colour remains a matter of individual taste. Colour issues are rarely discussed in a design studio review, and then almost never on an objective basis.

The challenge is to bring colour theory into a conceptual framework where its relevance is part of the design process. This challenge has become the point of departure for these investigations in colour-form interactions, and the subject for a number of graduate architectural design studios. Colour theory is used in these classes as a conceptual design tool to expand the means for clarifying the figural or hierarchical nature of building form. Colour theory is also used in the analytical or interpretative phase of the process as a critical tool in examining the integral relationships between the parts and the whole.

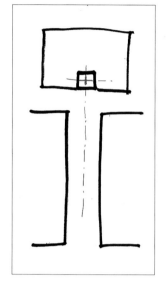

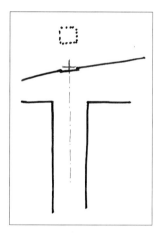

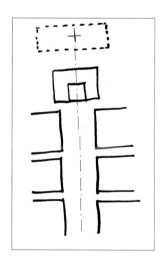

FROM ABOVE, L to R: Tower diagram I; streetscape, England; tower diagram II; streetscape, Liverpool, England; tower diagram III; Grand Central Station and the Pan Am Building, New York

Most formal analysis dismisses colour as transitory or treats it as a specific issue in the analysis of form. The preferred media for analytic studies are black and white drawings and photographs for elevational and perspectival studies. When colour is introduced it is not used in the critique of building form. Colour, however, is a powerful factor in the reading of form, as seen in the work of the De Stijl movement, and it is a major factor in clarifying the figure-ground relationships. Diagramming techniques used in formal analysis reveal the order of figure-ground, and these can be amplified by colour studies.

It is also clear that the perception of spatial phenomena is due in part to colour contracts, through juxtaposition of colour surfaces, and to the effects of atmospheric perspective upon colour. Certain colour phenomena such as these fall into categories that are recognisable and thus generalisable. These categories can be represented as part of the 'familiar' and 'general' world of colour interactions, and can also be represented through diagrammatic strategies. As with the formal analysis of buildings, a colour field can be named using the same terminology as architectural forms: centre, perimeter, figure and ground. For example, an abstract painting can be analysed, diagrammed, and interpreted in much the same way as a work of architecture, although colour juxtapositions become the only formal elements.

Since we understand the architectural diagram by means of black and white, solid and void, we neglect atmospheric reality in which colour is the variable which complicates and enriches the experience of figure, ground, solid and void. Colour has the capacity to clarify the figural components of form or confuse or obfuscate these elements causing multiple readings of architectural form.

Three examples of how building form and colour contrasts interact can be illustrated with these views of towers in an urban environment. The first example shows a distant tower as the clear terminus of an axis defined by the street and flanking buildings, and a diagram of the important plan relationships. Colour contrast does not play a major role in this view, although the relationship between the perimeter walls, building types, and the tower could be strengthened by colour.

The second example illustrates a distant tower, a square and an uncertain connection between the two. The diagram shows one set of relationships from a plan view, but the perspective view illustrates another interpretation. The bold facade created with strong colour contrast becomes clearly figural and takes the focus of the axis. The tower becomes a background element in the three-dimensional view.

The third example illustrates another clear tower-axis relationship in the plan diagram and in three dimensions. The tower is Grand Central Station in New York City, a major landmark and node in the city. The station's formal setting in the city was changed with the construction of the Pan American Building in the 1960s. This tower receives the attention of the axis of the avenue, rather than Grand Central Station. Colour contrast might alter the relationship between the Station and the Pan Am Building and restore the Station to its focal role at the end of the avenue by using a colour juxtaposition that makes the station figural and 'advances' it spatially.

An example of the interaction of building form with colour is the Portland Building in Portland, Oregon, by Michael Graves. If we compare the architect's line rendering of the building which portrays a clear cubic mass with delineated parts with the actual building, there are substantial differences. The actual building's

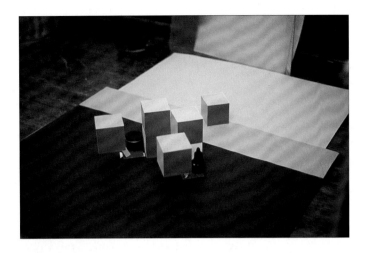

colours reveal another interpretation of the nature of the building. Here the cubic volume appears to bracket a second volume which appears as a dark mass in the centre of the building. Thus the actual volumetric characteristic of the building appears quite different from the drawn work.

The work which follows is a composite of experiments, observations, and student projects from a number of design studios taught by me, beginning in 1980, at the University of Washington. The students were graduate students in the professional degree program in architecture.

The first investigation was to explore the spatial effect of colour and create optical illusions using this effect in three-dimensional form. Students constructed three inch by three inch paper cubes with single planes of colour on their faces. Through colour juxtapositions and the spatial effect created by these juxtapositions students were asked to arrange these cubes in space and photograph them from a point of view which would create an optical illusion, misrepresenting the actual positions in space which the cubes occupied. It was interesting to note in these exercises the power and ambiguous characteristic of black. Black can be figural either as a solid or a void, and can easily deceive the eye as to its actual position in space. A black object in front of a lighter background can advance dramatically toward the viewer, or appear as a void in the background.

In the next exercise students were asked to find and photograph examples of the spatial effect in the urban environment with particular attention to the figure to ground interactions. These examples were numerous, and the variety of spatial effects observed were apparent in large spatial contexts as well as in fine detail. For example, light columns in slight relief on a darker background appeared from a distance as free-standing columns. Warmer coloured buildings appeared closer to the viewer than cooler buildings at approximately the same distance. The tops of towers from street level could deceive the eye as to their actual positions in space if colour contrasts were present.

In these initial studies we noticed specifically two factors which affected colour in urban settings: the importance of daylighting and climatic conditions on the perceived colour effects within the city, and the dominant presence of highly saturated colours in the environment. These two factors became subjects for further study in later design studio courses.

To study the effects of daylighting and climatic conditions upon colour in Seattle, we first photographed colour samples on bright and overcast days to observe colours which changed significantly with these conditions. We also photographed single family residential areas that had a variety of colour juxtapositions and could be viewed from a distance. Photography was done in differing weather conditions, and at different times of the day. From these exercises we observed the changes in the reds in the urban environment, particularly brick, in sunshine and in overcast skies. In sunshine, the red-orange hues dominated, usually making the building figural as the reds advanced when contrasted against a cooler field. On overcast days, the reds became dull and cool and retreated, into the background, changing sometimes from figure to ground spatially.

Blues, on the other hand, became vibrant and appeared more saturated on overcast days. This also was true of hues that contain blue such as blue-green, red-violet, etc. Yellows also became vibrant on overcast days, and colours with yellow components such as green could alternate between blue-green and yellow-green in differing light conditions. Guided by these initial

FROM ABOVE: First Street and Pike Street, Seattle, showing the focus on reds in buildings; First Street and Pike Street, Seattle on a cloudy day; warehouse in Seattle, showing the focus on saturated colour (red) at a distance.

observations, we photographed a number of buildings and objects in the red, blue and yellow range of colours on sunny, overcast and rainy days.

Another investigation focused on highly saturated colours on buildings within the city to observe their spatial effect. Of particular interest was to see how atmospheric perspective changed these colours and what spatial effects occurred at varying distances. Observations were made in different lighting conditions and these were photographed. Saturated reds and yellows were the most obvious colours on buildings observed. Both reds and yellows advanced dramatically from every point of view and seemed less affected by atmospheric perspective than the surrounding buildings. The strength of highly saturated colours, particularly on large surfaces such as building facades is obvious from this study, and these colours have an ability to exaggerate the spatial effect, advancing toward the viewer in nearly every example we observed.

In Washington DC, the Capitol Building, the White House, and the Washington Monument are all white, achieving figural status against the darker landscape, and advancing spatially. Against the sky the contrast is softened and makes the buildings appear to float in space. White also reveals detail in shadow often making the building appear larger than it really is. Buildings with a combination of very large scale contrasted with repetitive small scale elements make the building appear larger, exemplified in the drawings of the French neo-classical architect Ledoux. Many of the flanking institutional buildings are off-white, giving them equal status with one another, but of lesser rank than the primary buildings.

In comparing the planning of governmental and major institutional buildings in Seattle to Washington DC there is little similarity. In Seattle most institutional buildings are treated no differently from commercial buildings, occupying the same block pattern. There is no hierarchical intervention such as a central park, a mall, or a purposeful axis. The plan of the city reveals little information about where the governmental buildings are and how they achieve their status. In fact, they have no separate status: they occupy the same sized blocks as the commercial buildings, and have no plazas nor any special height.

Seattle contains a concentration of skyscrapers in the central business district where commercial, governmental and institutional buildings are located. The towers themselves are dominated by one massive black building, the Columbia Centre, the highest tower in the city. The coloration is designed to show minimal shadow and little detail, thereby creating a black monolith of great power within the city. The figural strength of this building is not because of its height alone or its position in the city but by its colour. However, it is really only another commercial office tower, which in most American cities are really background buildings in terms of their civic importance. The Seattle City Hall huddles at its feet directly adjacent to the Seattle Public Library which is also dwarfed, as are the court houses and the art museum a few blocks away.

In a design studio focusing on colour and urban form, students were given a building design project in the central business district near the Columbia Centre. As a sketch problem, students made a large painting from photographs of a view of the Columbia Centre in its urban context. Each student was asked to change the colour scheme of the Columbia Centre and paint an overlay to be attached to the original painting. It was interesting to see how the centre of gravity of skyline comprised of all the towers together was changed when the Columbia Centre was light grey or

ABOVE: Washington Monument, Washington DC; CENTRE: Seattle skyline showing black towers; Columbia Centre, Seattle, student project, rendering by John Kope; BELOW: King County Jail and Skybridge, Seattle, colour study by student Ann van Dyne; colour study by student Reese Kaufman.

silver and softened by the skyscape.

In the second part of the quarter, students were given a building design project for an office tower on a site in the central business district near the Columbia Centre. The new tower was not as high as the Columbia Centre but would be in a prominent position in front of the Columbia Centre when viewed approaching the city from the east, west or south. The students were asked to select colour schemes for their new towers which approached the figural status of the Columbia Centre.

The most interesting resulting design was a white tower which used colour to exaggerate its own height and stood as a strong counterpoint to the black tower. A more neutral colour scheme would have joined other neutral towers and become part of the background. A dark tower would become one of the family with the Columbia Centre and other dark towers, but a smaller sibling.

Another design project in the vicinity of the Columbia Centre addressed the new county jail, built adjacent to the major north-south freeway and just on the edge of the central business district at the south end of the city. As one approaches the city from the south, the jail becomes a gateway building. The new jail is a block away from the Columbia Centre and near City Hall and the County Courthouse. The jail is designed to look like a neutral beige office building. Through clever coloration, dark concrete panels give the appearance of large glass windows, however, at the base of these panels is a five inch slit which is the only real window to the cells behind. At night these slits become visible, and the building becomes a looming dark object with eerie thin slits of light, contrasted to the lofty, fully lit office towers.

Tight security is required when prisoners are moved from the jail to the county courthouse two blocks away. To provide this security a high skybridge extends from the top floor of the jail across a street over an entire block at the roof of an adjacent building, across another street, and into the courthouse. The bridge, intended to be innocuous and avoid notice, instead becomes a figural foreign object, and thus a sinister intrusion into the fabric of the city.

Students were asked to select a point of view from photographs which included the new jail and bridge with the city behind. A mural of this view was painted by the class. This exercise gave the students experience in mixing the greys and beiges which make up much of the urban palette. The students were then asked to take a point of view about the relationship of a jail to the commercial center of the city, and express this point of view in colouristic terms. This was recognised as an abstract exercise, knowing that a project like this in reality would need to consider more than one point of view.

Many students chose to accept the institution for what it was without disguising it. These projects made the building more figural in nature and treated the dark concrete panels as planes of colour rather than disguised as windows. Most solutions attempted to break the dominant scale and figural nature of the bridge with varying planes of colour. Some experimented with hues complementary to the warm grays and browns of the surrounding buildings for the purpose of creating a colour harmony with the urban context, but appearing as clearly distinct from the other buildings. The most unusual design was done by a student who abstracted the pattern of windows from the surrounding towers, and in bold black and white rectangles de-structured the cubic volume of the jail into a collage of fragments which blended with the rectangular patterns of the windows in the surrounding buildings.

In all these exercises, students used an analytical process to explore the relationship between their designs and the larger urban context. As part of this process, they made colour decisions that would clarify the formal and spatial properties of the designed buildings. This inevitably led to a broader understanding of how colour contrasts and, in particular, the spatial effect of colour become components in figure and ground and the perception of three-dimensional space. The students also learned that colour is part of the experiential nature of architectural awareness, and that its relevance in the design process is one of clarifying, complementing and enhancing rather than as an independent study.

Formal analysts feel it is impossible to fully 'know' a building. It can only be understood as a group of diverse abstractions. Likewise, it is impossible to fully 'know' a city, but the complexities and ambiguities which characterise the 'reading' of form and space are truly enriched by the diversity of colour, giving great variety to the creative interpretation of the city.

Galen Minah is Associate Professor of Architecture at the University of Washington.

Notes

1   Galen Minah, 'Colour Language', *Arcade* (Seattle), 1984, p3.
2   Peter Eisenman and Bernard Tschumi, *Deconstruction*, Architectural Design (New York), 1989, pp154-191.
3   Kenneth Frampton, *Modern Architecture, A Critical History* (London), 1992.
4   Frampton, *Modern Architecture*, pp124-126.
5   N Troy, 'De Stijl Manifesto', *The De Stijl Environment* (Boston), 1983, pp5-6.
6   Troy, *De Stijl Environment*, p83.
7   Chernikhov, J, 'The Harmony of Colours', *Deconstruction*, Architectural Design (New York), 1989, pp56-59.
8   W Pehnt, *Expressionist Architecture* (London), 1973, pp34-47.
9   C Alexander, *The Linz Café* (New York and Vienna), 1981, created an illusion of increased depth and occupied space beyond.

CLIFF MOUGHTIN, TANER OC AND STEVEN TIESDELL

COLOUR IN THE CITY

There is a renewed interest in the use of colour, one of the most effective methods of decorating the city. Colour should be used to strengthen the image of the city by giving emphasis to features such as landmarks, by developing colour schemes which are associated with particular districts, streets or squares and by colour coding street furniture.

There is great potential for polychromatic colour effects in the built environment. For much of this century the subject of colour in the city was not a matter for serious attention. A classical ideal, subscribed to by many designers, mistakenly associated with the architecture and sculpture of Ancient Greece, sees colour in architecture as a product only of natural finishes. The standing remains of ancient civilisations which have survived the ravages of time have been bleached of their original colouring by sun, wind and rain. They have, therefore, functioned as a monochromatic source of inspiration. To many the discovery that the great monuments of antiquity were stained or painted with bright pigments has proved quite unacceptable, particularly to those with a puritanical reverence for the expression of the inherent appearance of natural materials. The facts, however, are quite clear; 'Statuary was deeply dyed with garish pigments. The marble figure of a woman found on the Athenian Acropolis was tinctured red, green, blue and yellow. Quite often statues had red lips, glowing eyes made of precious stones and even artificial eyelashes.'[1] The Greek temple from the point of view of colour was closer in feeling to the Chinese temple, than to those pure but lifeless nineteenth-century copies found in many European cities.

The love of colour survives in the modern world. The church in its vestments retains a strong link with the past symbolic use of colour while colourful vivacity occasionally breaks out in the guise of the latest Parisian or Italian fashions in women's clothes. In the environment colour was kept alive by those not schooled in the centres of artistic excellence – the working class in the suburban home, the art of the bargee, the gypsy or fairground artist. In this spirit are the monuments to Art Deco of the late 1920s and 1930s. Such buildings as those by Wallis, Gilbert and Partners for suburban London fall neatly within this populist genre. Within the Modern Movement important experiments with colour were carried out. The De Stijl group in Holland in the early 1920s was one such group. While Mondrian used pure colours and white on canvas, containing them in a black grid of simple rectangles, Rietveld, following similar principles, decorated the internal and external planes of his architecture. Other notable modern exponents of colour in the environment include Le Corbusier who used flashes of intense primary colours to contrast with the white geometric frame of his architecture.

The legacy of the dogmatic views of Ruskin and the priggish taste in colour of those who followed abandoned the field of polychromy to the engineer. It was the engineer who embellished and protected with paint the ironwork of bridges, the coach work of the railway engine and the working parts of industrial and agricultural machinery. Arguably it was not until the building of the Pompidou Centre by Richard Rogers and Renzo Piano that a return was made to the more ancient architectural traditions of environmental colouring.

The natural colours of traditional settlements constructed from local materials delights the eye. The sophisticated and almost pristine colouring of De Stijl gives great intellectual and emotional satisfaction. They are, however, by no means the only ways in which colour can be introduced into the environment. The case being made here is the need for a more catholic and eclectic philosophy of colour in the environment. This is particularly true now when so much urban development is a concrete jungle. Given the current emphasis on sustainability, many local authorities attempt to humanise the built environment with paint, vegetation and sculpture instead of demolishing the concrete jungle.

Theory of colour

Before discussing colour in the environment it is useful to examine the general theory of colour and to define terms used to describe and specify colours. The term colour can be used in two main ways: to describe the hues of the rainbow, the constituent parts into which white light is broken (red, yellow, blue, etc), or, it can be used in its more popular form and include black, white and grey. The last three 'colours' can be obtained as paints for use in the home in the same way as red, blue or green. It is this populist definition of colour which is used in this text. It is, however, important to realise that the designer's use of colour in the environment differs from that of the painter. While following the same principle of colour harmony the urban designer is working in a field where the quality of light varies from city to city, from season to season, and from morning through to late evening. The painter, in his or her studio, attempts to mix and use colour in a constant daylight condition. The results of his or her work is exhibited in a gallery where optimum lighting conditions prevail. The painter has control over his or her palette and can chose to follow theoretical trains of thought in the abstract. The urban designer works with other actors in urban development, each following individual intentions. The urban designer works on a canvas which is three dimensional, of immense scale and in a constant process of growth and decay. The starting point for the urban designer must of necessity be the environment of the place in which he or she is working. Colour theory for the city, therefore, has to be seen in this greater context and used, where that is possible, for decorating the city by creating harmony where none may exist.

There are three sets of primary colours from which the other colours can be made. With light rays, red, green and blue (blue-violet) will form other hues when mixed. Red and green will form yellow: green and blue will form turquoise; red and blue will form magenta. Light primaries are additive so that all three light primaries when combined reform to produce white.

With pigments, red, yellow and blue are the primary colours which when combined will normally form other hues. Pigments tend to be subtractive, that is, red paint absorbs all light except red which is reflected from the surface. No pigments are pure mixtures, therefore, and combinations tend to deepen or subtract more of the light falling on the surface. A combination of all three pigment primaries will form black or deep brown: most light falling on the surface will be absorbed and very little reflected.

In vision, however, there are four primaries, red, yellow, green and blue. Each of these colours, perceptually, is quite distinct from each other. Any other colours tend towards one of the primaries. That is, a mix of yellow and green would look either 'greenish' or 'yellowish'. All four colours when spun on a wheel or mixed will form grey.

The three sets of primaries of the artist, the scientist and the psychologist, each produce different colour circles. While each colour circle can be used for deciding colour harmonies, this text, for convenience, will follow the traditional circle of the artist based upon the three primary colours: red, yellow and blue.

Figure 1 illustrates the three primary colour circle of the artist. It shows the distribution of primary, secondary and tertiary colours together with the division of the colour spectrum in terms of warm and cool hues. Ives, who brought this particular spectrum to perfection suggested that the red should be magenta (schlor), the yellow should be clear and clean (zanth) and the blue should be turquoise or peacock. These particular primaries when mixed will give a satisfactory spectrum of pure hues.

The use of colour harmony in painting or the built environment is founded on an understanding of simultaneous and successive contrast and of the phenomena of visual colour mixtures. M Chevreul described in his book the effect of simultaneous contrast as follows: 'If we look simultaneously upon two stripes of different tones of the same colour, or upon two stripes of the same tone of different colours placed side by side . . . the eye perceives certain modifications which in the first place influence the intensity of the colour, and in the second, the optical composition of the two juxtaposed colours respectively.'[2]

Figure 2 illustrates simultaneous contrast of brightness. Both greys are identical in brightness but the one seen against black appears lighter than the one seen on the white ground. Light colours will tend to heighten the depth of dark colour and dark colours will tend to make light colours lighter. Where colours of different value or brightness are placed side by side a fluted effect is produced (see figure 3). The edges of each tone will tend to be modified in contrary ways. The effect of 'afterimage' of contrasting colours is also quite noticeable. Figure 4 illustrates this using black and white (see overleaf). The effect of contrast is best demonstrated by staring at a given hue for a short time; when the gaze is transferred to a white wall the appearance or shadow of the opposite hue is stimulated. Referring to the full colour circle the contrasting colours are those that are diametri-

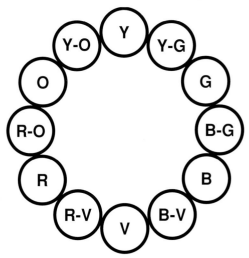

1. The red, yellow and blue colour circle

2. Simultaneous contrast: each grey star is identical in brightness

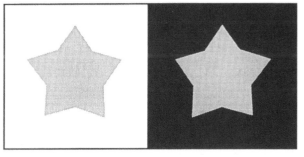

3. Simultaneous contrast: note the 'fluted' effect where the grey tones touch each other

cally opposite on the circle (see figure 5). The after-image of red is blue-green and vice versa; the after-image of yellow is violet and vice versa. Opposite or contrasting colours when used together tend to give brilliance and purity to each other without any change of hue.

Where non-complementary colours are placed side by side they are affected as if tinted by the light of the after-image of the neighbouring colour. When, for example, yellow and orange are placed together the violet after image of the yellow swings the apparent hue of the orange towards red while the blue after-image of the orange will make the yellow appear greenish.

Contrasting effects in value are stronger when light and dark colours are juxtaposed while contrasts in hue are most noticeable when the colours are close in value. However, the size of the colour panels is important for contrasting effects: large panels of colour are most effective for a startling visual contrast, particularly when the contrast is both in value and hue. Strong contrasting colours in minute areas such as spots or lines become diffused by the eye and tend to conceal each other resulting in an overall dullness. Opposite colours, therefore, are most effective in contrast when used in large panels of colour. Adjacent or analogous colours, on the other hand, are best displayed in different minute areas. The effective use of analogous colours can be found in many traditional stone or brick walls. Each stone though from the same quarry is a slightly different hue or shade of hue. They all blend naturally together. The foundation of colour harmony dates from the early nineteenth century and the work of M Chevreul. This theory established certain rules and principles. The first is that individual colours are beautiful in themselves; second, so are tones of the same hue; third, different hues, analogous or closely related on the colour circle, are in an harmonic relationship when they are seen in uniform or closely related tones; finally, complementary hues seen in strongly contrasting tones are also harmonious. Assorted colours when viewed through the medium of a feebly coloured glass take on an harmonic relationship.

The use of colour in the city

Until the nineteenth century, European cities developed slowly employing indigenous materials from their regions for the building envelope. Architectural styles changed but the building materials did not. The constant use of local materials produced streets, squares and whole cities with great visual harmony despite the varied forms. In this way the colour of the city was established and is an aspect of its history which has not been completely submerged by nineteenth- and twentieth-century developments. In Oxford's high street many styles are reflected but all have been unified by scale, material and especially colour. The colour of Oxford is derived from the ochres of the yellow sandstone. In the traditional city there was easy access to cheap earth pigments for painting stucco facades. Even in the nineteenth century it was only the wealthy who could afford the brighter 'imported' or 'foreign' colours for doors and windows. Cities and regions have come to be associated with particular colour ranges: 'For instance, the ochres and reds of Lyons; and, among the blues and reds, the predominance of a "Maria Theresa" yellow in central Vienna. There are also the brickdust reds and Georgian greens of a revamped Savannah, the pinks of Suffolk and Devon cottages, and the brilliant reds, blues and yellows of houses on the Adriatic island of Burano.'[3] The problem posed for the urban designer is how to recapture such colour schemes and give individuality and

distinction back to each centre.

Turin in 1800 set up a Council of Builders to devise and implement a colour plan for the city. The idea was to colour principal streets and squares characterised by a unified architecture in a coordinated scheme. The Council devised a series of chromatic pathways for the major processional routes to Turin's centre, Piazza Castello. The colour scheme for each route was based upon popular city colours and was implemented through permissions given for redecoration applications. It is not known how long the original colour scheme lasted but it was praised by Nietzsche in the late nineteenth century and by Henry James in the early twentieth century.

In his work on colour in the environment Jean Philippe Lenclos has developed the ideas found in Turin's earlier experiment. He has aimed to preserve a sense of place by devising a palette of colours relating to particular localities in France. Lenclos collects colour samples from sites within the region – fragments of paint, materials from walls, doors, shutters, together with natural elements such as moss, lichen, rock and earth. He analyses and structures the colours he finds to form a colour map for the region and a palette for intervention in the built environment.

The lessons that can be learnt from Turin and Lenclos are twofold. First an environmental survey is necessary to establish a colour map of the region or city and from that colour map palettes established as the basis for colour schemes. Second, any colour scheme for a city should be comprehensive and capable of implementation. From earlier sections of the chapter it would seem desirable that any colour scheme established should follow the laws of harmonic colour composition.

There are four different scales on which colour in the city can be seen: the scale of the city or of the district; the scale of the street or square, where colour can create various characteristics or moods depending on adjacent buildings, and at street corners or on diametrically opposed facades; the scale of the individual buildings; and the scale of details – windows, shutters, ironwork, street furnishings. Furthermore colour in streets and on buildings can be seen in four different ways: from the side; from the front; from above; and from below. It can be seen in deep shadow, in conditions of blazing sunshine or harshly against a bright sky. In each condition the same pigment may take on a different shade, tint or tone of the same hue.

Milan is a city which has a clearly defined colour pattern. It is a highly sophisticated and unique use of colour. Cities like Siena, Florence and Bologna depend for their colour on materials such as brick, terracotta and marble. In Florence, for example, dark colours abound including the dark green marble cladding of the cathedral. It is a city of shades and tones. In Siena the light and beautifully decorated cathedral decorates a totally different space from the dark coloured main square and the dark cliff-like streets that connect the cathedral and the main square. Dark brick and terracotta are the colours of the arcaded streets and squares in Bologna where rich gold is splashed on the soffit and arch of vaulted arcades. However, in Milan the experience of colour is quite different: here dark and light colours are juxtaposed. It is a city of light and shade. The highly decorated cathedral provides a white focus to the main square which has dark colours to the south and light pinks to the north. This highlighting of different areas in the city with white marble clad buildings is a theme repeated throughout the city.

In Vienna and Prague, yellow is the colour used to highlight Baroque landmarks. Small Baroque churches usually along narrow streets become visually significant when painted yellow. Colour of such intensity when combined with movements of surface shadows becomes highly decorative without being elaborate. In both Prague and Bratislava elaborately coloured decorations are common in Art Nouveau and Art Deco facades. Colour on buildings from both periods is widely used over facades, and while intricate and pleasing to the casual observer, it nevertheless misses the opportunity for the strategic use of colour and decoration which earlier and more disciplined periods achieved. For instance, the cathedral in Buda is a good example of colour used to highlight a landmark and important symbol of community solidarity. The cathedral stands out in contrast to the dark shades and tones of red, green and yellow used along the nearby medieval streets.

The two most common urban spaces are the street and square. The colour scheme of the street or square may have a considerable effect upon its character and appearance. It can contribute to the unity of the street or square, or it may destroy that unity. In addition, the colours used in the street have in themselves the ability to create character and mood. Taking the street for example, it is possible to emphasise the wall planes of the street by painting them a light tone. Alternatively the volume of the street can be emphasised by colouring the facades the same tone as the dark pavement, or the length of the street could be emphasised by horizontal strips along the facades. The street can also be broken down into units with vertical bands of colouring. Whichever scheme is followed the street should be viewed strategically as an element in the city, a path leading from node to node and interspersed with landmark features and street corners. It is features such as these which should influence the final distribution of colour within the street.

When developing a colour scheme for a building it must first be seen in its strategic relationship with its immediate surroundings. The building's visual function within the city or district should also be established. For example, is the building an important landmark or a closure to a vista? Does the building lie upon an important path with a particular colour coding? Having decided the strategic requirements then the building itself can be examined: if it is rich in decoration it will be articulated with relief – cornices, window frames, niches, projecting bays and oriels, stairwells, corner mouldings, overhanging roofs, balconies, etc. The relief lies in front of the main wall surface and is foreground colour, the wall becomes the ground or background colour. The background may be dark with pale relief or vice versa, but some distinction is necessary for articulation.

When choosing a colour scheme for a building it is the details that are the final constructional elements to receive consideration. It is only when we stop and concentrate the gaze that we notice the details and colour of fixtures and fittings but they are important for the overall effect of the street and where possible if flanking an important route they should be co-ordinated. The three zones of the building, the base, the middle zone and the roof zone, together with the relief and detailing make up the architectural treatment of the street. The planes, projections and ornamental work can be emphasised to create a lively pattern of decoration. In other areas where for strategic or master plan reasons the street can be bland and unassuming then the difference in elements can be masked by the subtle use of shades, tones or tints of the same colour.

Colour is one of the most important aspects of city life: it is one of the main factors in our description of a city's decorative effect. To be fully effective for city decoration requires some strategic policy which sets a colour agenda for the city and its main elements, districts, paths nodes, edges and landmarks. The city image from the point of view of colour is often formed over a long history and also strongly affected by its environmental setting. Determination of colour image requires a sensitive response from the urban designer. A response which should be based on a thorough survey of colour in the local environment. For the remainder of the city, colour can be used to highlight important buildings and landmarks, colour code important paths and give individuality within the overall pattern for important squares and meeting places.

Notes
1 Tom Porter, *Colour Outside*, The Architectural Press (New York), 1982.
2 ME Chevreul, *Principles of Harmony and Contrast of Colours*, reprinted by F Birren, Van Nostrand Reinhold (New York), 1967.
3 T Porter, *Colour Outside*, Architectural Press.

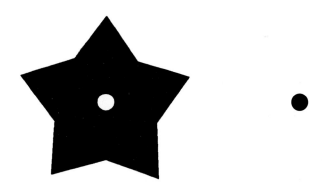

4. After-image: stare at the centre of the black star for several seconds then look steadily at the black dot

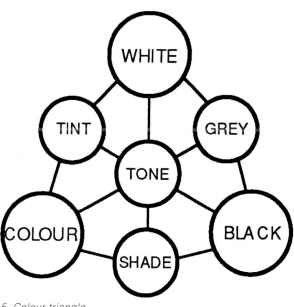

5. Colour triangle

MICHAEL LANCASTER
SEEING COLOUR

Two ways of seeing

We see colour principally in two different ways: as an attribute of objects, and as a separate sensory phenomenon. The surprising fact is that the first, regarded as natural and normal, is based not upon true colour appearance, but upon our experience and visual memory; what we know rather than what we actually 'see'. The 'true' or sensory view of colours is generally regarded as being the prerogative of painters, scientists, and those who work with colour. For the majority of us, most of the time, it is 'the object view' which prevails. The reasons for this are fairly obvious.

In order to negotiate objects and find our way in the world, we need to be able to identify things under a variety of different circumstances and in different light conditions. Colour constancy – in parallel with constancies of size, shape, texture and brightness – enables us to recognise objects and situations which experience has taught us to identify, thus freeing our perceptual faculties for detection of the new and the less unfamiliar. In this there is a direct similarity between the brain and the information processing mechanism of a computer, although the former is infinitely more sophisticated. The visual system is adapted to obtaining a maximum of information with a minimum of effort: that which is not immediately required, or can be taken for granted, can be considered redundant; 'the eye has evolved to see the world in unchanging colour, regardless of [the] always unpredictable, shifting and uneven illumination.'[1]

This dichotomy of colour vision (which Edwin Land suggests may be due to evaluation mechanisms operating within the visual process) seems to suggest answers to a number of questions which arise in attempting to analyse visual perception. First it must surely account for the fact that so many people seem generally unresponsive to colour, except for those credited with aptitude, intuition or 'flair'. It might well account for the common tendency to look so often at paintings in art galleries without registering their colour, and explain why the whole subject of painting can be divided between those whom we recognise as 'good colourists' and those for whom the academic process is more important. There is, for example, an accepted distinction between those schools of painting based upon drawing, such as the Florentine; and those for which colour was predominant, such as the Venetians. Ingres, writing in defence of the academic system claimed; '... drawing is everything, the whole of art lies there. The material processes of painting are very easy and can be learnt in a week or so.'[2]

Such relegation of the subject to the level of a child's colouring book is not untypical, and could well be applied to the study of colour in architecture today. Is it because of the perception that colour appears to belong to materials that architects customarily design in black and white, adding colour later? Certainly the Neo-Classical tradition was based upon the natural colours of materials, deriving from mistaken assumptions that the temples of Classical Greece were unadorned with colour. There are indications that colours applied in the form of paint – for whatever reason – were often in imitation of the colours of natural materials. The dichotomy certainly seems to account for many of the insensitive juxtapositions of colour in paint and natural materials that are increasingly common in our environment.

Although we are only beginning to understand the mechanisms of the two ways of seeing, it seems clear that they are not mutually exclusive, and it is likely that many intermediate stages exist. Gibson distinguishes them by location: 'filmy disembodied colours floating in a visual field (compared with) the colours of objective surfaces in a visual world. The former look filmy and insubstantial and appear at an indefinite distance, in contrast with the colours of objects in daylight illumination which appear to be localised on and be part of the surface of the object in question.'[3]

Given that perception is a very selective activity concerned with much more than just appearances it is necessary to examine how our concept of the visual world is formed. While it is clear that we can only survive in a functional environment, there is much disagreement on how these functions are expressed. Buildings, for example, are expected to be much more than forms following function. They are symbols, comforting or otherwise, of the places we live in. This raises the question of how a particular environment is perceived, and, more specifically, how we build up our images of the visual world. The visual process is one of scanning. The eyes move, the head, neck and body move, gathering images like the frames of a (movie) film. The rate of scanning is variable, but generally slow enough to make the illusion of movement in films possible. From these images (and other sensory impressions gathered simultaneously), the scene is constructed together with information already stored in our visual memories, redundant information being filtered out. To what extent cultural and social factors influence this 'editing' process is impossible to assess. In view of the ways in which we exercise taste and discrimination in describing our surroundings, it would appear that the picture of the world on which these judgments are based, is, in many ways, a product of our own imagination.

Learning to see colour

While the precise optical and neurological processes involved in perception are still largely obscure, we know that 'visual awareness' can be learnt. Learning to see – or perhaps more cynically, learning to see with the eyes of our teachers is a prerogative of all courses in art and design education. That there are many different interpretations of this process, at least in its applications, is all too apparent. Of these, colour is one of the most problematical.

The essential connection between colour and objects begins in infancy. As babies we are attracted by the lightness and brightness of things. But it is only later, probably with the beginning of the development of abstract concepts that are facilitated by language, that we learn to perceive colour as a separate sensation; identification is an aid to sight. Observations of a group of children revealed that this was occurring around the age of four and a half. Before then the majority matched objects according to shape rather than colour. But after that age, as culture demands, training in practical skills which rely more heavily on shape than colour the number of choices made according to colour decrease continuously into adulthood. This is perhaps not, in itself, surprising. The important distinction is that the colours of objects in the ordinary sunlit visual world are not the same as the patchwork (of colours) in the corresponding visual field.

Almost all of us have some capacity to sense colour in a detached way. The blue of the sky for example, is essentially filmy and insubstantial like that of the blue haze obscuring distant mountains; also the colours of the rainbow, although revealed by different means, are similarly insubstantial. Most people are aware of the shimmering mirage-like appearance of buildings seen at a distance. Rasmussen compares the view of Manhattan from a ship approaching over 13 miles of water with that of Venice seen across the lagoon, which he describes as 'architecture experienced as colour-planes'.[4] Such effects are typically expressed by the indistinct patches of colour in paintings by Nicholas de Stael (1914-1955). There are close parallels also in the 'dazzle-painting' effects of camouflage on ships during the First World War which made them appear to be steaming in different directions and some recent uses of the technique to disguise, or reduce the bulking effect of some buildings.

Another quite common effect is that in which natural light is seen to transform the visual world from its everyday appearance to one of light and colour. It occurs at its most impressive when the sun is low and the sky is dark with storm clouds. As the sun moves towards the horizon, more and more of the short blue wavelengths are absorbed by the atmosphere, which transmit mainly long ones. The intense red and yellow light turns everything to gold, transforming all objects. All colours: greens, reds, browns and greys, are united in the harmony of a single dominant hue, contrasting with the dark blue-grey of the sky.[5] The two 'modes of seeing' have been described by RH Thouless in 1931 as 'the object mode' and the 'illuminant mode'. The former refers to the everyday world in which we all live; which so often seems devoid of light and colour, that we seek compensation in artificial lighting effects and an extravagant use of applied colour.

Colour and light

Painters have always acknowledged the problem of painting light, but as an aspect of objects or their backgrounds. For Turner, after about 1820, luminosity and atmosphere began to predominate in his paintings, until, in the last years of his life, pictorial subjects seemed to dissolve in light and colour. Although rooted in the Romantic tradition of ideal landscapes peopled with images from antiquity, depicted in sombre melancholy colours, he

FROM ABOVE: Bruno Taut , Weissensee housing project, Berlin; Bruno Taut, Hufeisensiedlung housing project, Berlin; Waldsiedlung Zehlendorf (Onkel Tom's Hütte), Berlin

progressed towards a fresh and original view of nature and natural forces, not copied, but expressed by natural harmonies of colour. His palette changed to one of clear brilliant colours, anticipating many of the prescriptions of Goethe's *Theory of Colours*, which only came into his hands in translation in 1843.

Like Turner, Monet devoted the latter part of his life to portraying the atmosphere of colour. Figures almost disappear from his paintings. He stopped travelling and began to concentrate on a series of paintings of individual subjects: haystacks, poplars, Rouen Cathedral and the Gare St Lazare. The rural subjects are lacking in topographical interest and the paintings of buildings tell us little about the architecture. He had become absorbed, as Turner had more than half a century before, in the changing effects of light and colour to such an extent that the subject had ceased to be important; 'For me a landscape does not exist in its own right, since its appearance changes at every moment; but the surrounding atmosphere brings it to life – the air and the light which vary continually. For me, it is only the surrounding atmosphere which gives subjects their true value.'[6] He draws attention to the apparent difference in scale between buildings seen in direct sunlight with shadows, and seen in diffused light; an important distinction for those selecting colours for buildings.

Turner had worked mostly in isolation and developed his own theory of colours. The Impressionists – a loose association of avant-garde artists – had the benefits both of common interests and scientific and industrial backing. Industrial production included the synthesization and production of colours, the development of optics, photography, colour printing, and it included the development of colour theories. Of the latter, the volume by ME Chevreul entitled, *The Principles of Harmony and Contrast of Colours*, was outstanding for three main reasons; first, it was practical, setting out the uses of colour in every imaginable field from textiles to painting and from architecture to horticulture; second, it dealt sensibly with the subject of colour harmonies; and third, it provided explanations for such peculiarities as optical mixing and simultaneous contrast. Chevreul's explanation that orange sunlight produced violet shadows offered invaluable guidance to the Impressionist painters, providing an argument against those who were suspicious of the sensory approach to colour.

Colour expression

Turner and Monet had explored the atmosphere of light and colour in nature, the Expressionists turned away from the representation of nature as a primary purpose of art, towards the direct expression of feelings and emotions through line, form and colour. In 1908, Matisse wrote; 'What I am after, above all, is expression . . . The chief aim of colour should be to serve expression as well as possible . . . To paint an autumn landscape I will try to remember what colour suits the season; I will be inspired only by the sensation the season gives me'.[7]

Expressionist groups had appeared almost simultaneously in France and Germany, les Fauves having combined in their art the theories of Van Gogh and Gauguin and retained a certain harmony of design; die Brücke used form and colour to express drama and violence. 'We accept all the colours, which, directly or indirectly, reproduce the pure creative impulse.'[8]

This was no longer the atmospheric colour of Turner and Monet, but strong, highly-saturated colour imbued with meaning; and, as with most German art, the meaning was weighted with philosophical concepts. The process by which colours and forms themselves became the repositories of the pictorial ideas was carried to its

logical conclusion in abstraction. Attempts to reconcile the more anarchic impulses of Expressionism with the need for social reform were realised in the ideas of the activist movement, in particular, in the architecture of Bruno Taut (1880-1938), and in the principles on which the Bauhaus (1919-1933) was founded.

The importance of colour at the Bauhaus was ensured by the appointment of many artists and designers who had been connected with the Expressionist movement in painting; the links with form and space were confirmed by the foundation course, Colour and Form, taught by Johannes Itten, Paul Klee and Wassily Kandinsky. Each had a different approach, which become clear with the subsequent development. Itten and Kandinsky believed in a correlation between emotional states, colours and forms. The latter had derived his colour theory from Goethe via the anthroposophist Rudolf Steiner, and had published a paper in 1912 entitled, *Concerning the Spiritual in Art*. From an early age he had experienced synaesthesia (the association of colour with music), wanting colours to exist purely for their own sake, as sounds do. Klee, an accomplished violinist, considered that the pitch of colours functioned like major or minor keys, enabling a person to 'improvise freely on the chromatic keyboard'.[9] Characteristically, drawing for Klee was like 'a line going for a walk', changing its character according to what happened on the way, but he saw colour as the richest aspect of optical experience. While line is only measurement, tone is measurement and weight and colour is quality.

The building as art

Although the influence of the Bauhaus has been profound in all areas of design, it did not immediately stimulate the use of applied colour to the outsides of buildings. White was and remains in the common perception, the colour of the Modern Movement, as it had been the colour of Neo-Classicism. Apart from the elaborate and extensive uses in the social projects of Bruno Taut, applied colour was limited to a few individual buildings. Gerrit Rietveld's recently restored Schröder-Schräder house in Utrecht is a work of art. The purity of line and surface speak of a time when painters, sculptors and architects could work together to such an extent that their work seems interchangeable. With remarkable restraint strong saturated colours have been restricted to linear and structural elements – a lesson that might have been learnt from nature. Volumes resolve themselves into subtly coloured advancing and receding planes which seduce the eye with the elegance of their proportions: all of which reminds one that De Stijl is so much more suited to buildings than to chairs.

Le Corbusier's Pessac houses would seem also to have fitted the category of 'building as art'. Saying that he wanted to do something poetic, Corbusier chose a painter's approach. He embraced colour completely, seeking to achieve an effect of weightlessness by painting the surfaces in different colours which met at the corners, so that a light grey, for example, bordered on a light sky-blue without any hint of structural thickness. Rasmussen describes his experience of sitting in the shade of a maple tree in the roof garden of one of the houses;

I could see how the sun dappled the Havana-brown wall with blobs of light. The only purpose of the wall was to frame the view. The buildings opposite could be perceived as houses only with great difficulty. The one to the left was simply a light-green plane without cornice or gutter. An oblong hole was cut out of the plane exactly like the one I was looking through. Behind and to the right of the green house were row houses with coffee-brown facades and cream-coloured sides and behind them rose the tops of blue . . . [10]

Colour and social housing

Bruno Taut was also torn between painting and architecture. In his diary he wrote;

> thoughts about painting occupy me constantly. It seems to me that I can give my character its fullest expression in this medium . . . The idea . . . (of a) combination of my talents with regard to colour with my architectural ability. Spatial composition with colour, coloured architecture – these are areas in which I shall perhaps say something special . . . [11]

The opportunity to combine the rational and social skills of the architect with the vision of a painter came in 1914, when he was commissioned to design the small garden suburb of Falkenberg, near Grünau, in east Berlin. The colours selected were light red, dull olive-green, golden-brown, strong (saturated) blue, and white. Some contemporary observers interpreted the use of colours as a form of liberation, freeing working-men's housing from the tyranny of refined and alien forms. Taut saw it as a means of 'liberating German architecture from the strait-jacket of muddy grey styles.'[12]

When he won a place on the Board of Works of the industrial city of Magdeburg in March 1921, Taut immediately announced his intention to transform the city, 'tired of being regarded as a mere suburb of Berlin'. Unbroken colour (unmodified strong colour), he considered, was what the city needed, and Breiter Weg, the main business thoroughfare, was selected for the first phase. Although he succeeded in this and in having a number of public buildings painted, as a public experiment it was a failure. The air was too dirty, the cement render crumbled and the paint was of poor quality. The result, after little less than a year, was disastrous, and he resigned.

As artistic director of the planning division of GEHAG, Bruno Taut had more freedom to implement his ideas of colour without the need for public cooperation. With foreign capital supporting the building industry a number of estates was built throughout the city. These included a line of low-cost slab blocks of flats, in Prenslauer Berg in the district of Weissensee. They were boldly painted with broad bands of red and blue against white – an interesting early solution to the problem of giving identity to mass- and high-rise housing by means of colour. The two other main coloured developments were the Hufeisensiedlung (named after the horseshoe shaped central block) and the Waldsiedlung Zehlendorf (Onkel Tom's Hütte).

In the last of the five phases of the Waldsiedlung Zehlendorf the building authorities required a unified colour scheme to be submitted in advance for approval. The five parallel streets of off-set two-storey houses were painted in Pompeian red and bluish green, alternating left and right, with the complementary scheme being reversed on the backs of the houses. The facades were articulated with bands of glazed brick in the Mondrian manner and dividing walls of natural red brick; and the window, frames and doors carefully articulated in black and white, red and yellow. The use of the complementary red and green reflected the conditions of natural lighting: the east-facing facades being green, and the west-facing walls red. The colours of window frames were keyed in to the particular background wall colour in each case; and the ends of the streets were 'closed' with strategically coloured blocks. Taut described the colour choices in terms of space;

> colour should be used to underline the spatial character of the development. By means of variation in colour intensity and brilliance we can expand the space between the house rows in certain directions and compress it in others.[13]

The fact that applied colour has survived on the houses of all these estates is a measure of Taut's success. It has degenerated in the sense that weather has washed and bleached the paints and changes have been made. But this degeneration can be seen also as an aspect of human evolution, particularly now that restorations have been undertaken. It is becoming clear that, in addition to the planning framework for the use of colour, some degree of flexibility is desirable. But the message is clear, as Taut wrote in 1925;

> Everything in the world has colour of some sort. Nature has colour, even the grey of dust and soot, even gloom has colour of some kind. Where there is light, there must be colour. All man has to do is to give this phenomenon form . . . [14]

With the rise of National Socialism, as opposed to Taut's own version of Socialism, his work came to an end, and he took an appointment in Turkey. The Bauhaus was forced to close in 1933, and many of its teachers left for America; and there were serious suggestions that the flat-roofed buildings of the Weissenhofsiedlung – regarded as symbolic of degenerate eastern Mediterranean architecture – should have pitched roofs added.

Michael Lancaster is an architect and landscape architect. He has written Colourscape, *to be published by Academy Editions in 1996 and* Britain in View: Colour and the Landscape, *the subject of a BBC2 film series,* The Colour Eye.

Notes

1 Roy Osborne, *Lights and Pigments*, (Edwin Land quoted), John Murray Publishers (London), 1981.

2 Bomford, Kirby, Leighton, Roy, *Impressionism*, National Gallery and Yale University Press (London), 1990.

3 J J Gibson, *Perception of the Visual World*, Greenwood (Connecticut), 1977.

4 S E Rasmussen, *Experiencing Architecture*, MIT Press (Cambridge), 1959.

5 Michael Lancaster, *Britain in View: Colour and the Landscape*, Quiller Press (London), 1984.

6 J House, *Monet*, Phaidon (Oxford), 1981.

7 Harold Osborne ed, *Oxford Companion to Art*, Oxford University Press (Oxford), 1971-81 (Henri Matisse quoted 1908).

8 Harold Osborne (ed), *Oxford Companion to Art*, (Ludwig Kirchner quoted 1913).

9 Hope and Walch, *The Colour Compendium*, Van Nostrum Reinhold (New York), 1990.

10 S E Rasmussen, *Experiencing Architecture*, MIT Press (Cambridge), 1959.

11 B Whyte, *Architecture of Activism*, Cambridge University Press (Cambridge).

12 Düttmann, Schmuck, Uhl, *Color in Townscape*, Architectural Press (London), 1981.

13 Ibid.

14 Bruno Taut, Rebirth of Colour, 1925 lecture (quoted in Düttmann, Schmuck, Uhl, *Color in Townscape*).

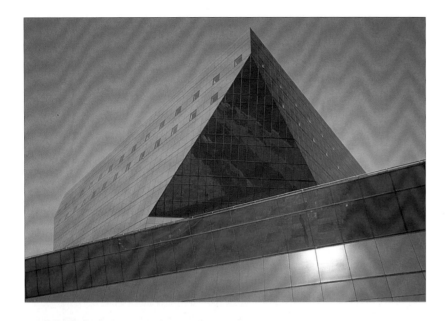

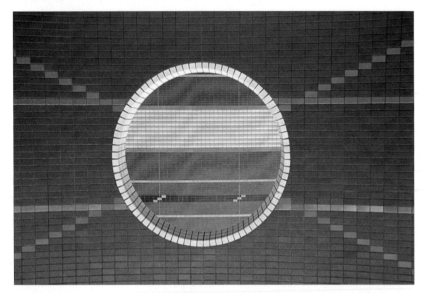

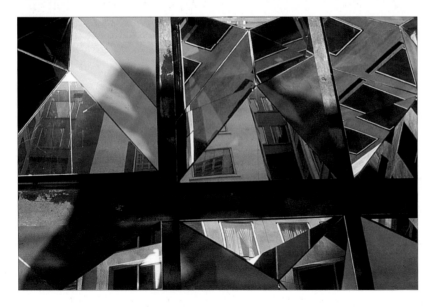

LEFT, FROM ABOVE: Pacific Design Centre, West Hollywood, California, 1988; Sea Hawk Hotel and Resort, Fukuoka, Japan, 1995; California Jewellery Mart, Los Angeles, California, 1968; RIGHT, FROM ABOVE: Pacific Design Centre, Sea Hawk Hotel and Resort

CESAR PELLI
DESIGNING WITH COLOUR

When I was asked to write an article on colour in architecture my first thought was that all materials have colour. Some are muted and some bright. Whites, greys and browns are colours as well as reds and yellows. The question is, what colours to use in each circumstance? I am also aware that by colour in architecture we normally mean colours as architectural elements in themselves, not only as definers of form. We also mean the use of saturated colours, contrasting colours, or colour used as a decorative element.

The use of bright, contrasting or decorative colours result from two traditions: one is an ancient tradition in many cultures of using only natural materials for the exterior of buildings – they tend to be mostly shades of grey and brown or stone and wood. Of course, there have been exceptions; red or orange brick buildings that were not seen as coloured because of local consistency. The same was true of the deep ochre of Tuscany. Some buildings were brightly coloured to mark them as exceptions, such as the vermilion shrines in Japan. The other tradition is that of Modernism which perceived architecture primarily as white, black or grey, with primary colours used only as accents.

I am primarily a designer–builder and not an academic scholar, and I believe that I can best explain my thoughts on this matter in terms of my experiences and through some of my projects.

When I was a student of architecture in Tucumán, Argentina, I learned that proper, serious Modern architecture should have no colour except for the colours of natural materials, whites or greys – anything else was frivolous or decadent. In the years after the Second World War, students of architecture in progressive schools all over the world must have learned the same lessons. There were several reasons for the avoidance of colour in Modernism: one was the opposition to the highly decorated eclectic architecture that Modernism was trying to replace; another was the personal preference of the main shaper of Modern architecture – Le Corbusier and his work as a Purist painter. In orthodox Modernism there was also a desire to go back to basics, to strip down architecture to its essentials in an ethical and formal cleansing. Perhaps the most pervasive reason was that orthodox Modernists believed in the imminent triumph of science, technology and reason and tried to base their architecture on rational design. Strong colours must have been seen as appealing directly to the senses, bypassing the prescribed filter of reason.

I started my career in architecture as an apprentice to Eero Saarinen. Saarinen used colour as a Modernist; his architecture took the colour of natural materials, or was finished in whites, greys and blacks with occasional bright coloured accents such as the glazed brick walls of the General Motors Technical Centre.

When I started practising on my own, although within larger firms such as DMJM and Gruen, I did not feel constrained by Modernist strictures although I was, and still consider myself to be, a Modern architect. One of the first projects I had at DMJM was the remodelling of an old office building on the corner of

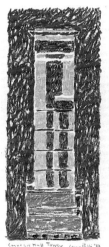

ABOVE: Sketch of Herring Hall, Rice University, Houston, Texas, 1984; CENTRE LEFT: Sketch of Sea Hawk Hotel and Resort, Fukuoka, Japan, 1995; CENTRE RIGHT: Sketch of Carnegie Hall Tower, New York, 1991; BELOW: Sketch of Pacific Design Centre, West Hollywood, California, 1988

Museum of Modern Art (MoMA) expansion and renovation sketches, New York, 1984

Pershing Square in Los Angeles that was being transformed into a jewellery mart. I had an extremely small budget. The areas for re-design were a lobby, where all I did was to clean it up, and a deep courtyard – nine storeys deep. To renovate the courtyard I was given a total construction budget of $16,000 which meant that I could afford little else besides paint. I designed a simple but strong pattern that transformed the dingy and unpleasant space into one that was bright and lively and a pleasure to look at. The forms were abstract and very much in tune with modern currents in the visual arts; therefore, I felt that I was only slightly stretching the artistic envelope of Modernism. This was my first built design to be recognised on the cover of an architectural magazine (*Progressive Architecture*, February 1968).

The Pacific Design Centre is a more instructive example, the form is simple, abstract and certainly Modern. By cladding the large building in bright blue ceramic glass I gave it a new quality, a direct impact to our senses. To me this meant adding another perceptual dimension to the artistic possibilities of architecture. There was something else of perhaps greater importance – if the building had been grey or brown (such as my earlier design for the San Bernadino City Hall) it would not have had the ability to engage the lay passer-by as completely as the Pacific Design Centre did. The building quickly gained an affectionate nickname, the Blue Whale. The colour established an emotional link between object and observer that is absent in many of the abstract colourless compositions we architects admire but are not understood or appreciated by the public at large. Some years later I had the opportunity to design an addition to the Pacific Design Centre, that appeared as a large, green sculptural form. The large-scale ensemble of coloured forms created an even more accessible and appreciated architecture, which was very rewarding for me.

A few years after the design of the Pacific Design Centre, I was commissioned to design the major renovation and expansion of the Museum of Modern Art in New York which included the design of a residential tower built on top of the museum addition. I was able to experiment with the use of colour for a more complex artistic purpose just as I had with two apartment buildings I designed in Houston (Four Leaf Towers) at approximately the same time. Glass towers have often been used to house office space, their abstract uniform nature can be justified because they enclose undifferentiated modular space for undetermined users –

every window on every floor is the same as any other. However, the MoMA Tower was a residential building with predetermined functions and it was important to express this character on its exterior and to express the changing sizes and relationships among living rooms, bedrooms and other functions. My design for MoMA started with saturated colours but I had to tone them down several times to have them approved. The building is now elegant, but not exuberant.

My work in ceramic glass progressed from the rational and somehow didactic gridded enclosure I designed for the San Bernardo City Hall to the addition of colour to a similarly gridded volume in the Pacific Design Centre, giving a new sensorial dimension to the MoMA and Four Leaf Towers. In these buildings the gridded glass wall became less abstract and more expressive of the functions it enclosed. This was not an issue of colour, but colour was the vehicle available to me. These designs represented my growing belief in the need for Modern architecture to evolve from a dogmatic and narrow position towards an architecture with a wider range of expressions capable of answering all of society's needs.

Herring Hall at Rice University, represented for me a further and critical elaboration of this line of thought. Herring Hall houses the school of business at Rice University. This is a small, beautiful and coherent campus designed by Ralph Adams Cram of the firm, Cram Goodhue and Ferguson of Boston, and by his disciple, William Ward Watkins, in the first and second decades of this century. The character of the Cram-Watkins buildings is romantic, colourful and very appropriate to its functions and to the climate of Houston. It was also based on materials and craftsmanship that were no longer affordable. The problem for Cesar Pelli & Associates was one of designing a suitable building to become part of an ensemble of buildings that I respected but could not imitate for intellectual and economical reasons. I resolved this dilemma by designing a contemporary building with colours and details of similar density to those of Cram. The basic colour is a salmon brick, with accents of limestone and glazed bricks and tiles. The sense of colour is achieved more by the juxtaposition of materials than by the use of highly saturated pigments. The lessons learned in Herring Hall gave me the tools with which to design the office tower for Carnegie Hall, a problem that would have been otherwise unmanageable.

One of my latest experiments in using colour on a building to

heighten its expressive and artistic qualities was in the Sea Hawk Resort Hotel that was recently built on Hakata Bay in the city of Fukuoka. The complex functions of a resort hotel require volumes of different dimensions and characteristics. I took advantage of the availability in Japan of beautiful and economical ceramic tiles and of a skilled work force well trained in their application. I developed the skin of ceramic tile as a critical element that gives character to the building, a character appropriate to a seaside resort hotel. The use of colours and patterns in this building allowed me to express, as I have in all the previous ones, the nature of contemporary buildings: air-conditioned spaces enclosed by thin, lightweight walls. These walls are two-dimensional surfaces defining three-dimensional hollow volumes. The patterns have a character-giving role and they also create what I call a 'supersurface' that guides our eyes across voids and around corners, strengthening the taut qualities of the building's envelope.

Colour in architecture is quite unlike that in painting; first of all it is colour in three dimensions. It is also subjected to changing sunlight and, most importantly, it requires the careful use of materials with necessary consideration to their ageing and weathering properties. Wood will grey and darken with age, copper will start its life as golden, turn dark brown, and in fifteen to twenty years will become bright green. Stone will grey and may acquire a green patina of moss. Ceramic materials in glass or glazed bricks and tiles will maintain their colour relatively unchanged through the years. Paint fades rapidly under sunlight and brightly painted coloured walls need repainting every three years or so. These considerations are essential to the craft and art of architecture. To produce good architecture, intuition is essential but is not enough, it also requires considerable doses of rational thought. It is this interplay of reason and intuition that I find most satisfying and often exhilarating in the practice of my art.

I have to qualify my enthusiasm for the use of colours in my designs. We must always bear in mind that sometimes colours are appropriate and sometimes they are not, it depends on the context. In a town or neighbourhood of buildings coloured only by natural materials a brightly coloured structure (or white or black) could do great harm to the total ensemble, and I believe the whole is always more important than one of its parts even if that part happens to be one of my buildings.

FROM ABOVE: Four Leaf Towers, Houston, Texas, 1992; Sea Hawk Hotel and Resort, Fukuoka, Japan, 1995

LEGORRETA ARCHITECTS

SAN ANTONIO LIBRARY

San Antonio, Texas

The City of San Antonio wanted a joyful building, far removed from the stuffy image of ordinary library facilities, a building the community would celebrate as its own, and a building that housed state-of-the-art technology for information access. In a traditional sense, the challenge of this project was to achieve a well developed architectural language which integrates the library functions and uses.

Described by local critics as an 'ingenious blending of design and function', the new facility can be compared with the old on only one level: both are places where books are kept. Books remain a critical element in the new facility, but it shows an appreciation for the other important elements in San Antonio's library facility: architecture, art and technology.

The capacity of the library has been doubled to 22,300 square metres, with space for up to 750,000 books.

The building's geometry of rotated, cut-away boxes, largely determined by the spatial restrictions of the site, allows people to view the library as a friendly, accessible and inviting building.

The exterior 'is a visual wonderland of shapes, angles, and openings that create an interplay of light and shadows, both inside and outside the building'.

The area is distributed on seven storeys, six of them above ground. The main mass is a six-storey box surrounding a yellow skylit atrium that serves as a focal point for each floor. Some terraces are accented by large geometric shapes. Triangular and rectangular baffle walls painted purple or yellow on the third floor terraces generate curiosity and invite people to go outside. Another terrace to the west is bordered by a slightly raised *acequia,* a water channel, that pours into a circular pool. Beyond the *acequia* stands a grove of palm trees. Exterior walls are finished with acrylic plaster. At street level, a stone wainscot gives scale to the building.

Blending natural light, shadow and geometric figures throughout the new library, creates a sense of mystery. Visitors discover something new at each visit, to entice them back, time after time.

The design evokes a sense of freedom, particularly in the use of space. This is accomplished by giving the library floors unique personalities by varying their shape and size. The differences encourage visitors to discover the building in all its variety.

Special features for children have been incorporated into the design of the third floor. Architectural elements and graduated child-size stacks, scaled-down furnishings and abundant natural light put young people at ease in an environment tailored to their needs.

Designed to incorporate many future innovations, the library's new card catalogue is on the cutting edge of computing technology; including a kid's card catalogue, a Spanish card catalogue, Internet access and a search system that allows access to libraries across the USA.

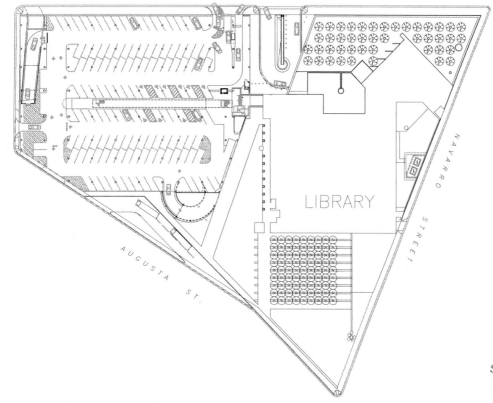

Site plan

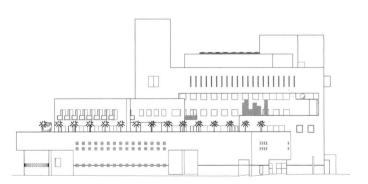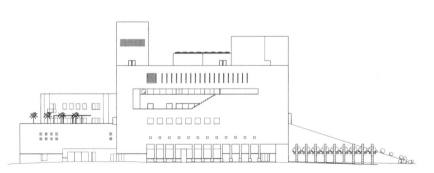

West elevation; south elevation

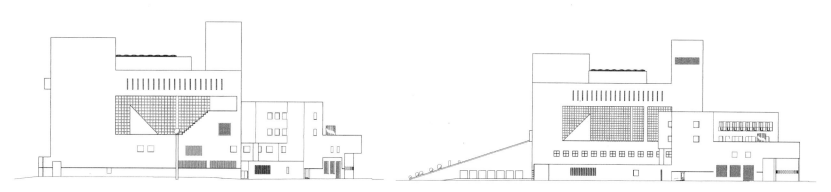

East elevation; north elevation

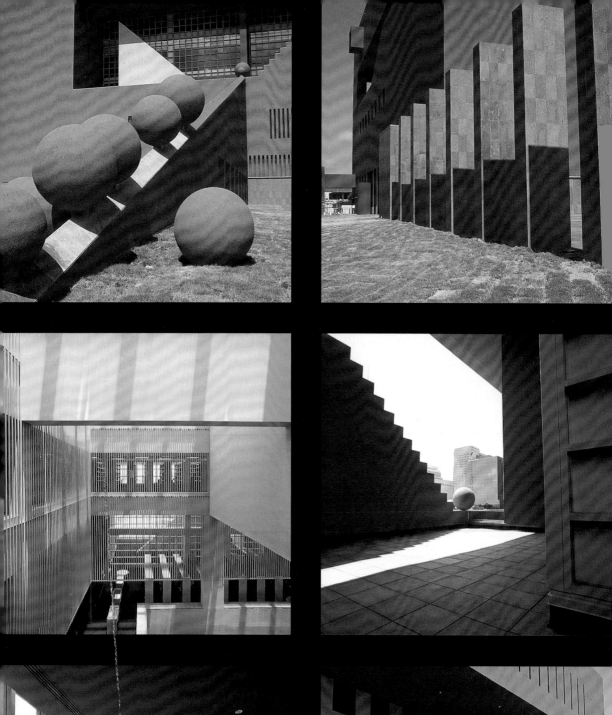

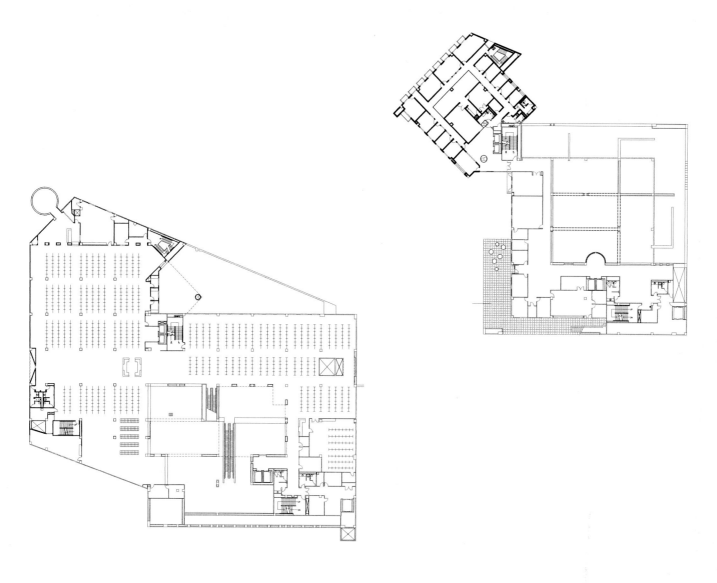

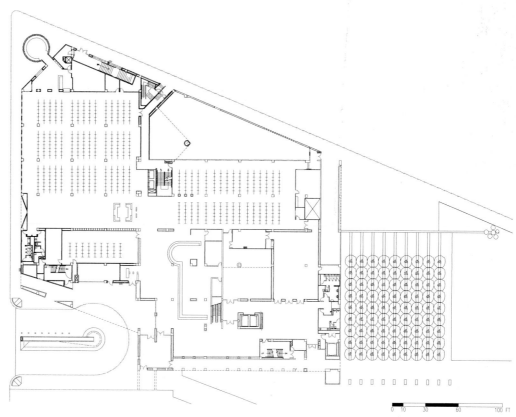

FROM ABOVE: Fourth floor plan;
second floor plan; ground floor plan

0 10   30   60   100 FT

SOLANA
Dallas, Texas

Solana, the 'sunny place', is a 900-acre business community just 10 minutes west of DFW International Airport in Dallas, Fort Worth. A team of three architectural firms, Mitchel Giurgola, Barton Mayers and Legorreta Architects along with landscape architect, Peter Walker, developed a simple scheme that took advantage of the highway that crossed the property. As a result, an underpass was designed to form part of the master plan. When complete in the late 1990s, it will encompass some seven million square feet of office space in a self-contained business community.

Unity was set by the interplay on walls, height, scale, materials and colour. Each architect was free to design and express his style, respecting simple guidelines, this allowed for a dialogue between the buildings.

The master plan preserves the natural beauty of the site's wild flower fields, prairie grasslands, and oak groves. It combines a low density, campus-style environment with the character of the southwest. Growth will be carefully controlled to ensure the quality of the environment long-term.

Solana contains two main office

spaces: Seven Village Circle and Nine Village Circle. These two buildings provide 300,000 square feet of office space. The distinctive architecture and exceptional interiors of these two five-storey buildings blend limestone, stucco, clear glass, and vibrant colours with porticoed entrances, arcades, interior atriums and outdoor balconies.

Vertical elements were created as directional entry symbols. The use of walls, plazas, textures and colour, contributed to create intimate spaces but, at the same time, humanise the almost unlimited scale of the Texas landscape.

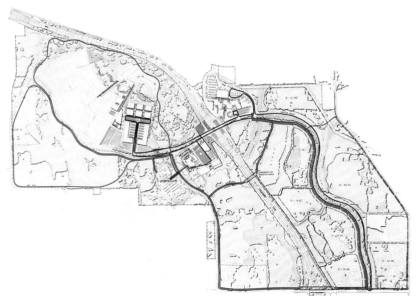

Master site plan

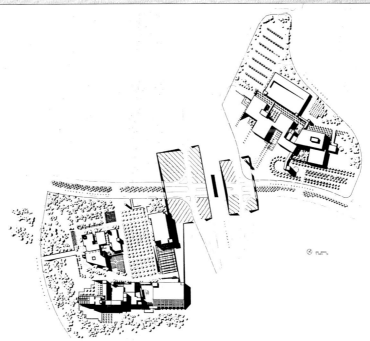

Village site plan

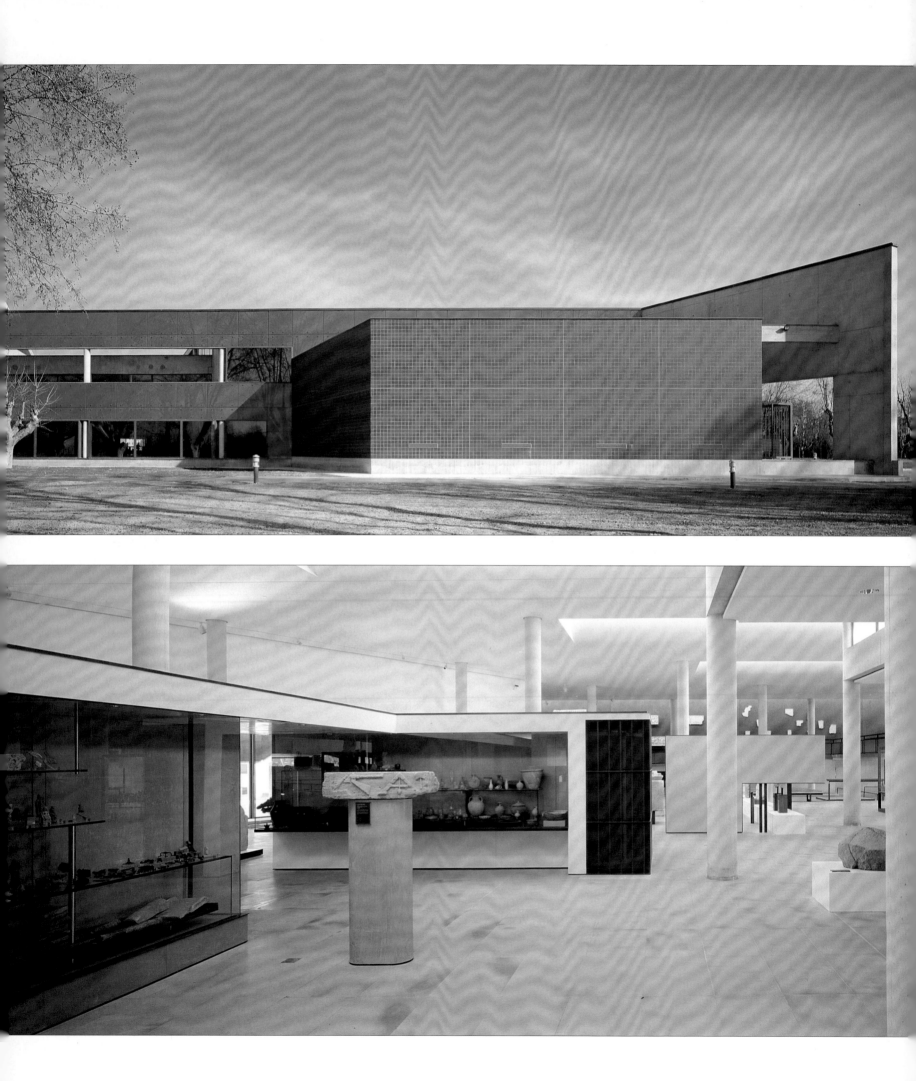

HENRI CIRIANI

MUSEUM OF ANCIENT ARLES
Arles, France

The concept of the museum has in effect only emerged in the last 80 years, although it has now developed to a much-heralded status. Hollein's project at Mönchengladbach, Meier's in Frankfurt, Pei's in Washington and Stirling's in Stuttgart opens the way for reflection on the edifice for which anterior references barely exist. The Museum of Ancient Arles was built to deal with the existing and increasing amount of Roman artefacts from the surrounding area in Southern France and set up sophisticated excavation projects and research groups.

The museum was to bring a new aspect of history to the town. Surrounded by water – the Rhone to the west, the Midi Canal to the east – this near-island, set on a triangle of land, is immediately imposing. Far removed from all things Roman, the triangular form responds, however, to the perfect oval of the amphitheatre of the old town, echoing the brutal geometries of the configurations of the new town. From a geographical point of view, the island harmonises with the urban context.

The triangle responds perfectly to the design which demanded both a short and a long route. The design is integrated logically in this form, with three sections: the scientific (catering operations, temporary exhibitions and stock, in addition to the school of excavation); the cultural (where teaching takes place, the library, conference room, administration, and foyer) and finally, the school for museum guides. These elements constitute two buildings which between them contain the museum proper.

The main facade is perpendicular to the sluice gate of the Midi canal, which enables the building to be anchored to an artificial element. This first wall, facing onto the old town, is not well-developed. It is the original element of the project as well as the facade of the immense juxtaposing circle in which the excavations are taking place. Behind lies the cultural wing, a white building, set against the heart of the city. The second facade looks onto the canal and dominates the scientific wing which is oriented towards the point of the near-island. This area, facing the Rhone, introduces the museum with its extension facing the town.

In the centre, the patio contains a grand staircase which is incorporated into the roof detail, thus completing the museographic route. This element fills the central void, giving direction to the helix while at the same time rendering it complete. The roof comprises the fourth facade of the building, as important as the three others and revealing in terms of internal organisation on account of the skyward lighting system.

The architecture as a whole is very dependent on the quality of light. A group of open shed-roofs to the north directs the light from the perimeter of the facade. This type of lighting, borrowed from the industrial world, has endowed the museum with architectural ingenuity. Here waves of white homogenous light seem to ripple, escaping to the ceiling. Another type of light is obtained by brackets which capture the sunlight and give it a more textured colour. Finally, the so-called 'view' lighting enters through openings framed by the countryside.

The blue building panels give this light a somewhat cold quality. This material and this colour were already present in the most ancient projects (notably that of the Opera-Bastille) where they conformed with a precise syntax (blue for the contextual elements, red for the functional areas). In Arles, the blue colour refers more simply to the intense colour of the provincial sky.

Since the time of the competition in 1983-84, the evolution of the design has confirmed the pertinence of the triangular form. What was the Museum of Ancient Arles has now become the Institute of Research for Ancient Provence. The museum has expanded from 6,000 to 7,400 square metres without detracting from the initial concept.

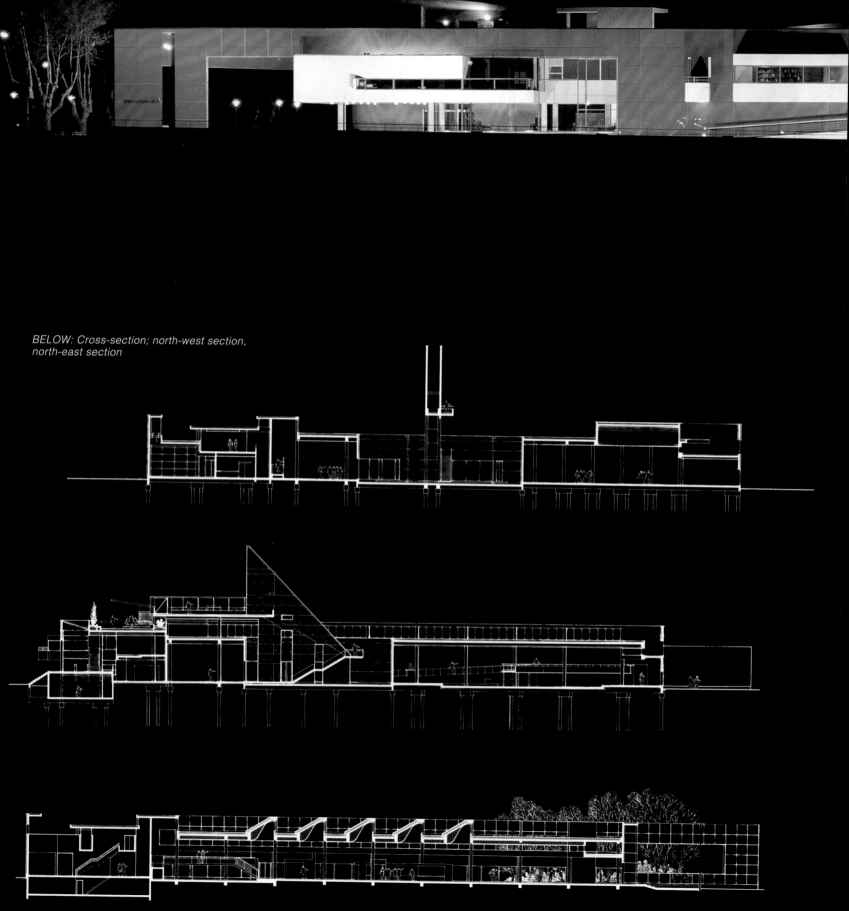

BELOW: Cross-section; north-west section,
north-east section

FRANK O GEHRY

VITRA INTERNATIONAL HEADQUARTERS
Basel, Switzerland

This project is a master-planned development with the first phase being a 62,000 square foot corporate office building. It is on a suburban site in Birsfelden, outside Basel, bounded by the low-rise Vitra manufacturing building on one side, and a small converted office structure on the other. The surrounding neighbourhood contains a mixture of light manufacturing, offices, houses and garden apartments. To the east is a dense forest reserve, visually tied to, but physically severed from, the site by an autobahn submerged well below grade. The existing zoning required a building of less than ten metres in height. Parking was required at a rate of one car for every three employees on site, including existing uses.

Programmatically, the building is to house various working groups which require 'changeable' office planning in a way which will allow them to demonstrate and experiment with their own furniture lines. The offices also become showrooms, so a relatively neutral space was designed for the programme element. Much research was done to investigate the state-of-the-art office space before the project began. As a result, 'combi office' and 'office landscape' types will be accommodated as well as more traditional closed and open offices. The strict energy codes of Switzerland do not allow air-conditioning in offices, so natural ventilation is accommodated by windows and the entirely shaded south wall under a large wing-shaped canopy.

In addition to the office block, there are more 'permanent' communal support areas such as the main entrance/reception, cafeteria, switchboard, mail, meeting and conference rooms. Since these spaces were thought of as less changeable and are used by all departments of the company, including off-site person-nel, it was decided that they should be located centrally and allow for future expansion of offices around them. The nature of these spaces also allowed them to take on richer, sculpted shapes. The size and proportion of this element is similar to the scale of some of the existing homes nearby; it thus became dubbed 'the villa'. The wing canopy houses a 'living room' atrium and formally mediates between the simple office block and the central, energetic villa.

Architecturally, the building responds to the varied scale and conditions of its context. It welcomes visitors and workers alike and provides a strong, unique image for the company within its own workspace/showroom. The structure of the building is concrete and masonry. The external materials are a combination of painted stucco, zinc metal panels, and wood-framed doors and operable windows.

FROM ABOVE: Concept drawing by Frank O Gehry; east elevation; west elevation

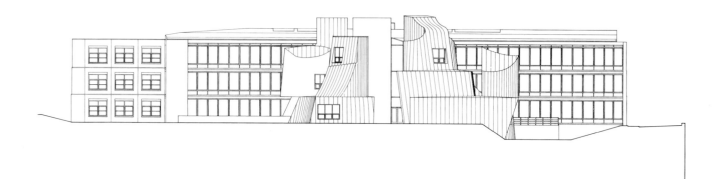

South elevation

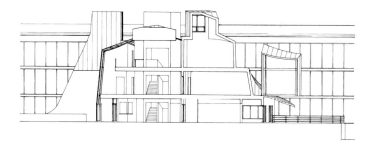
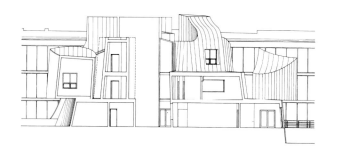

Cross-sections

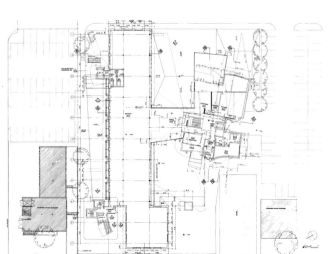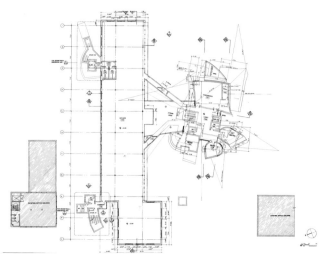

Ground floor plan; first floor plan

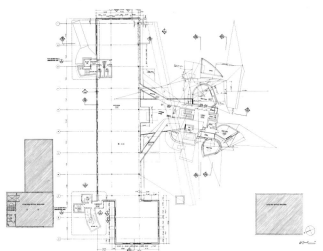
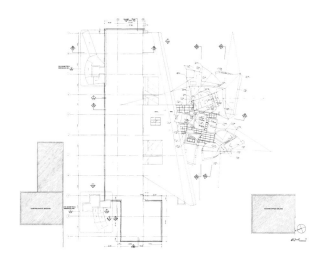

Second floor plan; roof plan

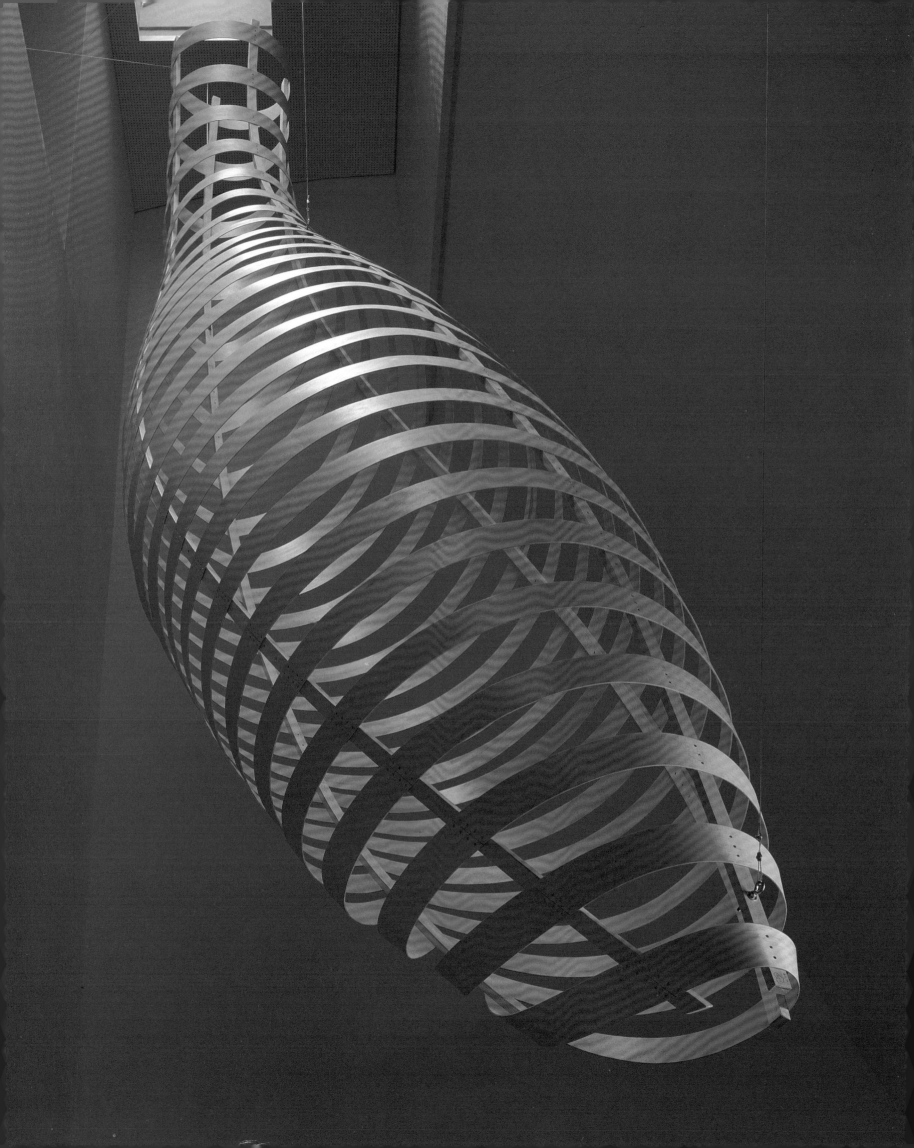

ANTOINE PREDOCK

MUSEUM OF SCIENCE AND INDUSTRY
Tampa, Florida

The spherical Omnimax Theatre becomes the key organising element of the entire facility and of the site. Contained in the museum is a lobby, major exhibit spaces, the Omnimax Theatre, education spaces, offices, and support spaces. Piers stretch to an existing facility and to the wetlands to the south creating an anchor for the site, unifying the assemblage of new and existing.

Visitors to the museum, travelling from heavily trafficked Fowler Avenue, are first struck by a shimmering, blue sphere – the new landmark/billboard for the Museum. The entry onto the site is marked by the glowing glass beacon (also doubling as a vertical circulation ramp) which guides the visitor under the building, allowing glimpses into the four-storey lobby and exhibit spaces. This drive follows the outstretched arm of the wetlands causeway, until it penetrates the thick wall and the woodlands beyond are revealed. Once parked and out of their automobile, the visitors are gathered along the edges of the 'Florida biomes' footpath, the first exhibit. This path becomes an experiential journey through several Florida biomes, from the low marshlands to the higher and drier live oak hummock at the Museum's front door.

A series of truncated 'legs' that define an outdoor adventure courtyard pen-etrates the building and leads the visitor into the lobby. The dining room, museum store, and library are all accessed from the entry at no charge. Views of the blue dome through the lobby to the west, and the reappearance of piers, lead the visitor beyond and into the four-storey lobby where the nested levels of exhibits seen earlier from the cars are once again visible. These overlapping levels allow exhibits to flow easily up through the facility where access is gained to the Omnimax Theatre.

Antoine Predock Architects worked in association with Robbins, Bell, Kuehelm Architects, and completed the Museum in 1995.

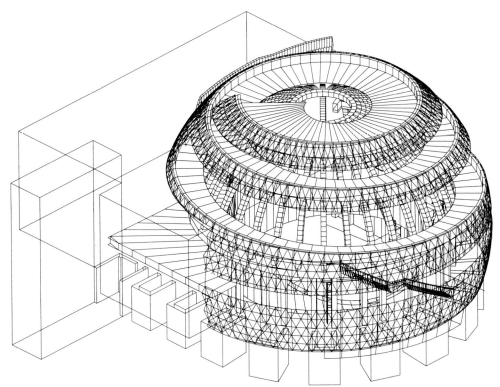

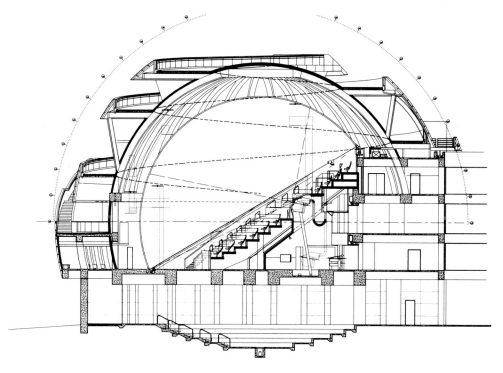

FROM ABOVE: Axonometric; section of Omnimax Theatre

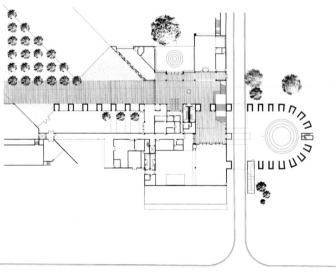
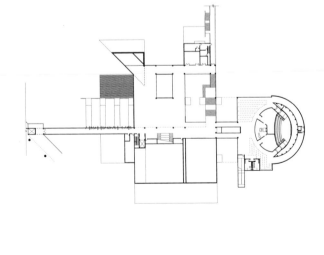

Ground floor plan; second floor plan

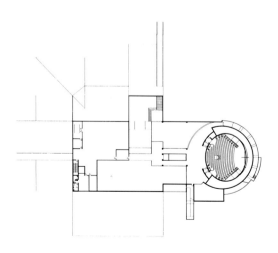

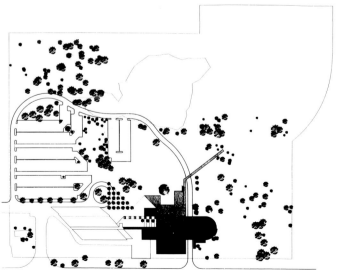

Fourth floor plan; site plan

FRANK GEHRY
IN COLLABORATION WITH CLAES OLDENBURG & COOSJE VAN BRUGGEN
CHIAT/DAY BUILDING, VENICE, CALIFORNIA

In Frank Gehry's own words, the new Chiat/Day/Mojo offices are 'designed to work urbanistically in a community that is practically formless. I wanted the building to have differentiation on the street line to break down the scale of the long frontage, and to punctuate the entrance with something special.' The building's special focus is a three-storey high pair of upright binoculars that are both functional and visually appealing. The eye pieces serve as skylights illuminating the interior of the binoculars, which open up into a large conference room. And, as if to inspire bright ideas in the room, huge lightbulb sculptures, designed by artists Oldenburg and Van Bruggen, hang from the ceiling. Oldenburg, who also collaborated on the binocular design with Van Bruggen and Gehry stated that the project was 'a departure from the usual antagonism between architect and artist. The beauty of it is that the sculpture is of equal weight with the other parts, acting as a pivot around which they revolve.'

The interior office design of this advertising company eliminates the usual hierarchies, with all offices and furnishings essentially the same. 'My hope in the interiors was to make the place comfortable' states Gehry, 'where people can feel relaxed while doing their work, and to create a place with a sense of humour.'

CHARLES JENCKS
Towards the Perfected Office

Main Street in Venice, California, is a mixture of Main Street USA, office park and seedy downtown trying to survive the recession. Right across from the binoculars of Frank Gehry's new offices for the advertising firm Chiat/Day/Mojo is a dosser's pad, a black mattress and garbage-pile set in the bushes as if beach bums had suddenly taken up industrial espionage. At the next road junction up the street is Jonathan Borofsky's *Hermaphroditic Clown*, its unofficial title, a running man-woman with ballerina-legs and moustache. Now Gehry's collage completes the scene – boat, binoculars, forest – a summary of the funky beach vernacular on a higher level.

Gehry will not like the compliment, but this is his most accomplished post-modern building to date. Small block planning at the right scale, a mixture of appropriate languages for an ad-agency in the commercial strip, explicit simile and implicit metaphor, high/low taste, symbolic collage and, on the interior, rich warm ironies. It's all here, almost the canonic PM formula conceived in the mid-1980s just as he was damning post-modernism and saying his 'fish' were meant as a response to and critique of the movement. As often happens in history, rejection of an approach becomes the sign of covert appropriation.

The contrasting images of the Main Street facades are superb even if at first, they seem a bit obvious. Second glance uncovers the relevant and multidimensional references: the 'white boat' is also a 'pointed fish' and in its metallic sleekness a comment on the boatyards and Pacific ocean nearby; the 'binoculars', designed by Claes Oldenburg and Coosje van Bruggen, while more representational, serve as a triumphal arch for automobile parking and the enclosure of the main conference room. This doubly-functioning object with its 'snake light' clearly advertises the purpose of this agency located in 'Venice'. The copper tree trunks lean towards the feminine binoculars like Duchamp's 'men' in *The Large Glass*, a clutch of wavering branches that also cut down the fierce Californian sunlight. These enigmatic shapes show the typical Gehry aesthetic that has evolved after ten years of skewing industrial and natural forms.

It's a chunky abstract representation positioned carefully between the requirements of architecture and communication. The chunkiness comes from the necessities of enclosing space with economy and using the geometric solids that architecture must employ, a direct result of articulating familiar shapes with flat metal panels – the fish, tree or boat. Mondrian, whose paintings of trees

from 1911-16 became successively more general, would find these angular struts midway in his series. This halfway position is the strength, not weakness, of Gehry's abstract representation and, of course, a key method of post-modernists (an issue of *Architectural Design* was devoted to the subject in 1983).

Even more convincing are the interiors – both the old refurbished warehouse on the back street and the new buildings on Main Street. Here a relaxed urbanity prevails, a grid of 'streets', major 'avenues' and 'monuments' set into the fabric. This transformation of the office into an interior city block – an idea that it has been around since Herman Hertzberger's work in the late 60s – finally takes the sting out of open planning. The open, flowing office-landscape no longer has to look like a military camp, or an assembly-line manned by well-paid zombies. The functional workstation is packaged repetitively here, as any office, but finally with intimacy, informality and surprise – precisely the qualities needed in our white-collar factories.

In the old warehouse a village landscape is structured around a Main Avenue organised north-south, and plugged into this grid are several enigmatic incidents – again abstract representations of fish and other objects that have acquired various affectionate euphemisms. Some are media rooms where complete silence and acoustical control are required. A set of three rammed together in a typical Gehry collage is constructed of contrasting materials: galvanised sheet metal versus corrugated cardboard versus dark-red-Finn-Ply.

The interior of the cardboard room is surfaced in corrugated blocks creating an acoustically zero-rated womb: you can hear your heart beat, naturally faster and faster. With its interior oculus allowing a shaft of Californian light to move around the conical dome this space – and I will stand by the comparison – is the equivalent of the Pantheon's. Magical, nicely perplexing in its mixing of wall, furniture and ceiling, it brings a space of contemplation and rest to the most pragmatic and restless of city functions.

If most of those in the First World are destined to spend 60 per cent of their waking hours toiling in factory-offices, then it is buildings like these that are going to make the experience equal to the full urban life of the cosmopolitan city. Along with the NMB Bank in Amsterdam, the Landeszentralbank in Frankfurt and recent work by Hiroshi Hara and Michael Hopkins, Gehry's buildings define the office paradigm of the 90s.

As Los Angeles, which is the parent city without a centre, increasingly yearns for an urban core that is synonymous with its new status as 'the capital of the West Coast', opinions are becoming more sharply divided over the part that architecture should play in its transformation. Joel Garrean, whose *Edge City* has been helpful in defining the urban type predicated by LA, has identified a key ingredient in this change, for as he says: 'Within the Sixty-Mile Circle one can find a stunning diversity of environments – ocean surf, rolling hills, canyons, mountains, lakes, deserts, and some of the most productive farmland on earth . . . The Edge Cities of the Los Angeles Basin contain a vibrant ethnic mix. America is going through the greatest wave of immigration since the turn of the century. It is absorbing more legal immigrants than the rest of the world combined. Los Angeles is its premier entrepot.'[1]

In the debate precipitated by this evolution, those who treat structures as a defensive weapon in an alien urban landscape are in strong contention with both the contextualists and the proponents of the single building as expressive sculpture, with each faction convinced it has the answer. Frank Gehry, who is recognised as an unparalleled medium to the subconscious of this city has now begun to display a decided social consciousness of his own, having recognised both the potential and danger of this diversity and the civil experiment it has engendered. His Disney Concert Hall, now under construction, is a dramatic example of the heightened status of his city and the marked change in his own stylistic direction that has resulted from his perception of that shift. Having begun in the same way as his houses, as a series of isolated pavilions that depended on the expressive individuality of each part to bring the whole composition together, the Concert Hall has since coalesced into a unified whole. While this change has admittedly been partially caused by an acoustician brought in at the client's request, it also reflects Gehry's recent move towards monumentality, as also seen in the American Centre in Paris and the Vitra Museum. As a sign of his awareness of the need for a more substantial symbol of the growing cultural base in LA, as well as his own artistic coming of age, the Disney Concert Hall marks a watershed in his career, and a *tour de force* in the joining of expression and function. Located on Bunker Hill, which is a prominent downtown site at the intersection of First Street and Grand Avenue adjacent to the existing Music Center of Los Angeles, the Concert Hall includes many innovative ideas, in respect to the legend it is dedicated to, the social agenda the architect has set for it, and his empathy with the artistic needs of the musicians who will play there. These include a fully accessible 'front door', joined to an entry plaza at the prime corner of First

and Grand, and a secondary entry plaza at Second and Grand leading into the gardens that will surround the Hall, which are visualised as an oasis of palm trees around the billowing curves of the exterior screen walls. Both entries reflect the sympathetic and inclusive sense that Gehry wants to convey, and his determination to avoid any hint that this is a bastion of the culturally elite. This accounts for the contrastingly human scale of the free-form arcade along Grand Avenue, and the fact that unlike most concert halls, the lobby here has purposefully been designed to relate to the street, and is intended to remain open all day, not just during performances. Large, operable glass panels will assist in this accessibility; a restaurant, the Museum of the Philharmonic, Disney memorabilia and a pre-concert amphitheatre will insure activity in the lobby. The amphitheatre will be used for lectures related to each performance, as well as educational programmes and impromptu events that will be scheduled throughout each day. With these egalitarian aims in mind, the 2,400 seat Concert Hall, has been designed to be visually and acoustically intimate, despite its necessarily large scale. The sail-like forms on the ceiling and the swooping curves of the side walls continue the image of closeness, and convey the feeling that the audience are all passengers on a ship heading into uncharted waters, bound for discoveries yet to be revealed.

Gehry's recently opened Chiat/Day/Mojo Office, which is the second of his larger projects in the Los Angeles area, offers another take on what he considers to be the proper architectural response to a dispersed urban field. Located in Venice, California, the offices occupy an L-shaped site, and have been designed in collaboration with the artist Claes Oldenburg and Coosje van Bruggen to be seen almost entirely as a facade best appreciated when seen through a windscreen on the way down Main Street. Reading from left to right, the principal elevation is divided into three different parts which have been named by Gehry's office, and subsequently referred to by company employees, as 'Boat', 'Binoculars' and 'Trees' with each part having a totally different character. While the notorious Binoculars, which in true LA fashion are intended as a gateway for cars rather than people, initially seem to be the centrepiece of this tripartite composition, the interaction between each part is a bit more subtle. When seen from the prime direction of travel along Main Street, from Los Angeles and Santa Monica towards Venice and the Pacific, the graceful curve of the 'Boat' first leads the eye towards Oldenburg's ocular gate, and then on to Gehry's 'Trees' which are its equal in scale and artistic impact. This pairing reinforces Gehry's self-image as artist-architect, which began with his own chain-link and raw plywood house-collage in 1978 and has continued on through early residential projects for many LA artists. As well as his recent Fish restaurant in Kobe, Japan, which is his most literal piece of architectural art prior to Main Street. In his Pritzker Prize acceptance speech Gehry openly referred to this identification when he said: 'My artist friends, people like Jasper Johns, Bob Rauschenberg, Ed Kienholz, Claes Oldenburg, were working with very inexpensive materials . . . broken wood and paper, and they were making beauty, these were not superficial details, they were direct, it raised the question of what was beautiful. I chose to use the craft available, and to work with the craftsmen and make a virtue out of their limitations. Painting had an immediacy which I craved for architecture. I explored the processes of raw construction materials to try giving feeling and spirit to form. In trying to find the essence of my own expression, I fantasised the artist standing before the white canvas deciding what was the first move. I called it the moment of truth. Architecture must solve complex problems . . . But then what? The moment of truth, the composition of elements, the selection of forms, scale, materials, colour, finally, all the same issues facing the painter and sculptor. Architecture is surely an art, and those who practise the art of architecture ·are surely architects.'2

Binoculars apart, Chiat/Day/Mojo is an intriguing addition to Gehry's oeuvre in another sense, in that it is intended to be more lyrically metaphorical than the tissue thin French limestone wrapper around the Disney Concert Hall. It evokes images of the glamour days of Hollywood and the Pacific, in the 'Boat' and the dendritic carpet that once covered the California coastline in the 'Trees'. The stylised trunks, branches and canopy of this copper-clad part of the building, which houses chief executive officers in democratically apportioned, open-landscaped style, is also an intentionally graphic reminder that the natural beauty being replaced by asphalt all over Los Angeles is impossible to replace. As Joyce Kilmer said, 'Only God can make a tree'.

If the Disney Concert Hall is the unified monumental gesture that is meant to signify the arrival of LA as the premier commercial and cultural centre on the West Coast, Chiat/Day/Mojo perpetuates the attention getting, scenographic approach that Gehry still senses to be a valid representation of the fragmented urban landscape surrounding the downtown area. Each is an equally germane prototype of a different aspect of the city's character, fit to serve as a guide while LA reinvents itself. The fact that each model also functions well is further proof that this particular architect resists categorisation. At the same ceremony in which he described architecture as an art, jury member Ada Louise Huxtable said that 'he has reconciled art and utility in a handsome, workable and intensely personal synthesis of form and function [that] is his singular achievement . . . Gehry's work goes to the heart of the art of our time, carrying the conceptual and technological achievements of Modernism (as real and instructive as its much better-publicised failures) to the spectacularly enriched vision that characterises the 1990s.'3

These latest additions to those explorations in pure form and sculpture continue to delight offering the promise of an almost inexhaustible imagination that is sure to survive future changes in architectural fashion.

Notes

I Joel Garreaux, *Edge City*, Doubleday, New York, 1991, p 283.

2 & 3 *The Pritzer Architecture Prize Presentation Book*, 1989.

ROBERT AM STERN
THE POP AND THE POPULAR AT DISNEY

Lang Residence, Washington, Connecticut

This talk has a curious history. It was prepared in response to a request of my publisher and master, Andreas Papadakis, who called me and said, 'We're talking about Pop, please do something. Goodbye.' Now Pop has been very far from the front of my mind for quite some time – or so I thought. But when I began to think about my assignment, I realised that a great deal of what I've done and a great deal of what I've learned, especially from my early mentor, Bob Venturi, comes out of the Pop sensibility. So what I will try to do today is to illustrate the effect of Pop on a few early projects of mine and on some of the recent things I've done for Disney, which run in that vein.

It's 25 years since I began to practise independently as an architect. My first house, the Wiseman House in Montauk, New York (1966-67), was an attempt not only to kick the teeth out of the dull conformism of late Modernism and to reflect on what I had learned from Bob Venturi but also, and I believe naturally enough for a beginning architect, to cut a little swath of my own. Venturi's house for his mother set the agenda for me and probably quite a few other architects who wanted to change things as they were. But though in many ways it can be seen as a refection of Pop, it was not that aspect which interested me. I was impressed with the Vanna Venturi house because it used history.

On reflection, Pop seems to have meant a great deal more to me than I thought it did at the time. At the very least it was important as an energy jolt; on a more profound level, because it looked at things as they are in the world and took pleasure in them, it helped me find my way around the Modernism I had come to regard as overburdened by empty rhetoric. Modernism saw the world in ideal terms; Pop-ists saw it as very real. Modernist buildings were designed not for the world as it was, but for the world as Modernist architects wanted it to become. Take the Modernist argument about technology, for example, or should I say, applied engineering, which was what it really was about. Given that Modernism was so obsessed with technology, it's amazing how little real understanding of actual construction its proponents exhibited. The major figures of the inter-war and postwar era had ideas about the way architecture should be built, but from the American perspective these ideas, like their ideas about function, had precious little to do with how buildings were actually built or how things really worked.

So Venturi's house for his mother, like the Wiseman house for my college roommate and his beginning family, tried to answer Modernism's windy calls for a brave new world with an architecture completely ordinary in construction, and familiar in form, if not typical in the way the form was manipulated. So it was that the conscious play with imagery – the use of historical forms in bold, iconographic and/or iconological ways, as well as the parodying of history, were Pop's particular influence on my first work.

The parodied Brillo box seen in Warhol's then and still famous show at the Stable Gallery set the agenda for the nascent Post-Modernism of the 1960s. But with the passage of time, the interest in the world-as-it-is has evolved from the shock value of the banal container into a more scholarly exploration of the architecture of tradition and of traditional architecture, which are not necessarily the same. In architecture, an example of this maturing approach is the idea that the gable roof is at once a paradigm of domesticity and an iconographic representation of the sacred mountain. I think such double readings certainly intrigued Palladio – for example when he put the Nymphaeum behind the Villa Barbaro. As a student of Vincent Scully's, I was early on introduced to this way of thinking and seeing. His existential approach to Greek architecture stressed the relationship of form to site in ways no other commentator had yet done. In a little temporary golf club in the middle of the Rocky mountains, nothing more than two trailers pulled up where somebody said 'Can you make something of it?', I thought of Palladio's Nymphaeum and its split gable and of the Greekness of the gable that evokes the mountain landscapes behind it.

The Lang House in 1974 was built at the point in time when Modernism was really on the run. The idea was to take a very ordinary building and with it to comment on the great works of the past, using hyper-bold colour and exaggerated detail, deliberately revealed as added-on rather than integral to the construction process.

Pop was a liberator, making it possible for me to look at things as they are and to see what might be made of them without worrying about what we were told in school, or better still, not worrying about what other architects would say, which was that the past was dead and therefore of no real interest to the creative process, and that to be new one had to be abstract and discontinuous. When the Best Products Company, seeking an alternative to the surrealism of their SITE-designed catalogue showrooms, turned to the Museum of Modern Art for advice, six architects were commissioned to prepare new prototypes. These architects were Allan Greenberg and Michael Graves at the beginning of their Classical phases, Charles Moore, Stanley Tigerman, Robert Venturi, and myself. My proposal for Best Products was a temple of consumerism. Best's buildings typically were built on flat sites on commercial strips facing major highways. I chose to develop an iconography to describe the kinds of goods that were sold inside, describing a life cycle of consumerism, each stage represented by a familiar item, such as an engagement ring or a camera. Our Best building was imagined for a site on the strip. It was a box with signs on it – reflecting Venturi's Las Vegas-inspired typology. It used bold colours. It made a cartoon of Classicism. For these reasons it was Pop.

Our proposal for the second Chicago Tribune competition was a column, the same form that Adolf Loos used in the 1921 competition. Pop enabled me to see Loos' 1921 design for the Chicago Tribune Competition for itself, made it possible for me to take it as a serious joke. Our Classical column was sheathed in glass, so as to demonstrate that traditional firmness of shape could be sustained even in an age of thin-skinned buildings. From the technological point of view, our column was comparable to the one that Mies projected in 1919, but his had no rhetoric outside that which proclaimed itself. In Mies' case, the design was the thing itself, but in ours, the rhetoric was added on as a commentary on Chicago, on the client, on the very nature of newspapers.

I think we're fated to see Disney over and over again today, because the work commissioned by that company since the mid-1980s puts a new spin on the discussion of the relationship between Pop and popular and populist. My first introduction to Disney came not through a visit to one of the theme parks but through an experience of my architectural education. When I edited *Perspecta* as a student at Yale, Charles Moore proposed, and we published, an article about Disneyland in California, 'You Have To Pay for the Public Life', in which he made the fundamental observation that people go, and pay for the experience to go, to Disneyland in Anaheim, California (as they now also go to Walt Disney World in Florida, to Tokyo Disneyland, and as they will soon go via TGV or RER to Euro Disney outside Paris) because it satisfies a need unfulfilled in their everyday lives, one which seems increasingly unavailable to them in the places they live and work in. That need is to be safe and secure yet amongst strangers in a public place, to have a sense of a town or a city, to have choice and variety in hyperabundance in the environment around them. Disney's appeal is rooted in Walt Disney's sure sense of what binds people together in an atomised world. Disney is very complex, far more so than many give it credit for being. It is about place and symbol; but what of values? For Bob Venturi it is a secular religion of the 20th century, nobody knows what Mickey Mouse means but everybody knows he's some sort of important, almost godlike figure.

Our projects for Disney fall into two categories. Our hotels – the Yacht and Beach Clubs at Walt Disney World and the Newport Bay Club and Cheyenne Hotels at Euro Disney – are 'themed'. They represent an effort to be popular but not Pop. In designing the hotels, architectural traditions deemed dead by the Modernists but very much alive to the public are evoked. These hotels take a Disney programme which specifies not quantity and cost but also character and tries to recapture the past in the present. Our hotels are not reproductions. They are inventions. The Beach Club invents a resort of the 1870s on the New

Jersey shore. The Yacht Club invents one that could have been built anywhere along the Atlantic coast from Maine to Rhode Island between the 1880s and the early 1900s. The plans of the two hotels are identical. They share kitchens and other 'back-of-the-house' services but they *look* different. The plan is not the generator of form – at least not in these cases (and indeed most hotels are planned pretty much the same way everywhere, are they not?) So you have the 1870s 'stick style' as Vincent Scully labelled it, in the Beach Club, and what he named the 'shingle style' in the Yacht Club. Neither is used in a jokey or ironic or Pop way at all. Neither has much to do with Pop except for one significant thing: Pop made it possible for me to see these past styles for what they are – not dead curiosities but living actualities. Pop made it possible to accept them as on-going and valid rather than to see them as only sentimental manifestations of a faulty vision unable to come to terms with the 'constituent facts' of that damnable eternal present that Gideon, in particular, loved so much.

Each of our 'themed' hotels is a whole world within the cluster of worlds that Disney creates as environmental entertainment. Disney's worlds are live-in movies, and visitors are able to roam from one scene to another just as they are able to flip the channels on their television sets. But each world is coherent, inhabitable and real on its own terms. It's dead-pan and straightforward and in that sense it is very much like Warhol's vision of Pop.

Disney is about the movies and Pop, which, with its serial imagery, is also closely connected to the movies. The connection to movies is particularly clear in the work of Warhol. But there is also a connection in the work of Rosenquist and other Pop artists to the movies. In Disney, while they were willing to set up an environment in a very coherent and convincing way, at the same time they never let the visitor forget that there are many different worlds. Disney's theme parks and resorts offer a wonderful juxtaposition of worlds. Earlier this afternoon Charles Jencks noted that Michael Graves' dolphins can be seen 'sitting' on the roof of my Yacht Club Hotel. In the movies, these crazy juxtapositions are often cultivated to great effect – think of fast cutting. Nowhere is that more clear than in the heart of the so-called Magic Kingdom where a mere craning of the neck will shift one's gaze from Cinderella's castle to Disney's now charmingly frozen 1950's view of the future.

In designing the Casting Building for Disney, which represents the second direction of our approach, and the one we also pursued in Espace Euro Disney, we confronted the issue of Pop more directly in our effort to transform an ordinary office building into an expression of the Disney enterprise as a whole. Facing the interstate highway, but on land belonging to Disney at the edge of the private realm of Disney World itself, the Casting Building is the only facility that bears Disney's identity in the public realm. If you haven't been to Florida, I should point out that Disney owns some 26,000 acres of land which it administers as a kind of independent fiefdom under a quirk of Florida law. An enterprise district, Walt Disney World has its own government governed by a handful of employee-residents who, out of what might best be called enlightened self-interest, tend to see things the

Rear view of villa in New Jersey

Residence, Hewlett Harbour, New York

Entrance rotunda, Disney Casting Center, Florida

Disney way.

In that district, the Casting Building is the one building facing on the public realm that is identifiably Disney's. The Casting Building was built for the single purpose of attracting people to work for the Disney Company – not to work as presidents of major divisions, but to work in the 'cast' of the theme park. Disney calls people who work for them the 'cast', the paying guests are alternately the 'audience' or the 'guests'. The Casting Building was to be an ambassador of good will for Disney as an employer. It was to express Disney's vision; to make people smile and to encourage some among them to consider working for Disney. On a real movie lot, casting is definitely a 'backlot' activity, but at Orlando, the Casting Building, though budgeted as a backlot facility, was put on-stage in a front and centre position.

Every move in the Casting Building was thought through in functional and representational terms. The spirit of Pop was never far from my mind as the design unfolded. Yet, the Casting Building is a conventional office building as well, containing all the clerks and executives who take care of the welfare of the approximately 20,000 people who work for Disney in Florida. The Casting Building is a conventional office building with a twist. Instead of the typical situation of offices wrapping a solid core filled with toilets, elevators and fire stairs, the Casting Building has been pulled apart, leaving a void through the centre into which a ramp is threaded connecting the ground floor entry at one end with the main reception room a floor above at the other. The ramp simulates the experience that everyone has when they visit Disney, or any theme park, that of waiting in line on ramps leading to an attraction. Though most of the building houses office space devoted to routine activities, its heart is a singular sequence of space designed to effortlessly lead the arriving would-be employee to his objective, a job interview.

Employees enter the building through an inconspicuous door located near their section of the parking lot. But job-seekers enter under a 'futuristic', 'airfoil' canopy, then pass through an oval rotunda, before they make one left turn and head up the ramp. At the top, a person sits whose sole job is to ask the job-seekers to perform the supreme rite of initiation – which is to write his or her name down on an application card. Let me emphasise one thing: by and large, the people seeking employment are not carrying briefcases; they are not dressed for success in smartly tailored business attire; they are kids, some of whom are not even old enough to drive themselves to the interview; they are unwed mothers or fathers, but it's the unwed mothers that seem more the tragedy; and they are also old people who are returning to the job market because they've either bored themselves to death in retirement or can't make ends meet. It's an extraordinary cross section of post-industrial society, American style.

Venice is the point of departure for the building's exterior, it can be seen in a stucco box overlayed by a diaper pattern of muted cream and golden brown squares. Forming a bridge between unemployment and employment, the Casting Building was to have 'spanned' a lagoon. But the water feature was 'value engineered' out of the project. Venice, also evoked in the glass campanile, is

not a chance reference: a reproduction of the campanile at San Marco is one of the major attractions of Walt Disney World's Epcot Center; and the light and abundance of water in Central Florida also makes a Venetian point as well as the juxtaposition of cultures in a previously bland place, Orlando (which has become a focus for migration into the United States, as well as a major destination for vacationers from Europe and South America). The company's traditional iconography is not ignored. Mickey Mouse's profile forms the scuppers needed to carry the rain from the building during the downpours that so frequently and forcefully flood central Florida. Cinderella's castle plays a role in our design as well; a kind of unattainable goal, it sits above the 'airfoil' entrance and is reprised as a false balcony outside the second floor waiting room.

Because executives want corner windows, we created the Gothic framed enclosures that trap, Rapunzel-like, the most powerful bureaucrats in their towers of power. The executives occupying the corners get the best views from their windows – of the parking lots and roadways which necessarily surround our building.

Back to the arriving job seekers: they enter the building through imposing bronze doors, pulling on doorknobs which represent characters from Alice's Wonderland, rubbing them so often for good luck that they have to be replaced periodically. Inside, the rotunda is surrounded by the Disney Pantheon, dedicated to important characters represented by gilded statues carried aloft on columns and bathed in light coming down from a dome of heaven underneath the glass campanile. There is but one way to turn. There is no need for signs because you are now part of a ritual of movement familiar to you because it is so similar to the movement pattern of the park attractions themselves, which most job-seekers know from their visits to the park. You move up a ramp towards your destination, to the right you look out through *trompe l'oeil* windows to freeway scenes where, instead of tourists from Iowa and Ohio, you see the great Disney characters having a lot of fun in crazy cars. Now you, the anxious job-seeker, are elevated to the same position as the high executive looking through those Gothic-style windows – but yours are views of ideal versions of Disney World while they have to settle for the realities of roadside living. Isn't it wonderful what you can do with paint? Looking through the *trompe l'oeil* windows on your left, you look into the park itself – that is into evocative vignettes of some of its key environmental scenes, places where you will be performing on stage should you get a job.

You continue under a bridge of sighs above which a dome offers a childlike view of heaven with Peter Pan and Wendy flying above. Your journey concludes at the top where a fresh-faced, perfectly scrubbed and groomed person says, 'May I help you?' and asks you to fill out an application form. Some 50 percent of the people melt down at this moment and have to leave because they cannot provide the information required. The rest are asked to sit down and wait . . . and wait. You are then interviewed in confession-like booths, where you are asked to give away such intimate facts as how fast you can type and what your previous jobs have been. Some of you are then asked to stay longer. If you are lucky enough to get a 'call-back', as the movie business calls it, you are asked to come back the next day for further interviews – and get a second glimpse of our building. For those of you who are the lucky ones, as you wait, the bright light dims from the sky to be replaced by the dramatic spotlighting of the theatre world illuminating Disney's representation of hope, Cinderella's castle.

Were it not for Pop, the building would not have been possible. The corporate iconography has been hyped up, mixed up, scrambled up, but in a way that can be easily understood by the people who actually use the building. True, on some levels it is an intellectual's version of Disney. Maybe it is elitist as some suggested this afternoon. But it is also very popular – it's easily understood; and it is fun.

Now, Disney is coming to France. The project is not only challenging because of its size but also because of issues of cultural exchange and meaning. I am the architect for two hotel projects at Euro Disney, the Newport Bay Club, which shares many ideas with our Yacht Club in Orlando, and the Hotel Cheyenne, which I will discuss with you today because it is somewhat different. The Hotel Cheyenne is a two-star hotel with 1,000 rooms. Some 4,000 people will occupy 14 two-storey buildings, arranged along a street, that will also contain some other buildings to provide the guests with food, entertainment, and other services. The hotel is based on the idea of an American Western town: not the Western town in its reality, but in its hyper-reality, the Western town as seen through the movies, the Western town as built on studio backlots. As in the movie backlots, our main street bends to contain the view. You can't really have the open vista of the real Western town on a backlot.

The buildings that line our Main Street are essentially identical, two floors of guest rooms lining double-loaded corridors. But each building is treated as a different design problem, so that the total effect is that of a town. Not a real town, but an environmental prop, a set dressed for a movie, one in which the overnight guest is the star.

Lastly, we were asked to do the building which has turned out to be the first building representing Disney in Europe. It is a little information centre called Espace Euro Disney and it is perhaps the most 'Pop' of our buildings to date. For this temporary building, hardly more than a facade in front of some trailers, I had the opportunity to play a Pop game in a way that could bring together my interests in iconography and contextual reference. The building sits in open fields, easily viewed from the A-4 superhighway that leads past it. It's a billboard. While the building's conelike roof undoubtedly represents the hat Mickey wears in The Sorcerer's Apprentice, it is also the typical tower of the kind of farmhouse groups one finds in northern France, some of which can be found very near the Euro Disney site.

Pop has become a 'constituent fact' of the late 20th century way of seeing. Not *the* fact, but a fact. In my work, there is much that is Pop but I know that there is more. Pop is, but it is not all.

Two Venture Plaza, Irvine, California

Pool House, Llewelyn Park, New Jersey

MARK FISHER

SOME THOUGHTS ON POP AND PERMANENT ARCHITECTURE

As a high-brow pursuit, Pop architecture has a problem. Popular culture is ephemeral, but most architecture is designed to be permanent. The high-brow dredging of popular culture to make Pop Art is OK for paintings. They can be hidden when they go out of fashion, and then rehung from time to time as historical curiosities. For architecture the only escape from old fashion is demolition. Long-life buildings are anathema to Pop architecture.

In the late 50s Reyner Banham contradicted Sir Hugh Casson's fallacious argument that Pop Art presaged Pop architecture. Banham demonstrated that Pop architecture had existed before Pop Art. He proposed Albert Kahn's Ford Pavilion at the New York World's Fair of 1939 as the first example of Pop architecture because it was an advertisement, the precursor of all 'exclamatory hamburger bars and other roadside retail outlets'.[1] An essential feature of popular culture was the disposability of everything including its aesthetic qualities. He quotes Leslie Fiedler: '. . . the articles of popular culture are made, not to be treasured, but to be thrown away'.[2] Leaving aside his academic preference for crediting an architect with the invention of the genre, his thesis was that once architecture embraces commerce, it becomes Pop, subject to 'the same set of Madison Avenue rules' as popular culture – including, by implication, being thrown away .

He also noted that 'the collage-effect of violent juxtaposition of advertising matter with older art forms . . . was being widely discussed in architectural circles around the time of the Festival of Britain'. In a manner which today seems rather precious, this mixing of graphics and form can be seen in the temporary buildings of the Festival itself, which were far more exuberant than the permanent architecture of the period. The certainty of demolition must have been a liberation for the architects involved.

Many of the early examples of what Banham called Pop architecture borrowed their forms from the Modern Movement. Stanley Meston, the architect of the original Golden Arches for McDonalds, introduced the parabolic arches to give the building a 'futuristic' look in 1953. He wasn't bothered that the arches had no structural function. Richard McDonald, one of the franchise's brothers, said later that 'it was fortunate the arches were not structural, since if a vehicle had run into one of them, it might have done serious damage to the building!'[3] The life expectancy of Pop architecture has always been short. Commercial buildings like hotels and exhibition pavilions, or the interiors of shops and clubs, are really advertisements, built to last as long as the products they contain will sell. Harrison and Fouilhoux's Trylon and Perisphere, the centrepieces of the 1939-40 World's Fair, were copied in a whole range of consumer goods which today command good prices in antique shops. But the buildings themselves barely made it to the end of the fair. As *The New York Times* put it: 'If the builders of the Trylon were counting on a single season Fair, it might be argued that they timed themselves with one hundred percent precision.'[4]

The survival test for things in popular culture is whether or not people will buy them. In the purest form, these things are unnecessary, like fashion or entertainment. New styles are constantly invented to exploit the natural habit of consumers to become bored. Even when things are not improved by technical development, they are restyled to excite jaded palates. Permanent architecture cannot survive in this commercial environment; it's too durable.

One of the most transient forms of Pop architecture can be found in the world of popular music. The stage sets for outdoor rock concerts are conversion kits which change the use of space on an architectural scale. With equal ease they turn sports facilities and wastelands into transitory theatres for popular entertainment. They are large and expensive, incorporating technical equipment, decoration and weather protection, in structures which it can take more than 20 trucks to transport from show to show. For the bands which perform on them they are distress purchases, brought about by the lack of facilities at the venues where they play, and the competitive need to add value to the tickets they sell. Greed and ambition drive bands to sell as many tickets as possible. These vices are endorsed by the huge public demand for tickets to the most successful shows; the Rolling Stones sold 6 million $35.00 tickets to their concerts during 1989-90. Left to themselves, the bands would present the cheapest shows they could get away with in the largest venues they could sell out. The fact that they present extravagant spectacles instead, is a response to public demand.

The economic pressure on stage set design means that the materials and technology employed are just sufficient for the job. The sets are ephemeral; they have no use after the final concert. This is why, underneath the decorated surface, they are built from commonplace sub-structures of scaffolding and timber, assembled by hand from rented components. They are an entirely commercial architecture, sustained by voluntary public subscription and discarded as soon as they have passed their sell-by date.

Notes

1 Reyner Banham, 'Towards a Pop Architecture', in *Design by Choice*, Academy, 1981.

2 Reyner Banham, 'Throw-Away Aesthetic', in *Design by Choice*, Academy, 1981.

3 Philip Langdon, 'Burgers! Shakes!', *Atlantic Monthly*, 1985.

4 Quoted in Cohen, *Trylon and Perisphere*, Abrams, 1989.

PREVIOUS PAGE: Rolling Stones, 'Steel Wheels' US Tour; OPPOSITE & ABOVE: Roger Waters, 'The Wall', Berlin

NIKOS GEORGIADIS
TRACING ARCHITECTURE

'Tracing' in architectural experience has a practical meaning as a design technique transforming ideas to drawings and eventually to real space. In contrast to the metaphoric use of trace (in so-called marginal philosophy) architects' tracing paper engenders a process of controlling opacity, rather than transparency, which strives to bring to the fore what is 'underneath', in its maximum possible formal richness. 'Tracing architecture' focuses on *trace* as a dialectical process as opposed to trace as a metaphor for leftoverness, dismantling or dispersion. 'Unsculpting' architecture, or 'the extended site of architecture', are concepts which also drive the work of this issue in the same direction. The term trace, however, best encapsulates the *foundness* of architectural experience both as analytic and propositional form. The debate this issue hosts constitutes a response to the way the emerging condition of objective realism in the visual arts is often casually imported into the field of architecture. It aims to foreground architecture's spatial identity rather than subordinate it to an object–spectator viewing process, to regard trace as an active, real design procedure and tool.

'Trace', 'texture', 'minimalist forms' – the object in pieces, the bare object, the blurred object, and even the obstructing object – are all leading sculptural metaphors, as witnessed in a series of examples: from various unfortunate translations of Rodin's concepts into contemporary art, to Richard Serra's sculptural propositions, and to schemes of applied negativity in architecture. Even the idea of the 'complexity' (or ontology) of the object seems to relate architecture as subservient to the visual arts and to the latest objective or counterobjective (textual, literary, etc) idealisms. The theoretical back-up to these can be found in the positivisation of psychoanalytic concepts in the context of their straightforward visual application in art and architecture, which celebrates the idea that the Freudian symptom (whether termed 'object', 'real', or 'uncanny') can be inserted as 'disturbance critique' in the course of its mere visual appearance. Deleuze and Guattari's counteroedipal 'spatial' philosophy, Derrida's 'trace', and certain misreadings (mistaking undasein for anti-dasein) of Adorno's critique of Heidegger, seem to hint towards that direction, which not only reinstates the philosophical subject (a philosophical alibi or replica borrowing its imaginary clothes from 'place' or 'object' – counter-Platonic and Kantian in essence) but also seems to produce and actually needs a 'new' morphological style: that of spatial poverty.

In parallel, it appears that the metaphor of archaeology *for* knowledge (the Foucaultian paradigm, combined with Habermasian communicational universal pragmatics) has largely contributed to recent postmodern sculptural-philosophical aesthetics, and now becomes a metaphor for practice, as seen in the production of amorphous, fragmented, deformed (yet nonetheless finite, singular and self-referential) objects in the field of architecture

and the visual arts – 'communicational' objects whose function and reason of communication are untraceable and elusive. Architecture thus becomes an area of the bizarre application of naive and crude *anti*-architectural metaphors from which designers are meant to take their references and inspiration. Ruins, remnants, dilapidated and abandoned spaces become leading aesthetic guides in design, in a celebration of 'de-determinist', dysfunctional and unusable spaces. The architectural event, then, has a tendency to be abandoned to the user, whereas the work's real functional course is often shrunk to mere appreciation and non-discourse. But while such a *spatial aporia* (spatial poverty and privation) is easily recycled as a sophisticated concept in contemporary architectural debates, its manifestation in real cases (bombarded cities, under-utilised sites, wastelands, peripheral non-spaces, to name but a few) is never recognised as an architectural problem as such – 'minimalism', 'deconstruction', 'desolation' are in fact real experiences in war zones long before their translation into architectural style. The archaeological metaphor, in keeping with the modernist tradition, appears to exchange, yet again, the real site of architecture with the a priori site of the plastic arts – a (non)site, whose morphological parameters are at best ignored, or at worst taken into negative consideration (with the built work operating as a 'site specific' obstacle or rendering a 'ship in a bottle' effect), in a condition celebrating the morphological autonomy of the built work and the inevitable 'gallerisation' of public space.

The aestheticisation of ruins (already dating back to Piranesi) reappearing in the context of a new romanticism, as well as neo-functional cyber-objective pluralism and the delirious proliferation of singular objects in space, all serve to contextualise architecture in a new frame of ultra-functionalism (and ultra-exhibitionism). Here, spatial relationships simply become the ecstatic witnesses of the vicissitudes of a highly self-referential functionalist condition, which cancels out and optionalises itself at a symbolic level, before function can be tested in real forms. While in archaeological practice, traces, ruins and findings constitute the epistemological material itself, in recent deconstructive design such 'findings' are meant to be constructed anew to suggest forms that already appear antiquated, yet do not inform one another; dismantled or irresistibly swept away in style (with their original meaning designed to be foreclosed and unrecognisable). And while in archaeology, determinist relations between culture and space are actually sought after and seen as important localisations of culture and life, in archaeology's metaphorisation into design, such relations are negated from the outset at a programmatic level.

Nevertheless, at an experiential level, architecture does seem to resist such objective realism, and qualifies a possible field of criteria in relation to which such realism is naive, even primitive. The unequivocal urgency of function in architecture brings to the

Anamorphosis Architects, 'Spatial Cast' – spatial multitude of the New Acropolis Museum project

fore the question of form, but form as a raw, undisputed *realness of a spatially extended – both inwardly and outwardly – condition*; the real site of architecture. Such a site may appear unelaborated when considered through the criteria of sculpture and the visual arts; after all, it is neither objectively autonomous nor blurred. However, such a symptomatic but simultaneously active recurrence of 'function as form' becomes the crucial point of differentiation between sculpture and architecture; indeed, it reflects the problematic way in which the visual arts develop their discursive certainty by dismissing function and instrumentality.

Moreover, it seems that such a resistance today has the political character of a reclaim rather than a mere return. Seen from the spatial (non)point of view, architectural experience recurs today not as a question of objective or discursive identity but as a (personal/public) reclaiming of spatial culture, exceeding the limits of 'physical' or 'livable' space (or its opposites); a *bon symptome*. The main question raised here is about how the real (by returning to itself) is processed as location-specific; about the 'specific-ness' of the real, rather than the 'realness' (or non-realness) of the specific; not about the return of the irrupting real but about *how* the real returns as spatial practice – as a question of the dialecticisation of the historic rather than as a query in the field of visual philosophy (women's traditional domestic space, migration, homelessness, agoraphobia, citizenship, are all problematics which have already raised this point).

Perhaps the above discussion might also be regarded as a response to certain points developed by such theorists as Rosalind Krauss, Anthony Vidler, Hal Foster, Andrew Benjamin and others. In the context of an architectural journal, however, the intention is to open up a *spatial* dialogue of critique both through the concepts elaborated in the essays and the architectural works presented herein.

The dialectics of trace-in-practice specifies a kind of inverted archaeology: a design tool that introduces the discourse of the real as presencing. The 'accomplishedness' and 'pastness' of the trace hints at a way of conceptualising form in a state of irreducibility and plenitude. Trace is therefore to be seen as a critique of the ruling symbolic environment, which can introduce the political value and economy (to paraphrase Henri Lefebvre) of the return of the familiar objectal world in a state of morphological affluence, not in order to disturb but to re-relate to us as users.

A direct environmental problematic is hereby introduced in the context of spatial anticipation and association. Environment does not appear, however, as an externality, liable to 'adjustment', 'protection' etc at a general conceptual level. Instead of being a shapeless ideology, environment is reintroduced in design at the level of the problematic of *form*, involving the specific spatial reality which constitutes the *extended architectural site*. It develops through relations of spatial detachment and immediacy beyond 'micro'–'macro', 'built-space'–'landscape' distinctions and visual/perceptual reductionisms. The question of plasticity reappears in a context other to that of isolated – finite or deformed – 'objects in space'. Furthermore, the realness of the object in the context of architectural experience reopens the question of how form, as a direct environmental concept (and not as a neutral or autonomous objective property), informs design to become a critical instrument. It is also in this context that the long degraded issue of *function* enters the discussion. Far from the paradigm of functionalism (or counter- or neo-functionalism), function is tested as that which substantiates architectural experience in the field of agitated spatiality or extended form. Trace is proposed at the

point at which *function* and *environment* in architectural experience converge, to produce dense and uncompromising morphological propositions. Such an engagement of function seems able to activate a psychoanalytic dimension Other to that of subject as individual: the dialectics of the *person* – a so-far repressed subjectivity able to enact rich performative countertransferential processes into the *social*, by proposing localisations of its symbolic images (as opposed to the individual's enreasoning of its most remote symptoms).[1]

Tracing architecture means to *trace architecture* as the missing paradigm of unsymbolic/unvisual conditioning; as a possibility and urge for spatial contextualisations, involving unfashioned and impure morphological propositions for radical reallocations of function. Tracing architecture entails specifying the real architectural site in its full formic dimension as a process which expands the limits of 'physical' space (hence as fantasy), and acknowledges the dialectics of environmental immediacy occurring across 'close' and 'remote' spatial relations. The texts included in this issue from the fields of architecture, archaeology, psychoanalysis, communication, political theory, philosophy and the humanities argue for the necessity of a problematic of location and customised reality seen as a potential field of critique. They all share a political awareness of the limitations (in terms of poverty and expiration rather than 'crisis') of certain ruling symbolic contextualisations of space subject to: the building as representative of the brief; historicalisation of the past; user-friendly discursification (fragmentation) of sensuality and object-relating; spatial retirement (privacy) of the reindividualised 'psychoanalysed subject' and urban living as a-political wandering; after-image mediation of urban communication; visual (and interpretative) discursification of artwork; familiarisation (or defamiliarisation) of domestic space; and architectural authorship and copyrighted design. Respectively, *trace*, in an anti-Derridean manner, appears as spatial engagement rather than abandonment in concepts such as: the unfinished/unbuilt (as opposed to non-built); the historic as a total diachronic spatial experience; sensuality as body-objectal dialectical resistance; the countertransferential public spatial projection of the domestic; unmediated collective communication; spatial figuration of the artwork's allocation; the politics of undasein; and uninflected stubborn architecture.

Tracing architecture also means conceptualising *architecture as a tracing process*; to de-metaphorise *trace* and engineer it as a proper *realising* design method that has the ability to engage with form at an uncompromising operational state of plenitude. In contrast to the sculptural paradigm, form-synthesis is an effect of the way the extended locality/site principles the scheme and opens it up to spatial intelligibility rather than objective finiteness or counterfiniteness. Function, or the brief, is hereby seen not as an imperative to be accurately implemented, but as an 'objective' body of meaning hinted at by the morphology. This allows for the presentation of a diversity of architectural projects which all have the *real* as their starting point. Their concern is to permit the expression of the morphology of the real – both as given and manipulable – rather than the architects' viewpoints. The projects do not aspire to create new environments but instead take on board and respond to existing ones. They consist of small, medium and large (or S, M, L, XL!) morphological engagements of the site concerning landscape features, climatic conditions, monumental integrations in dense urban space, pre-existing structures and locational characteristics, idiosyncratic natural conditioning at an urban level, strong building tradition, specific materials and construction methods. If the theoretical texts presented in the first part of this issue propose a rethinking of spatiality, these projects propose a *non-ideas* condition which is of practical but also of theoretical importance yet to be developed.

Necdet Teymur's 'unbuilt' environment suggests that unfinished architecture can never be overlooked. The *unfinished building* is neither disrupting nor 'backgrounding' our perceptions but comes as a state of plenitude of form (and educational value) impregnated with possibilities of functions rather than of individual buildings. The unfinished building is not an unfinished object; it is rather a tautology – a condition synonymous with the building-process itself. 'Unfinished Buildings' introduces us to a condition of overstatement of real built form freed from its original symbolic enclosure and associated with the urgency (rather than the establishment) of function – a condition critical of the idea of 'bricolage' or 'collage city'.

Philippos Oreopoulos introduces us to an inverted archaeological context in a fundamentally anti-Derridean reading of the concept of 'trace'. The *labyrinth* indicates what the trace is really capable of. Remaining in the positive, he discusses the specificness of the local, how the 'past' returns as a historic-real and total design tool. Perhaps what is equally important with his approach of this spatial model is its safeguarding from any symbolic remodelling or positivisation. So a distinction between the *spatial* and the *visual* labyrinth has to be drawn here: the former leading to a *total design* experience and practice encompassing a range of objectal processes from garments to urban space, the latter, merely a visual appropriation of the spatiality of the former, leading to disorder.

Richard Sennett's *touch* or *resistance* introduces spatiality as a critical subjectivity occurring on the side of the object. In the audio discourse, the body-microsite is re-organised in a process of the realisation of musical sound; the latter is not a given but a quested sense, occurring at a micro-dialectics between finger and instrument. This is in contrast to dasein-minded space that de-organises the body by individualising it as a comfortable whole, applying the subject's taste catholically to the world and committing itself 'freely' to discourses requiring spatial fragmentation. Resistance seems to be generated in the difference between procedural space and the (ideally expected) dasein place (a user-friendly operation) of a discourse (it is on these grounds that Anamorphosis Architects introduce the concept of inverted narcissism and attempt a visual introduction of Sennett's text).

In Andreas Empirikos/Andrew Samuels' countertransferential paradigm the site/trace acquires a psychoanalytic dimension. Psychoanalysis 'ends' as linguistic practice, but continues through the spatial field, at once social and personal, real/factual and poetic, domestic and public, modern and ancient. Space as both 'here and there' enables and maps the politics of reclaimed subjectivity and a redefinition of the personal in terms of the social. 'Notions of objectivity' or *urban fantasies* (visually developed by Anamorphosis Architects) have nothing in common with the privacy of imagination; they are spatial propositions enabling the politicisation of the Freudian symptom. The person/individual difference recurs here; but this is as old as the difference between spatial and symbolic cultural processes, or between citizenship (polis) and aimless flâneuring (a-polis).

Pavel Büchler's *crowd* affords a *shadow* full of spatial meaning, reminding us of Lyotard's fully spatial absence of truth. In a strong un-wandering manner, the crowd is seeking un-symbolic cohesions (which eventually may radicalise it); making a case for the quest for an internal, un-individuated, human-to-human, body-to-body solidifying 'resistance', rather than for physical expansion to abstract space. A different kind of 'uncanny' appears here: the site appears as an *urban body*; the crowd is the medium of spatial communication – traditionally unsymbolic – an urban fantasy perhaps, reclaiming lost citizenship; it is the collective symptom of private symbolic activity. The Red Flag is an urban-conscious artwork radically realising a symbolic situation of total gravity – 'architecture becomes an active paradox of the show'.

Jean-François Lyotard's extract from *Discours, figure* bridges the gap between visual artwork and spatial experience. Spatiality, rather than entropic (ie accidental, flâneuring) interpretation, brings us closer to Rodin's intentions. The 'visual art object' is never placed at the same place (as the 'real'), but placeness itself becomes a discourse exposing visuality as a whole. The Imaginary activates site-relations beyond the visuality of the Real. Artwork acquires a radically different meaning from some contemporary art critics/historians' interpretations; it is not here to signify the absence of the real object but the absence of truth strictly speaking; more importantly it enfigures the actual *allocation process*, introducing a critical distance between the original symbolic discourse and the spatial environment in which it operates.

In Doreen Massey's reading of the inverted House artwork, spatiality is highlighted as a major political dimension. Unlike some postmodern historical approaches (from architecture or art), her *politics of location* points at neither anti-dasein (uncanny) design strategies, nor entropic interpretations. Massey's House is not that of Whiteread's, but is yet further inverted; it challenges the responsibility of forms – standing there radically bare and empty, but rich enough to *cast* real living. The politics of location specifies an agitated site engaging: *nostos* as a spatial mode of presencing (as opposed to a symbolic nostalgic 'past'), *socialisation of the familiar* (as opposed to privatisation) and the *tradition of locality/history-making* (as opposed to the familiarisation with 'heritage' and tradition). Agitated 'private' space – the space that 'women have lived in' – and to that extent the space of agoraphobia, migration etc, is not a symptom but a problematic of spatial instrumentation for the re-allocation of function.

In Roger Connah's discussion of ARRAK's architecture, the concept of the *uninflected* – an invisible uncanny – addresses the architect's internalisation of the site of architecture. Neither expressionism nor impressionism, a real-space problematic is inscribed in the architect's personal design exploration. Here is a non-attitude, a sought-and-lost style, an honest uncovering of that torturous feeling we practising architects have when, in the middle of nowhere, we are asked to build. A 'nowhere' that can be anywhere; a problematic perhaps more real than a theoretical 'non-place'. For some it is a spatial virus in the healthy body of the expected place (homely or unhomely); for others it is a *spatial alertness,* a spatial montage – a report of somebody's personal engagement with architecture.

In terms of the projects presented in this issue, *territorialising architecture* is a description that best reflects the built work of Ian Ritchie and the conceptual work of François Roche. It signifies a morphological engagement of the site (whether rural or urban) often leading to seemingly 'high-tech' but essentially modest solutions that are based on the engineering of nature itself. The greenhouse microclimate is not 'a building' but a local duplication of nature, operating as a design principle for schemes hosting cultural activities. *Chameleon architecture* is thus not a metaphor but a working concept based on the deep awareness of the morphological potential of nature and of the spatial economy produced out of the processes of the redirection of nature to itself. Technology – surely 'high' – emerges as an effect of such processes rather than as an imposed model pre-developed elsewhere.

Janek Bielski's *desertscape* and Livady Architects' *nightscape* introduce us to the discourse of *Other* urbanities. Their morphological propositions activate the urban/collective 'natural' a priori, proposing possibilities of spatial cultures in large urban schemes. The desert or nightlight are not discomforting symptoms of the 'green city' or 'daylight city culture'; neither are they settings, neutral conditions or design metaphors. They are instead considered as the *Other* urban site(s) of the town – sites so far repressed by specific urban cultures but highly constitutive of them. What was formerly exurban (desert and night), is now dialecticised as a 'large scale' design problematic. Urban space is called upon to refer to itself – *at the same place* – in an act of spatial engineering and economy, anticipating and doubly realising culture and life.

In Jim Taggart's presentation, Patkau Architects' *particular pragmatism* (or *found potential*) and their general–particular, interior–exterior, spatial dialectics orients design towards the localisation of strong community, educational, etc, values (not surprisingly, their big school buildings lack graffiti). Far from being a style, such a principle appears in a variety of forms according to the specific requirements of the project. The apparent similarities with certain deconstructive styles of our time, whereby a 'freedom of forms' is effected after the imposition of the metaphor of a free play of bodily movements or actions, raise a good critical point. The morphological complexity in their work is indeed manifestly un-sculptural and construction- and site-minded, whereas in deconstructive examples it is a style, a non-tool, a leftover or redundancy of the building process (not surprisingly, often demanding high-tech solutions for its realisation).

Jones Partners and Lapeña–Torres Tur propose a 'surrealist' *excessive use of a singular material or construction method* in an act of over-realisation of function. Here the material recurring to itself *is* the active site. In their cabins Jones Partners incorporate the morphological principle of yet another site quality involving not just natural environment but the very experience of distancing. Their design bears a kind of *spatial awareness of transportation*, offering a structure that is at once stable and firm but also removable. Flâneur-style architecture seems out of question; transportation, including that of the construction material, is, rather, mapped in a reversed way, as a firm anti-metaphorisation/anti-intellectualisation of physical distance, travelling or visiting.

In Clare Design and Antithesis Architecture's projects, *casual* architecture means a spatial incorporation of all site and landscape aspects, reworking spaces on the traces of pre-existing building structures. Cheap and handy materials are used within the logic of quick construction, durability and recycling. In contrast to other work that espouses the 'monumentalisation' of the casual (eg corrugated panel style), and the delirious hijacking of architectural 'scrap parts' used in proposals entertaining

unrelatedness and dysfunctionality (in the same breath, amazingly, as 'hypercommunicability'), forms and materials in the work of both teams are functionally busy and destined to realise much more than one purpose in uncompromising compositions. Indicative of this is also their simulatory use of colour which appears to be an integral part of the extended site. In Antithesis' schemes, *modernity* (as *object/site – excess*) is revealed as the underlying architectural principle not only of the traditional settlement of Santorini but also of its figurative, self-referential landscape – a principle apparently inhabiting the island for the last 4,000 years.

Nikos Georgiadis/Anamorphosis Architects propose the concept of *negative space* at the level of technique in analysis and practice. In their museum proposal, *building in process* activates a site consisting of the historic/'past' as exhibited object, pre-Renaissance spatial tradition and the urban quality of the social subject *vis-à-vis* the symbolic load of the Acropolis monument. As a critique of flâneuring and negativist architecture, the project covers a design field ranging from the micro-level of the allocation/exhibition of the sculptures to the urban role of the museum building. Spatial technique is hereby employed as a *total design* approach that encompasses urban space, architecture, art, even graphics – an early modern design concept revitalised via a spatial contextualisation of psychoanalytic principles.

What associates all of these works is not their uniformity of style or their thematic similarities but the fact that they have the potential to anticipate one another at a spatial level, acting as spatial reminders of one another. So, for example, one could associate Patkau Architects' interiors with Jones Partners' overworked staircase; the Acropolis museum with Rodin's statue of Balzac; Sennett's 'resistance' with ARRAK's 'stubborn' architecture. Equally, the 'unfinished' buildings of Teymur and Jones Partners' 'overfinished' buildings afford the same morphological affluence and exaggeration, while they can also meet the unsculptural reading of Massey, and so on and so forth. Indeed, one of the aims of this issue is to enable free spatial associations amongst the contributors' works, rather than to 'style up' a 'trace' discourse. It also aims to challenge the reader to encounter the featured architectural work in terms of its public usability. Far from being a discursive principle, this condition of architecture as a tracing process signifies an open procedure whereby more projects can be invited and presented. For these works allow no space for authorcentricity but belong to a kind of active spatial tradition – an international unconscious architecture, the main characteristic of which is the generosity of space.

Nikos Georgiadis is an independent researcher in psychoanalytic theory and a practising architect, founder member of Anamorphosis Architects.

Note

1 The conceptual framework of this issue is informed by the author's spatial, symptomatic reading of Lacanian psychoanalysis. Moreover, the research of Anamorphosis Architects in the field of what is termed traditional (contemporary and past) architectural experience, as well as work in urban design, architecture and graphics, have greatly contributed to the work presented in this issue.

NECDET TEYMUR
'UNFINISHED BUILDINGS'

An (unfinished) introduction

The unspoken assumption in almost all design and building activity is that it must end up with a 'finished' product. After all, if, as popular wisdom declares, starting a task is one half of finishing it, a finished task must be the two halves of the whole – nothing less, nothing more. But can there ever be such a 'whole' that is 'complete'? And outside the domain of the proverbial generalities is there an end-product in design and building processes that represents a definitive *full-stop* to them? The moment when dignitaries cut the ribbon or when the contractors deliver the keys, the 'construction' phase is assumed to have stopped and 'habitation', criticism and aging phases are assumed to begin. But can any building, or anything for that matter, ever finish in absolute terms? It may of course be asked whether it really matters, especially if the architects' or the builders' ultimate aim appears to be to deliver the keys – real or metaphorical.

The end of which beginning?

Seen from a scientific point of view, there is no *beginning* as such that can be pinpointed and no *end* that we can be certain of. As everything changes all the time, there is never a fixed state. Photographs tell the story only of the state in 1/250th of a second. What may appear to be finished is but one stage in the development of the matter – whether it is Mount Fuji in its perfect proportions, an industrial product that comes off the assembly line, or an architectural or urban product that is designed on drawing board and put together on site. Besides, the chemical, physical and social forces ensure that the lives of cities and buildings go on forever.

Buildings, or all artefacts for that matter, are made up of previously existing or produced 'ingredients' – soil, water, air, timber, metal, glass, plastic, but also human knowledge, skills, culture, social norms and rules, resources and human labour. They include physical and other fragments from *previous* artefacts, including previous buildings. Their built history is nothing if not *intertextual* and uneven.

They even incorporate within themselves organic remains from thousands of years of natural history. There could plausibly be dinosaurs in baked bricks! However, in designing and constructing, we also pass into the building the *genotypes*, the inherited knowledge, the patterns of space, form and behaviour that we, as designers and members of a culture, may have inherited over the years.

Seen in this way, the role of the designers or planners as members of the building team becomes that of a *participant* who contributes in some respects, rather than that of a *master* who conceives the final composition and applies the finishing brushstrokes before declaring it ready for execution and use. But that is another story.

The multi-variant, multi-dimensional, complex and uneven lives of buildings thus continue after they are assumed to have finished. They variously become old, dilapidated, damaged, altered, added to, abandoned, or are worn out, left to the ravages of time, bacteria or climate, burned down, or partly or wholly destroyed by nature or by conscious acts of vandalism, war or 'ethnic cleansing'.

In short, buildings become ruined by use or by intention. Human ingenuity tries to ensure that bombs are created which will kill people without damaging buildings, but often 'precision bombing' misses the target by a few millimetres – with disastrous consequences for the inhabitants and profit for others.

Some ruins are later built upon – the foundations holding up more than one superstructure in their lifetime; others are cleared completely to make way for new buildings, or salvaged only to reincarnate in other places and times. Buildings that have been left to their own fate may become significant ruins of historic interest, often ending up as objects of holiday tourism or as sterile sculptures in museums (such as the Pergamon Altar in the Berlin Museum).

Some buildings, on the other hand, are left unfinished or half unfinished – more by accident than by design. They may be accepted as they are, namely as (un)finished 'normal' buildings. In other words, unfinished buildings can be buildings too – in form or in use.

After all, if 'Unfinished Symphonies' count as music, unfinished paintings hang in galleries, unfinished poems cause serious debates among scholars, and unfinished social and political projects produce an unfinished society that fails to dislodge even the most incompetent governments, why

Wet Paint, *Les Coleman*

'Unfinished Building', student work

Ruins, Palmyra

is it that it is not possible to have an 'Unfinished Building' (UB) as the 'final' product? What is 'final' anyway?

It is known that in olden times artists were not supposed to declare their work fully finished as this would be tantamount to competing with God's perfection. In parts of Anatolia, for example, finishing a house would signal the time of completing one's mission in this world and of passing to the 'Other' one.

Of course, some buildings become progressively 'unfinished' due to uncontrollable, unnegotiable, if slowly exercised, forces of nature.

Other UBs may variously become ruins of another type – sources of criticism, ridicule or inspiration, havens for rats and cats or, in societies which appear to have solved all their problems, shelter for the homeless. Or they may be seen as accidental masterpieces or stylistic innovation, hiding their 'finishedness' behind an unfinished surface (a common question to the architects of the Pompidou Centre could easily be, 'When are you going to finish this building?'). 'Deconised' architecture could be described as avoiding the question by designing-in unfinishedness – with an admittedly uneven degree of success!

Some architectural questions

Some theoretical and polemical questions emerge from the above observations:
– can one design or build a 'ruin'?
– can one design an 'unfinished building'?
– can one unfinish a building?
– can an unfinished building be an object of knowledge?

Compared with the theoretical, professional and educational implications of such questions, would it be unfair to suggest that some of the concerns of so-called 'deconstructivist architecture' might look somewhat less than significant?

A serious interrogation of architecture and design along these lines could not only suggest some truly new possibilities, but also new insights into the design process. What is the 'problem' that is to be analysed, studied, designed and evaluated (to refer back to the stages defined by the design methods movement) in a process the result of which is to be necessarily and profoundly unfinished?

Is 'absence' something to be ignored, avoided, filled up, or celebrated (à la Zen)? Isn't space an absence that should necessarily remain unfilled? Is it not the case that a filled-up space can no longer be accessible, hence describable as social or architectural space? Moreover, understanding finished buildings as somewhat unfinished could reveal much that might probably have been hidden from our conditioned eyes.

Finally, in education, can we teach and learn what is not there from what is?

Educational objectives (and possible objections)

In line with the concept of 'educational project', an unfinished building (UB) project could have the explicit aim of provoking thoughts around two seemingly opposite possibilities:
– doing something to finish an UB, or/and
– designing a ruin, completing an UB, or further, unfinishing an UB.

By forcing us to think of the paradoxical or the impossible, it might free ourselves from some of the conventions that organise our responses to given historical, architectural or urban problems.

From an educational point of view, it also aims to test the hypothesis that design projects do not have to be (poor) imitations of what architectural offices do out there, or that they must start with a hypothetical site, brief and client, yet finish up with a 'realistic' and 'complete' project.

Why, for example, can't a seemingly unfinished project be theoretically valid and educationally useful? Isn't the world bound to remain unfinished however many finished buildings we may construct?

Or, if education is supposed to be responsive to the 'real world', why should it be something that finishes at the end of four or five years of schooling? So, what about a truly 'unfinished education'? Can we not therefore imagine a curriculum, a course or a project that is unfinished by design, and not simply by a failure to complete the requirements? Would this not then be another word for 'open-ended learning', 'open(-ended) education', 'open-ended design' or, indeed, an 'open(-ended) society'?

A studio(us) problem

The project is based on a sad little story. There is an 'unfinished building' (really and literally) that lies to the south-east of a university Architecture Building. Those who are old enough to remember its inception might have a faint memory that it was originally designed as an annex to the existing Building. However, as a result of various economic measures, there was never enough money to finish it.

The architect became disillusioned with architectural practice, taught in the school for a few years, but left big city life in favour of a peaceful retreat somewhere in the country, reportedly growing sunflowers, rearing chickens and training horses. He did not leave a forwarding address for his mail, nor is he connected to the rest of the world by telephone, fax or e-mail (he refuses the Internet and the Internet refuses him!).

As if that was not enough, the only remaining set of drawings submitted to the municipality for planning permission was burnt during the civil riots in Gaziosmanpanpafia a few years ago.

Cappadocia, Turkey

Pergamon Altar, Berlin Museum

Finished?

Unfinished?

In short, we have no information as to how the building was intended to be completed. The task therefore is to finish it or/and further unfinish it or/and do something with it.

Methods and possibilities

The starting point is the present state of our UB with its exposed columns, formwork, reinforcement bars, leftover building materials, the water that is creating puddles and the natural growth. However, the material, site, brief, plan, programme, and, by implication, possible range of responses are all there (or, perhaps, to a fresh mind, waiting to be released). One may deduce the type of structure that was intended from what exists, or its latent potential; or, one may ignore its given history or limitations and construct anew.

In tackling this problem, it is possible to be as conventional as one likes just as much as unconventional. A functional solution may be considered as much as one that is not functional!

The imagination may be allowed to run wild in all directions, or the ruins may be placed in a box and sold to architectural tourists (remember the Berlin Wall!).

Or the structure may be thought of as an extension to the present Architecture Building, or as a deconstruction, explosion, baby, clone or clown of this building; perhaps even as its antithesis, full-stop or semi-colon.

One may decide to make the UB a symbol of the end of 'architecture' (or 'Architecture') as we know it, or the beginning of a new architectural movement (especially now that deconstructivism is 'old hat', even in Sarajevo School of Architecture).

The building may become a lasting monument to all unfinished projects, unthought-of projects, projects that were never begun, or those that were killed off before they got off the ground. Indeed, it may become a shrine to the unfulfilled aspirations of all humankind, the clipped wings

of beautiful birds, or commemorate broken pediments and promises.

The UB may become a testing ground for the ideas that were not able to be realised in the studio, the building that one always knew one could design, the drawings that one never got round to doing, the painting that one always wanted to hang in a prestigious gallery, the sonata that one always wanted to compose, the poem that one felt was trying to come out, or the story that one wished to tell one day.

It may become the embodiment of one's fantasies that was never manageable on a scale of 1:100.

A haven may be created for oneself, one's friends, profession, culture, hobby, obsessions, concerns, people, language, T-square, paintbrush or computer!

Or, a new construction method could be experimented with, a new settlement plan, a new lifestyle, a new fast-food chain, a new type of bookstore, disco or travel agent, a swimming pool, a tropical jungle, or a cultural, worship or meditation centre, or a zapping centre with 32 channels, a bicycle shed or a cathedral, a decorated or, probably, a 'neo-post-deconclassical' shed.

It is possible that members of the School of Architecture with this particular UB in such proximity may be dying to undertake an *educational* experiment to improve their education (even their teachers'), to prove that there is more to architecture than Architecture, and more to education than schooling. Or, being so close to a School of Architecture that is bursting at its seams, they may decide to do a new and 'real' alternative to their present building.

Or, failing to do all or any of these, one may simply do an 'Unfinished Building'!

Necdet Teymur is Dean of the Faculty of Architecture and Professor of Architecture at METU, Ankara.

References

The thoughts expressed in this paper were inspired by a half-finished extension to the Architecture Building (designed by Behruz Çinici and completed in 1963) at METU, Ankara. The project referred to was originally designed in sketch form in 1995. At the time of preparing this article, the building was, finally (and hopefully) being 'finished'!

An earlier and shorter version of the complete programme with instructions to students was published in *Architectural History and the Studio*, Adam Hardy and Necdet Teymur (eds), Question Press (London), 1996. For the concepts of 'educational object' and 'educational project' see the aforementioned book.

For the concepts of 'unevenness', 'uniqueness' and 'complexity', see Necdet Teymur, 'Uneven Development of People and Places: An Outline of a Theory of Built Form', in A Awotona and N Teymur (eds), *Tradition, Location and Community*, Aldershot (Avebury), 1997, pp27-33.

The theme picture *Wet Paint* by Les Coleman is published by Artists' Cards, London. I thank the artist for the inspiration.

Progressively unfinished – sketch of church in 1750, 1904, 1912, 1919

PHILIPPOS OREOPOULOS
THE SPATIAL MODEL OF THE LABYRINTH

This paper will address a theme that is both central to my own theoretical research and appears to be part of a more general problematic in the theory of the built environment. I would like to focus on what I term the Spatial Model of the Eastern Greek World,[1] a little known area in the context of architectural theory and urban planning. This brief, rather schematic presentation will develop at both paradigmatic and methodological levels, describing the production process of the built environment in order to see how a conceptual framework might be generated in relation to it.

My research in this area was instigated by a 10th-century legal document by the architect Juliano Askalonites (although recent studies have suggested that Askalonites lived as early as the sixth century AD). This text is itself located on the border of antiquity and the Middle Ages, appearing as it does at the moment when the crucial split between the Greek East and the Latin West began, where two respective, fundamentally different philosophical models originated. A short 'theoretical' text that accompanies the main legal document led my analysis to the uncovering of a cosmological framework, which as well as appearing as an ecological model of the earth, air, fire and water, shapes an anthropological model (concerning human relations at a spatial level), which in turn defines a spatial model 'logicised' by relations of neighbouring, adjacent and communal living.

The main characteristics of this spatial model are abstraction, permanency and universality: the basis of the production of similar permanent structures of settlements during a period that lasted about 10 centuries and extended throughout the Mediterranean, the Balkans and the Near East. The settlements appeared to develop from what I term the principle of the *primary element*. A similar principle can be found in Aristotle's theory of kinesis (*Metaphysics*, 1073a) whereby the original/primary element, even though it does not move, sets in motion the structure of the universe. Excavations have revealed that the creation and reproduction of these settlements were not structured according to a particular urban plan; rather, their development, in both small- and large-scale terms, was based on the principle that each built unit emerges from pre-existing, neighbouring spatial rules. The primary element is that which, through its own function and random character,* defines the way the spatial sequence gives structure to the urban fabric as a whole. Consequently, building blocks are not shaped by predesigned roads; rather, elementary neighbouring structures are shaped by six orientations, together forming a cohesive built environment. The distinction in Western theoretical discourse between 'architecture' and 'urban space' therefore does not apply here – instead, the two are unified in the built environment – and what we have found here is a theoretical and practical tectonic discourse that is shared among various fields of knowledge (including philosophy, law, medicine, combat, farming, music, mathematics and engineering). Indeed, the pattern produced by these settlements defined

by the primary element takes on a labyrinthine form. Basic types of the primary element in settlements,[2] including villages, private land, suburbs, towns and cities, identified in Byzantine documentation are:[3] the church (the church itself and the parish), the military (the fortress and the palace), and production (the diocese and the square),[4] which corresponds with the church, military and agriculture: the three typical components of medieval society in the East and the West. They are also quoted in the *Geoponica*, a 10th-century Byzantine text that states 'kind-wise, three are the basic divisions of the state: military, church, agriculture',[5] and can be found in the classic Western medieval social division of *oratores, bellatores, laboratores*.[6] Thus the labyrinthine structure of medieval settlements is related to the deeper organisational structure of medieval Western and Eastern society as a whole; and this is due to a common tradition in Greco-Roman law on the built environment.[7]

In order to have a clearer idea of the elements that constitute this spatial model and that validate its use in contemporary architectural theory, we need to examine where it originated, taking into account that 'origin' is an extended cultural process rather than an absolute attainable point. The moment of origin can be seen as a period of transition in which 'nature' develops into 'culture'; this will also entail an archaeological analysis of prehistoric settlements and an examination of mythology. An archaeological approach necessitates moving back and forth in time and weaving a path through various fields of knowledge in order to pass from the empirical world of history to the transcendental space of theory, and thereby from the specific to the typological, the local to the global, the particular to the general – in sum, to common compositional principles.[8]

For example, the Neolithic tripartite structure of permanent dwelling, agriculture and stock rearing which relates to an elementary social order and introduces nature into the cultural process first appears in Greece in settlements in Thessaly, northern Greece, in the preceramic Neolithic period (around 7,000 BC). (It is also identifiable in other areas of the Mediterranean and the Balkans,[9] and can be traced back to prehistoric Mesopotamian civilisations.) In Thessaly, clearly organised settlements can be found in the middle-Neolithic period in Sesklo (fifth to fourth centuries BC), and in the late Neolithic period in Dhimini. Their layout is almost identical to the form of a labyrinth, consisting of courtyards with entrances/exits, dwellings, and a central square in which is located a 'public house' which appears to be the starting point of the labyrinthine shape. According to recent research by Hourmouziadis, the towns of Sesklo and Dhimini of the middle and late Neolithic period, and the ancient period to some extent, do not constitute citadels (as Theocharis and Tsountas maintain);[10] rather, their world-famous courtyards (three in Sesklo and six in Dhimini, as excavations have shown) are architectural elements that form basic structures (similar to the courtyard walls of the Greek islands), whose function is

Village of Pyrgos in Thera

Capital settlement of Astypalea

dependent on general planning regulations mediating the overall process of production in society.[11]

A rigorous and cohesive spatial arrangement of the settlements is created by the circular courtyards whose contiguity forms a kind of continuing spiralling wall, either side of which the houses and work places are articulated, and by the fact that all the settlement is organised through one imperfect spiral beginning at the central public house. Indeed, the fact that this public house functions either as a storage space, palace,[12] or shrine (as in the Neolithic building discovered at Nea Nikomedeia),[13] would suggest that the first core feature organising the Neolithic settlements of Thessaly into different phases of their rudimentary transformation follows the tripartite division of daily life of farming, power and the sacred. During the Bronze Age, between 1600 and 1100 BC, these three elements are to be found again in the labyrinthine citadel of Mycenae, comprised of royal tombs (the sacred), a fortification (the palace), and storage space for cultivated produce (farming), and furthermore in mythology.[14] This structure appears to govern all Indo-European societies, as shown by Dumézil's studies on the tripartite belief system of Indo-Europeans, substantiated in the comparative analysis of myths on deities.[15]

Before introducing the aspect of mythical thought in relation to the fundamental aspects of a labyrinthine settlement, it is important to note that even in Dumézil's tripartite ideology, which governs Eastern and Western medieval settlements, we can identify primary aspects that are found in Neolithic settlements (of labyrinthine structure, following the principle of the primary aspect) with basic structural aspects of both Greek (Eastern) and Latin (Western) medieval settlements. Yet by identifying them as such the spatial model of the Greek East begins to take on a more archetypal character, as it is directed into the more primordial and universal aspects of our civilisation, while its features – ecological connection/awareness/concern, labyrinthine structure, courtyard wall function, centrality, principle of the primary aspect, contiguous built mass, free geometry, socio-spatial cohesion – all seem to acquire a continuity and overall compositional character.[16]

In addition to tracing back the Greek spatial model to archetypical structures in Neolithic settlements, a further link with mythical thought might strengthen the possibility of discovery as an even more general compositional principle, which also has an archetypical attribute.

In Indo-European mythology, the labyrinth is identified with birth,[17] and more particularly with the archetypical symbols and functions relating to Mother Earth. Entering a labyrinth, for example, is identified with a return to Mother Earth. The labyrinth also takes on a cave-like function, in that it is a place of initiation and for the burial of the dead (ie a sacred place), a place of divine intercourse (ie the origination of the universe and of life), a place of wielding power (such as the Minoan labyrinth). Therefore the labyrinth in myth appears to follow the tripartite Indo-European belief structure echoed in both medieval and prehistoric spatial

Sesklo

Byzantine city

Western Medieval city

Medieval city of Thebes

Dhimini

Muslim city

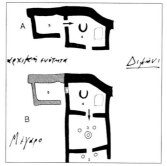

Dhimini storage space and palace

Mycenae

models. The labyrinth archetype is directly linked to the archetypical image of the 'tekton' (the artisan, craftsman) Daedalus,[18] and they both seem to form an integral conceptual system. However, the Daedalus archetype reflects its *tectonic*, rather than its *archi*-tectonic abilities (in the etymological sense of 'archi' as 'leading'): so it is related to the craftsman of the Eastern and Western Middle Ages, rather than to the notion of the architect of the Classical period or the Western Renaissance.

Moreover, the myth of the labyrinth reflects aspects of practical Reason, and more specifically, the issue of representation. Indeed, if in the Neolithic ceramics the spiral, the graphic representation of the labyrinth at a social communicational level, reproduces the archetype of the spatial system of the settlements of the time, then the disk of Phaestos, with its spiral-shaped writing, appears to be the first archetype which combines the spatial system (the labyrinth), the system of representation (the spiral) and the system of writing (iconographic spiral). I will refer to a particular application of this combination where the engraved writing refers to the ploughshare that ploughs from right to left and left to right, and to the road – via rupta – of the settlements. We thus have three primary operations with which we pass from Nature to Culture: the ploughshare (farming, a system of production), the road (building, a system of organising space) and writing (representation, a system of communication and aesthetics). Here we have a 'representation' of space as its simple writing/drawing, and not its imitation, and therefore 'inaccurate' representation. It is also important to note the archetypical negative relation within the language–space framework, as witnessed in the Judaic tradition of the Tower of Babel, whose spiralling labyrinthine shape is paralleled with disorder and chaos.**

So far we have introduced the fundamental, constant characteristics of the spatial model (its labyrinthine logic, principle of the primary element, masonry and representation) at the level of the universality of primordial and archetypical structures. But it is also necessary to describe what gives rise to the basic differences between the aspects that constitute the labyrinthine form described above and their transformations in the entire spatial, archetypical model, when this applies in the particular conditions of an era. We will shift emphasis from the description of a still, stable structure to the structure in motion, adding the dimension of time. This foundational archetypical meaning of *difference* will be searched for at the core of the spatial model, in the aspects that constitute the principle of the primary element (which, as we have seen, in every case reflects the Indo-European tripartite arrangement of production/agriculture, power/military, culture/sacred) and its equivalent spatial structure. This difference will be sought for paradigmatically via the appearance of the labyrinth, in the myth of the Minotaur and Theseus.

The Minotaur who inhabits the labyrinth is the result of a teratogenesis, the union of human and bull; his existence is therefore an example of the outcome of production's negative aspect. King Minos uses Daedalus' construction to exercise a vindictive form of power in his war against the Athenians; his abuse of sovereignty is compounded by inhuman consecration in forcing the Athenians to yield a tribute of 14 Athenian youths to be fed to the Minotaur. So in this structure of the myth of the labyrinth, the barbarian aspects of production, military power and culture come to the fore – that is, the three central aspects structuring Indo-European civilisation, which so far we have seen to be defining both the medieval and prehistoric (Neolithic and middle Helladic) spatial models. By enlisting the help of Daedalus,

Theseus succeeds in killing the Minotaur, thereby overthrowing the three barbarian aspects that structure the core of social life (production, military power and culture). On his return to Athens from Crete Theseus joins all the dwellings surrounding the city, placing the Agora at their centre. Indeed, Theseus is the first to apply this structure and therefore considered to be the founder of democracy and possibly, even, according to Lévêque and Vidal-Naquet, a rival model for Clisthenes' own political and spatial model[19] – one in which geometry coincides with the political theorisation of the city-state whereby the common hearth ('hestia koine') is the centre of the city, the state and its legislation.[20] This is not a precise geometrical centre, but an arithmetical one which, according to Vernant, Lévêque and Vidal-Naquet,[21] declares an absence of sovereignty and restates the civil equality of citizens. The same applies to the rational, simplified, strict geometrical order that is proposed for the city by the political theorist and astronomer Hippodamos. By contrast, in the Platonic city the centre is not the Agora, but rather a hilltop on which are located temples, military residences, gymnasia and eating places.[22]

As for the public space and time, according to these scholars these are supposed to operate as mirror image of heavenly 'reality'; thus the microcosm of the city, through absolute geometric symmetry and harmony,[23] (following classical aesthetics) can participate in the macrocosm of the universe. This is a typical example of Platonic idealism, which in the Western and Eastern Middle Ages will again be manifested through the category of the *Unbuilt* [24] (reflecting divine religious utopias), but maintaining as we have seen, in the category of the *Built* – that is, the space of mortals – the logic of the labyrinth and its anti-classical aesthetic which, once again, will be destroyed by the neoplatonic Classicism of the Renaissance at both theoretical[25] and practical discourse[26] and continued by neoclassicism.[27]

By shifting from the myth of the labyrinth and the Minotaur to the political and spatial reality of Clisthenes, and then to the Platonic utopia, it can be seen that the genetic difference of the core, or more specifically the *archetypical*, principle of the primary element, which is determined by the triadic categories of the Indo-European peoples, gives rise to the transformations in both the structure of space and social life.

The *labyrinth* is therefore not simply a formalistic shape, but an archetypical compositional and organising principle that deconstructs yet also structures life and space in a generic, comprehensive way. It is an important conceptual key in the criticism of works of architecture and theoretical interpretations as well as in their recomposition. Viewed within this framework, various penetrating contemporary analyses in environmental psychology, such as Moles and Rohmer's *Labyrinthes du vécu* (1982) appear culturally poor; by contrast the labyrinth – as an aspect of spatial culture – provides an insight into a cultural world and can serve as an inspiration to the architect – the poet catharsising our guilty everyday life. Comprehensive notions such as ecological concern, labyrinthine structures, the function of the courtyard wall, centrality, the principle of the primary element, a contiguous building mass, free geometry and socio-spatial cohesion are the origins and the foundations of a continuum which extend through time to provide a conceptual system applicable in architectural practice today.

Philippos Oreopoulos is consultant Architect and Historian for the Archaeological Department of the Greek Ministry of Culture. This article was translated by Vivian Constantinopoulos.

Notes

1 P Oreopoulos, 'Histoire de la pensée sur la ville et l'architecture en Grèce du XVe au XIXe siècle', Thèse de Doctorat de l'Université de Paris I, 1990, vol 1, pp 19, 136, 166, 246.

2 W Ashburner, 'A Byzantine Treatise on Taxation', *Journal of Hellenic Studies* 35 (1915). See also A Thomadaki, *The Farming Community in the Late Byzantine Age*, MIET (Athens), 1987, p71.

3 See C Bouras, 'Residences and Buildings in Byzantine Greece', in *Shelter in Greece: Architecture in Greece* magazine (Athens), 1979, pp30-52. See also Oreopoulos, op cit, p311 for an analysis of Muslim architectural documentation; and for a 15th-19th century study see A Refik, *Onuncu Asr-i Hicri' de Istanbul Hayati*, 1988, vols I-IV, vol I, pp144-45.

4 See G Ralli and M Potli, *The Gods and Sacred Rules* (G Chartophylacos), Athens, 1852, pp536, 538; R Janin, *Constantinople Byzantine, Archives de l'Orient Chrétien, 4A*, Institut Français d'Etudes Byzantines (Paris), 1964, pp138, 304; Ralli and Potli, op cit, vol B, pp41, 395; W Enselin, 'Government and Administration in the Byzantine Empire' in *Cambridge Medieval History*, Vol IV, Cambridge University Press (Cambridge), 1966; W Ashburner, 'A Byzantine Treatise on Taxation', op cit, p77.

5 *Geoponica sive Cassiani Basi scholastici de re rustica ecologae*, ed H Beckh, Lipsia (Teubner), 1895, p2.

6 J Le Golf, *La Civilisation de l'Occident Médieval*, Artaut (Paris), 1984.

7 P Oreopoulos, 'The Legal Question of the Built Environment from the Roman to Late Byzantine Periods', in Gerolymbou, Iordanoglou, Lavvas and Oreopoulos, *The Legislation of Greek Town Planning*, unpublished, 1994.

8 Useful references for this method of approach are: J Derrida, *Le Problème de la genèse dans la philosophie de Husserl*, PUF (Paris), 1990; J Derrida, *L'Origine de la géometrie*, PUF (Paris) 1962; and J-F Lyotard, *La Phénoménologie*, PUF (Paris), 1954.

9 K Kotsakis, 'The Use of Habitational Space in Neolithic Sesklo', in *La Théssalie, 15 années de recherches archéologiques, 1975-1990, Bilans et Perspectives*, actes du colloque international de Lyon, 17-22 Avril 1990.

10 See D Theocharis, *Neolithic Civilisation*, MIET (Athens), 1989, pp88-96 and H Tsountas, *Prehistoric Acropoleis of Dhimini and Sesklo*, Archaelogical Society (Athens), 1908, pp27-65, 69-107.

11 G Hourmouziadis, *Neolithic Dhimini*, Vanias (Thessalonika), 1993, pp88, 93-94.

12 Ibid, pp100-102, 104.

13 D Theocharis, op cit, pp58, 62-63, 149.

14 A Kyriakidou-Nestoros, 'The Interpretation of Myths from Ancient Times to the Present', in *Greek Mythology*, Ekdotiki (Athens), 1986, vol I p295.

15 G Dumézil, *Mythes et Dieux des Indo-Européens*, ed H Couteau-Bégarie, Flammarion (Paris), 1992.

16 G Hourmouziadis, op cit, pp123, 128, 163.

17 For a general discussion of the labyrinth, see P Santarcangeli, *Le Livre des labyrinthes*, Gallimard (Paris), 1972. For an analysis of labyrinthine archetypes and symbols see M Eliade, *Mythes, rêves et mystères*, Gallimard (Paris), 1957, pp211, 212.

18 For the origins of the myth of the labyrinth see S Morris, *Daidalos and the Origins of Greek Art*, Princeton University Press (New York), 1992; for a discussion of the myth itself see F Frontisi-Ducroux, *Dédale – Mythology de l'artisan en Grèce ancienne*, Maspero (Paris), 1975; for a contemporary interpretation see J-P Le Dantec, *Dédale le héros*, Balland (Paris), 1992.

19 P Lévêque and P Vidal-Naquet, *Clisthène l'Athénien*, Macula (Paris), 1964, p119.

20 J-P Vernant, *Myth and Thought in Ancient Greece*, Maspero (Paris), 1965.

21 Ibid, and Lévêque and Vidal-Naquet, op cit, pp32, 89.

22 Lévêque and Vidal-Naquet, op cit, pp127, 134.

23 Ibid, p146.

24 N Matsouka, *History of Byzantine Philosophy*, Vanias (Thessalonika), 1994, p195.

25 See Alberti's text: *De Re Aedificatoria*, Rome, 1452.

26 As it appears in the austere geometricity of star-shape cities.

27 The appearance of neoclassicism in modern Greek culture coincided with the constitution of the New Greek State and was widely imposed as a substitute for the aesthetic culture of the Greek middle ages. See P Oreopoulos, 'Histoire de la pensée sur la ville et l'architecture en Grèce du XVe au XIXe siècle', op cit.

Guest-editor: * *Randomness here appears more as a process of an ongoing spatial self-reference, of technical significance, rather than as randomness of a logical/combinatory character, free choice etc.*

** *An important distinction needs to be made between the Labyrinth operating in the 'positive' and the 'negative' Labyrinth. It might be worth testing the hypothesis that the latter could be seen as the visual appropriation of the spatial principle of the former. Indeed, the Tower of Babel's erection is guided by mortals' need to visualise their access to God and the connection between the earth and heavens.*

Disk of Phaestos

Tower of Babel

Experimental conceptual drawing by the author, employing the leading spatialities of medieval aesthetics: the wall, the labyrinth and the complexity of volumes. Spatial logic is hereby highlighted as a critique vis-à-vis *conventional perspectival laws*

Anamorphosis Architects, 'I am not the man you think I am', spatial multitude

RICHARD SENNETT
THE SENSE OF TOUCH

In memory of Gunther Busch

The sense of the senses is an ancient issue in philosophy, and a frustrating one – at least to me. Discussions of the senses often lack much direct engagement in physical realities. But the physical world contains secrets of its own which cannot be unlocked through dry speculation; this is particularly true of the physical secrets of the body. To try to unlock one of these secrets, the meaning of touch, I am going to write not as a social philosopher but as a musician. I do so because I have had another life as a cellist, mostly performing chamber music. Theodor Adorno once remarked that musicians who become intellectuals are haunted by the fear of abandoning their real selves. Perhaps; but the sensate, bodily experience of making music has something to reveal about the condition of society.

Every cellist learns the sense of touch through mastering movements like vibrato. Vibrato is the rocking motion of the left hand on a string which colours a note around its precise pitch. Vibrato does not start with the contact of the fingertip and the string; it begins further back at the elbow, the impulse to rock starting from that anchor, passing through the forearm into the palm of the hand and then through the finger.

Vibrato is a physical capacity which ripens in the course of a cellist's formation. Freedom to rock requires that a cellist masters the capacity to play perfectly in tune. If a young cellist lacks that mastery, every time he or she vibrates, the note will sound sour, accentuating the inaccuracy of pitch. There are acoustical reasons for this distinction between the sour and the vibrant, relating to the overtones set going by a string. But the need for mastery of pitch in order to vibrate well tells an elementary truth: freedom depends on control, whereas purely impulsive expression produces just mess. This piece of common wisdom is as true of the hand as it is of the heart. But even once this technical mastery is gained, vibrato poses a danger to cellists, especially young ones, when they begin to perform in public. For most of us, adrenalin flows when faced with performing; the stomach tightens; we need to withdraw before the event into a concentrated silence. When we walk on stage, we enter into a peculiar state of relaxation, a trance in which we become hyper-alert. In this trance our bodies can betray us, and no more so than in the work of vibrato. I can describe what happens fairly concretely. The vibrating forearm suddenly promises to release the tensions we have built up in preparing ourselves to perform; energy flows into the forearm and away from the hand. Often the wrist begins to flex, further cutting off the transmission of energy from elbow to finger. The result of this short-circuit is that the weakened hand begins pushing too hard on the string in order to recover strength; the fingers lock on to the fingerboard beneath the string; movement then becomes jerky rather than fluid. These concrete events are what may make a musician sound 'nervous' to you, even in the midst of technical pyrotechnics.

Of course nerves are the culprit – fear – beckoning the body into a false promise of release. But the cellist who loses control of vibrato generates, on stage, a division between conviction and expression. Again there is a physical foundation; the touch of the fingertip to the strings has ceased to be the performer's focus, the contact between flesh, steel and wood has ceased to define a zone of hyper-alert attention. But now the musician's own perceptions of her or himself performing split in two; one is the domain of conviction, of what the music should sound like, the other an inferior domain of achieved expression, the music as it is. Physical fear and the false promise of release generate in this way a divide between subjective and objective expression. Once set going, the divide may last only a few moments, in which the artist is aware that the music does not sound as it should, and then disappears as the body takes over and the artist's inner 'it should be other' fades away. Or, this divided consciousness of oneself making music can last, fatally, all evening.

I describe this danger in order to focus our attention on the phenomenon of resistance. We might say that the nervous musician has encountered physical resistance to his or her desires. But that sort of resistance is something the musician has generated him- or herself; only after losing control does he or she hear in the domain of conviction, of what it should sound like, of desire. Even more important is where resistance originates in a musician good enough to perform in public: in a crisis of vibrato resistance originates in the musician's body rather than in a struggle with the instrument he or she plays.

The paradox of release through encountering resistance can originate when a cellist deals with the E and F notes on the G string. To vibrate under these conditions risks an even worse ugly sound. Yet, when the nervous cellist is faced with this challenge he or she may suddenly connect; the scene of difficulty shifts from the human body to the wood; the body is set free.

For instance, when I first performed the Schubert Cello Quintet with the great cellist Jacqueline du Pré – who was barely adolescent at the time – she was gripped by a crisis of nerves until the famous moment in the first movement when the second cello becomes mired in this danger zone. Her F bleated for a fraction of a second, but then she conquered it: she began making a richly vibrant, generous sound, her body relaxed, and she entered into the music with that wide, ardent smile which came over her whenever she was inside the music.

The sense of touch thus is all about the dialectics of resistance. Contact and resistance are expressively inseparable. The resistance of physical objects can both arouse the body yet relax it as well. The experience of touching, as in a successful vibrato, overcomes the division of conviction and expression. When we are 'in touch', as American slang puts it, we do not dwell in a state of wholeness, conflict and danger free. Difficulties and resistances confront us, but the territory of struggle has shifted from within the human being to the world, to grappling with inert physical objects. Expression occurs through that physical struggle. When performing well, every musician feels the poet Wallace Steven's famous declaration, 'no truth but in things'.

As a cultural analyst, I have perhaps paid too much attention to 'things' at the expense of theory. I have written about the history of wigs, chairs, bathtubs, street lights, earrings, herbs, condoms, and most of all, buildings. I allude to this musical example, though, not just to stress the importance of grounding cultural theory concretely. The work of making musical vibrato conveys a general truth: expression occurs when human beings address the resistances of material reality; we then make contact with the world, we literally touch it in all its roughness, hardness and difficulty. This rough terrain is the landscape in which expression occurs.

Many modern efforts to shape the physical world seek, however, to flee this landscape. Society aims, in the creation of physical things, to reduce resistance, for example in 'user-friendly' computers or street layouts where traffic flows smoothly. Social and political practices submit to the same principle. We like our identities clear-cut and easy to use: German versus Turk; heterosexual versus homosexual; successful versus failure. It could be said that this is only a matter of functionality and practicality; a computer with a dysfunctional program like Windows 95 is of little value to anyone. More largely, it could be argued that reducing resistance is one way to measure the divide between social life and culture; we cannot use the world in the same spirit we might play the cello, searching out experiences of resistance or ambiguity, dwelling in them in a Heideggerian sense.

This practical argument seems to me, in fact, all wrong. The result of diminishing resistance in the daily environment, I want on the contrary to argue, weakens connection to reality. Ease of use erodes engagement, a yielding physical world diminishes arousal.

Permit me just once more to recur to the cello. One way of teaching beginners to play is to plaster little bands of tape across the fingerboard, so that children know exactly where to put their fingers. This, the foundation of the so-called 'Suzuki' method, seems to make fingering easy. But once the tape is removed, the children are surprised and chagrined. They find they haven't really been making good contact between fingertip, string and wood; the tape weakened solid contact at that crucial intersection. I want to argue that the everyday world is increasingly 'taped over' in a similar manner, with ease of use dulling the sense of material connection.

Weakening the sense of touch in daily life takes two forms: one political, the other cultural. Physical disconnection serves a regime of power and a regime of subjectivity.

To understand the political regime, let us begin with the most solid element of our everyday reality, a building. All buildings have programmes which define the particular uses of space. Modern buildings tend to have particularly definitive programmes. Every square metre has its allotted function, and functions in modern buildings, even in small structures, are tied tightly to physical properties like energy consumption, plumbing, lighting or heating. In the past, a creator of highly integrated structures, such as Palladio, would marvel at this physical coherence; all of which makes buildings easy to use: the programme lays out what you should do, the coordination of function to properties how it should occur. You know the object from the moment the doors of the building open.

However, such highly defined, user-friendly structures tend to be rigid as habitations; the spaces can only be used in one way, unvarying in time. You can made an 18th-century palace into a modern art museum, but it is not so easy to make a museum into a palace, a hospital, or a church. At a more mundane level, Georgian row architecture of two centuries ago adapts fairly easily to the shifting needs of offices, residential housing and commercial stores in the course of time; shopping malls are hard to put to any other use than as theatres of consumption.

These easy-to-use, fixed-function objects ask for submission in use rather than engagement. You are meant to do what the object tells you so clearly to do. That is the obvious disciplinary regime built into user-friendly objects. But what is the actual role of the subject, the user, in this regime? Rather than focus on great architecture, we might reflect for an answer on more mundane structures, like social housing, factories and offices. The discipline of ease induces apathy; the apathy or aversion of residents in regard to the highly formal, well-designed ghettos of social housing is both obvious and profound. The user's response in the sphere of work is more subtle.

The modern workplace may well have flexible inner spaces, but there is usually no provision for spaces where workers might find shelter from the demands made upon them by employers. Of course architects are employed by owners, not workers; they make workplaces of surveillance, of imposed discipline. The result of this functional, disciplinary space has been studied by myself and many other sociologists. Such spaces of power produce a reaction of physical indifference and disconnection among the servants directed and controlled. Dulling your physical awareness in a highly controlled or hostile environment is a natural defence mechanism; you retreat inside yourself, where others can't get at you. But you also suffer due to that defence mechanism; you have no way to concretise your discontent or objectify your anger. Domination succeeds when it produces this kind of material indifference to one's surroundings among the subjects of power.

Modern architects are often blamed for the neutral spaces and dull buildings which populate our environment. But I want to argue against aesthetic blame. The issue is power. A well-ordered regime of power produces dematerialisation; indifference to one's surroundings is one way in which domination is consummated. Architecture becomes complicit in that domination when designs for clarity and ease of use, to recur to the Suzuki analogy, 'tape over' human conflicts rather than open up physical possibilities for visceral resistance, commitment and expression. The dulled 'sense of touch' encodes a regime of power.

Let me emphasise that this weakening of the sense of touch is no mere metaphor. Our streets are infinitely easier to use, safer and cleaner than the streets of the 18th century, while crowd life is infinitely weaker, and the knowledge of other human beings to be gained through street life has radically diminished. The behaviour of modern urban crowds, as Erving Goffman so brilliantly demonstrated, is disciplined so that physical contact is repressed in elaborate ballets of bodily movement. Silence between strangers on the street enforces this discipline, so does avoidance of prolonged eye contact. Actual touching among strangers on the street arouses fear. Modern crowds are organised into shopping crowds, crowds at sports events, or crowds in cars on highways, each a functional density rather than a physical human mass generating dissonance or ambiguity.

In my own studies of street movement I have been struck by the way in which the organisation of motion in the modern city has dulled the sense of touch. The great highway system erected in New York City by the planner Robert Moses in the 1940s and 1950s sought explicitly to use the automobile as a tool to relieve the pressure of crowding at the city's centre. He imagined people compacted together to resemble a nuclear reaction, sure to explode through its own density. This fear of the undisciplined urban mass has its roots in Baron Haussmann's reconstruction of Paris in the 19th century, when rapid transit movement was first conceived as escape from physical contact with the poor, the enraged, or simply the unknown. And that fear of unregulated physical contact has been carried forward into current urban planning. The redesign of contemporary Berlin is a prime example of a regime of spatial power in which ease of use, definition of function, discipline of crowds, all dull physical arousal, resulting in a neutral city of the known and the safe, which is anything but innocent in its neutrality.

On the cultural side, this repressive regime may seem to have no parallel. Walk into any New York gallery today and you are likely to see plaster vaginas or photographs of cocks; go to a movie and you are likely to watch bodies blasted to bits, blood and gore smearing the screen. Fashion has become an art of striptease. The erotic body, rather than constructs of steel and glass, seems to be the locus of our sense of touch in the realm of culture. But try taking one of those plaster vaginas off the wall to study it better and guards in the gallery will immediately shout at you; try caressing a fashionably exposed crotch on the street and, in America at least, you will be arrested for sexual harassment. You made a mistake in confusing display with touch, you have tried to cross a forbidden barrier between image and object, the barrier between eye and hand.

In America there has been a long and exhausting argument about that barrier, debate about whether the depiction of pornographic scenes in magazines like *Hustler* indeed encourages voyeurs to commit pornographic acts, or whether the pervasive entertainment-culture of violence encourages violence on the streets. This argument, though it has perhaps uniquely American and puritanical overtones, concerns the sheer fear of touching, touch as violation of another human being, and it is important to explore its construction a little more.

Only a very few of the millions who watch bloody war films exit the theatre determined to become killers themselves; but what about the others? The mass of viewers emerges from these orgies of violence or sex to become again law-abiding citizens or mild bed-mates. The fear of touch and the discharge into fantasy seems, therefore, a kind of beneficent discipline and discharge to many psychologists. From a substantive point of view, though, the content of the fantasy remains compelling, even if not expressed. To put the matter a little more strongly, that inner state of arousal has been protected by being organised in such a way that it cannot be challenged by others. Fantasy is sheathed in a condom.

The mass-media-protected fantasy offers a clue to understanding a larger cultural regime which regulates the sense of touch: withdrawal from physical contact occurs for the sake of stimulating inner life. The issue of inner-ness and withdrawal seems to me the crucial element of this regime of protected fantasy.

Ghostly presences lurk in this withdrawal; these presences are desire and longing. And these are subjective formations of a particular kind: longing for what is absent, desire for an ideal which cannot be consummated. The erotic, as Freud himself was the first to argue, concerns a different order of time from immediate sensate pleasure. In his formulation, desire withers in the course of physical consummation; or as Lacan put the matter, desire is the dreaming of absence. Touch is inferior to the imagination. Proust, in *Albertine Disparue*, shows again and again how his narrator's desire for Albertine grows strong when she is absent, and weakens when her own body lies in fact close to his.

So the withdrawal from touch might be seen as an act conserving desire, indeed the imagination itself. But once we step outside the erotic realm, the psychiatric belief that this protected domain is beneficent becomes completely untenable. A privatisation of subjectivity occurs in which individuals lose touch both literally and figuratively with reality.

In a way, this may seem an odd abstraction: what else could subjectivity be other than private? In fact, it could be quite other, quite public. The religious convictions of Christians, Muslims, and Jews can be entirely public forms of subjectivity, nothing hidden in the movements of the heart, longing for the Ideal directly connected to religious ritual and law. In the Enlightenment, what Voltaire, Jefferson, or Adam Smith called 'moral sentiments' were also public forms of subjectivity. They were not puzzles of individuality, and they most certainly were not fantasies. A moral sentiment comes into being only when practised; intentions count for little. The strength of compassion or wit (wit was a moral sentiment for Voltaire) depends upon pressing that impulse hard into the dense, resistant clay of human society.

A privatised subjectivity, however, treats inner life as a transcendent, individual condition, and the contents of that inner life as a secret, hidden from others – and often also, if not a secret, at least a puzzle to the individual. In one of his most moving letters, light in tone but rich in substance, Voltaire wrote to Madame de Pompadour that he was often amazed by his own behaviour but seldom surprised; 'I had a fair conception of who I was when I reached the age of reason, perhaps more talented than other men but like them; I had only to study their characters to know myself and read my own heart to find there the evidences of all humanity.' Which of us today would dare make a similar statement? I know I wouldn't dare. For us – if you permit me that generic liberty – we spend our lives trying to unravel what we desire, what we are longing to be, in this inwardness of becoming.

This regime of subjectivity is just the danger of a society which eschews the embrace of resistance. Difficulties which are 'taped over' hardly disappear; contradiction, ambivalence and confusion are the intractable ingredients of resistance to desire in human affairs. But like a young cellist losing touch, these difficulties can be introjected within, gathered into the self in a time of becoming which promises their transcendence. The domain of the objective world, the world of realisation, will grow ever further apart from this unfolding and ever so promising domain of intention and desire. Psychologically, this sort of subjectivity often disposes people to imagine that reality is failing them, failing to measure up; or again, the actual self with its constraints and limits seems inferior to that idealised being whose existence is a wistful possibility. 'If only', 'I should have', 'I had hoped' are key phrases in this language of privatisation. It is a language which subverts engagement in the world's difficulties, prevents these engagements from doing their work of freeing the self from the self; a door closes on the insistent, dissonant noises outside.

Many modern philosophers and social scientists have written on the perils of subjectivity in this privatised form, from Arendt and Habermas on the philosophical side to Robert Bellah and Anthony Giddens on the social side. And yet I must confess to a certain discomfort about the conclusions often drawn from these critiques of privatised subjectivity. They are often quite conservative, as in the case of Theodor Adorno; or they contain rather emotionally bloodless ideas about the act of connection and engagement itself, as I think is the case with Jürgen Habermas. Subjectivity is contested; objectivity remains equally disembodied.

We could not, indeed, recover from that privatised subjectivity without re-embedding ourselves in the physical world, and this is where the realm of artistic practice is a helpful guide; it shows something of general value about how embedding occurs. Adorno's fears of the anarchic, naked youth of the 1960s as icons of physical freedom misunderstood, for instance, the discipline required to make any physical gesture expressive. In vibrato, as we have seen, the sense of touch has to be precise in order to be expressive; again, as any good striptease artist will attest, you have to learn the art of taking off your clothes *well*.

One thing that stands in the way of embedding the physical world now is the confusion between erotic desire and physical expression. Take an artist like Cindy Sherman who recalculates sexuality over and over in her work. We respond not only to the symbolism of her masks and body armour, but also to the care with which the masks or armoured suits are made, the use of unlikely materials, and the difficulties she resolves in joining these unlikely materials together. These materials are her labour site, and thanks to these labours with recalcitrant material we become aware not of a feminist act but of a feminist art. Yet most of the critical reception of her work focuses on her intentions, the symbolism of her masks, as if divorcing the meaning from the labour of production.

That divorce of meaning from labour signals a privatised consciousness. To explain this, permit me to recur once more to the peculiar labour involved in performing a piece of music. I have described Jacqueline du Pré suddenly encountering through nerves a block to her formidable technique; she told me some years later about this traumatic concert, relating how she began then to hear two pieces of music: one in her head where everything is beautiful and just right, and the other in her ears, neither right nor beautiful. She had, in the language I have just used, at this moment entered the eroticised world of longing, of desire for what is absent. She said in fact she felt within herself an ideal impossible to realise. But as a working cellist she knew her listeners at the concert were not consoled; they could not hear her inner music. Aroused as she was by desire, at worst she bored them. But that experience of hearing music as it ought to be, an ideal music, later served to warn her, as a working artist, that she wasn't performing well.

All artistic labour encounters barriers, from writer's block to performers suddenly going blank on stage; like all other workers, we are constantly confronted with the frailty of our own powers. It is at these moments of troubled practice that the erotics of longing and inwardness threaten to seduce us. Thanks to a Romantic legacy which continues to colour modern attitudes, however, the gap between conviction and expression appears as a heroic division, with the blocked artist dwelling in a colossal trauma. The paradox of vibrato suggests how relief comes from this trauma through the dialectics of resistance and connection, which have nothing to do with the Romantic taint of heroism in artistic struggle. The real struggle in art is not to generate an inner vision, but to work without one. This happens by displacing energy from self to object.

Much of the art I am now seeing, reading and hearing made by very young people, in their late teens and early 20s, has taken an encouraging direction; it emphasises craft and materials. In America, at least, we are in the midst of a repudiation of theory-driven art, a repudiation which is not conservative, I think, but driven instead by a renewed appreciation of the labour process. In new music, especially, I am hearing work designed to be played, rather than scores to be read. New cross-over music, for instance, demands that jazz musicians revise the way they blow, finger and bow their instruments, and that classical musicians like myself also revise the use of our instruments. What I would like to see is a cultural discourse equally enmeshed in the qualities of things, and further, a politics of objects which opens them up to divergent performances and truly flexible uses. Embedding the senses in a resistant world is a political project, one which, as I have tried to indicate, would have the consequence of challenging the disciplinary regimes of ease and clarity of use. A physical world more available to touch might help lift the cursed regime of inward desire.

It might appear that the regime of power and the regime of subjectivity I have sketched have little in common. One is a domain of the explicit; the other is a domain of the ambiguous. What unites these two domains though, making power and subjectivity two sides of the same whole, is the crisis of expression they engender: both regimes deprive individuals of a medium of expression. The first induces a kind of numb, defensive withdrawal from one's surroundings, the second drives one ever further within, away from others, in order to find oneself. The regime of power deploys neutrality; the regime of subjectivity deploys desire. Neither aspires to action through resistance: both lack the arousal of touch.

I acknowledge that the arguments I have made are biased because mine is an art of performance. The music I make comes from someone else; the cello I play is not my own invention. Were I a composer or an inventor, the erotics of longing might perhaps be a fruitful starting point; I might struggle to translate the desired ideal into something concrete and physical – and that achievement would extinguish my desire, at least for the moment. But the cellist must instead make someone else's world come to life.

The performance problem, however, is much closer to the difficulty people face in the everyday world than is the composer's longing. Like me on stage, people in the street do not create the social roles of family, work and community in which they engage. Those roles are enshrined in social texts which may make vivid performance difficult, powerful texts like those encoded in buildings and urban designs which repress engagement. In *The Paradox of Acting*, Diderot argues that the good performer, on stage or in the street, cannot be the simple servant of these texts; interpretation always entails a process of translating the immaterial into the material. Within the confines of translation, though, enormous freedom is possible. That freedom, ever available in art, remains little explored in society.

Richard Sennett teaches at the University of New York. His many publications include The Conscience of the Eye, *and* Flesh and Stone.

Guest-editor: 'Touch' and 'resistance' could be understood as a process of inverted narcissism: as a dialectical subjectivity, occurring on the side of the object in the course of raw advent of function. Function appears as form, or rather as form plenitude. We could recognise here the production of form – as one binding process – as opposed to (discursively conducted) fragmentation or deformation. Finger–instrument 'become one', in a dialectical instance where the form of the instrument lends its form to that of the finger. At the level of the body, we should make the distinction between deformation (object/real metaphorisation of the subject) and spatial figuration (subjectification of the real).

Resistance as joyful persistence of form introduces the latter in its anticipatory critical power; which should not be confused with any deformation and ugliness – ie abandonment of the dialectics of form. If deformation or de-organisation is individualist sublime transcendence, visually discursifying its solitary encounter with death (Real), then spatial figuration produces re-organisations and overrealises symbolic conducts (even death) producing laughter in an (un)visual real condition.

If we extend this argument to a spatial level we could perhaps find similarities with distinct body organ-isations introduced by comic figures in old slapstick films – characters spatially figured with a minimum symbolic identity whose physical attributes often appear as morphological anticipations of objects or specific spatial conditions; fat bodies stuck in doors, objects falling on to bald heads, thin bodies swept by the wind or run over by a car but then standing up and walking off. Fat, thin, hunchbacked bodies, flat feet, long noses, etc, are not signs of individuals' characteristics but signs of re-organisation, constantly in touch with domestic space and surrounding objects; their limbs are not to be looked at but to be touched and in physical touch with objects; furthermore, their role is to domesticise space even if the latter is alien or hostile.

'I am not the man you think I am' is a spatial multitude designed by Anamorphosis Architects aiming to introduce Sennett's concepts in association with the spatial problematic of inverted narcissism. This synthesis also aims to be a critical response to Dali's The Metamorphosis of Narcissus (1937). The attempt here is to extend further the surrealist paradigm, beyond the mere employment of dream-work or the paranoiac visual matière, and operationalise it in the dimension of function. The advent of function should be understood as a symptomatic operation rather than a symptomatic irruption within the frame of the visual canvas, and be recognised as an objectal overstatement directly involving visual framing – an effect of unity or oneness disappointing the sculptural/visual as the latter becomes open to a broader field of collocations and spatial associations.

An inverted oedipal relation occurs at the level of the object. A process of spatial repetition is introduced as a critique of symbolic repetition or duplication. It opens a binding process not on the basis of similarity but on that of sameness and oneness doubting the symbolic field altogether, hence including morphological imperfection (rather than replication or distortion) and also performative gestures of completion of meaning (rather than mimetic processes). Here, what becomes critical of the narcissistic instance is neither its repetition nor its deformation. Inverted narcissism does not imply an anti-narcissus (deformed or ugly) but a narcissus 'seen' from the non-point of view of a spatial configuration of symbolic wholes. Such a configuration crosses oppositions, like those between background and foreground, material or metric/scale, elaborate and raw. It also gives emphasis to the heterogeneity between the space of access and the space of visual consciousness. In an advanced Fort-Da context, as it were, the body's re-organisation feels and registers with the 'break' or 'disappearance' of the object with which it comes to terms, by seeing it as formal affluence in the course of realisation of symbolic meaning.

The spatial 'you' (both singular and plural; conveying the spatial intimacy of psychotic dialogue but also being a personal calling to the public) objectifies the 'I am, or I am not, what I think I am' – who cares really! – as a purely verbal, symbolic question. At the level of synthesis though, it introduces form, no longer as a property of humans' objects but as the dialectic through which such familiar 'objects' re-encounter (as an extended spatial site) our symbolic preoccupations – now becoming beautifully naked (empty) discursive fixations; yet enabling and articulating new symbolic and cultural inscriptions through spatial syntheses of the local.

Beyond the Proustian paradigm, the spatial event is here to be challenged out of its solitude as a mere 'unwelcome memory'. Spatial synthesis, instead, welcomes and articulates a plurality of discourses, introducing relations of identification, affiliation and disappointment amongst them, on the basis of the spatial bind. The spatial bind is presented as unfinite (in terms of visual consciousness, formalisation, background-foreground, gravity etc) and also as an associative function-minded (ie welcomed and familiar) processed place, not simply engaged with the mapping of one single symbolic myth, truth or scenario. Resistance here is to be understood precisely in the context of associative ease and comfort which forms have in relating to one another in the course of sameness and placeness, and, simultaneously, in the context of the symbolic difficulty forms go through in this process of anticipation and association. Resistance, therefore, seems to be our own symbolic problem of understanding and making such a spatial condition operational. NG

ANDREW SAMUELS
CITIZENS AS THERAPISTS

I was on the subway. It was crowded and hot. I had a sudden fantasy of staying all day with the people who were in the carriage. We would go to lunch as a group and become friends. I wanted to call out and suggest this plan. I really felt in love! I wanted to embrace everyone. I had an erection. I don't think this was just polymorphous sexuality or a manic response to underground miseries. For, if we take my bodily reactions and my fantasies as a kind of countertransference to the social issue of transport, then perhaps this was one way of embodying my need and desire for movement with my need and desire for stasis and continuity.

Watching the regular TV report of parliament one evening, I

How can we translate our emotional, bodily and imaginative responses to Bosnia, to ecological disaster, to homelessness, to poverty worldwide, into action? How can we begin to make political use of people's private reactions to public events?

There is a sense in which this is the key political issue of our times: how we might translate passionately-held political convictions – shall we call them political dreams? – into practical realities. I think it is possible to take a subjective approach to a political problem, maybe one that has been fashioned out of personal experience, and refashion that response into something that works – actually works – in the corridors of power.

In common with many analysts and therapists, I would like to see politics become more 'psychological', taking on board a deeper understanding of people's emotions and what goes on inside them. In this piece, I would like to make a contribution from the professional world of psychology and therapy towards a strategy for empowering the powerless.

But, before that, there are a couple of important caveats to make, sort of health warnings and dampers on excessive enthusiasm.

First, we must concede and recognise the limitations of a psychological approach to politics. Freud, Jung and the founders of humanistic psychology like Maslow had ambitions to be of use in the political world. But they and their followers have, on occasion, gone in for ridiculous psychological reductionism. Hence, objections to psychological theorising about politics cannot all be put down to resistance. The impression one gets that some analysts think that everything would be OK with the world if only the world would attain 'the depressive position' reveals nothing more than the maddening rectitude and mechanistic, circular thinking of some psychoanalytic critics of culture (myself included, sometimes).

Second, it is equally important to renegotiate what can be meant by 'politics' so we can engage with the issue of empowerment and disempowerment in a more psychological way. In the late modern world (to use Giddens' phrase), politics and questions of psychological identity are linked as never before. This is because of a myriad other interminglings: ethnic, socio-economic, national. The whole mongrel picture is made more dense by the exciting and rapid course of events in

screamed at the parliamentarians, 'shut up!'. This total response was concordant with what I now see as their desire that we, who are outside the charmed circles of power, should stay shut up. Certainly, this could be taken as an example of my own authoritarian tendencies. Or I could have been merely expressing a general unease with the nightly spectacle. But my reaction gave some unthought but known specificity to the unease: Parliament as tending to silence and marginalize other fora for debate – for instance, at the workplace or within groups defined by common interests – not to mention other styles of debate, more modular and conversational and less adversarial.[1]

the coruscating realms of gender and sexuality.

The emergence of feminism as a political movement introduced us to this new kind of politics. It is sometimes a feeling-level politics, or a politics of subjectivity, that encompasses a nodal interplay between the public and the private dimensions of power. For political power is also manifested in family organisation, gender and race relations, in connections between wealth and health, in control of processes of information and representation, and in religious and artistic assumptions.

Citizens as therapists

I will turn now to my main point which is to suggest a strategy for the empowerment of citizens as therapists of the political world.

It is clear that everyone, and I think I do mean everyone, reacts to either the political issues of the day or to the political dimension of experience in a private and often heartfelt way. But most of us diffidently assume that our cloistered responses are not really of much use in the objective world of 'real' politics. Even though we all know there is no objectivity when it comes to politics, we behave as if there were, in obedience to an ideology of civic virtue that cannot abide passion in the public sphere. For the powerful fear the dissident fantasies of the radical imagination.

Clinical analysis and therapy ponder the same kind of problem: how to translate the practitioner's private and subjective responses to the client (what gets called in jargon the 'countertransference') into something that can, eventually, be fashioned into a useful intervention?

In their widely differing ways, therapists and analysts have managed to do this – and this is my point. Therapists and analysts have already managed to give value to their subjectivity, seeing that its very construction within the therapy relationship can provide a basis for useful intervention.

Analysts and therapists already have texts that teach them how to translate their impressions, intuitions, gut responses, bodily reactions, fantasies and dreams about clients into hard-nosed professional treatment approaches. They already have the idea that their subjective responses are precious, valid, relevant, effective – and there is some knowledge about how to do something with those responses.

So perhaps without realising it, we in the world of psychology and therapy do possibly have something we could share with the disempowered, with political activists – or make use of when we ourselves become politically active. For example, most clinicians know that their bodily reactions to the client's material are a highly important pathway to the client's psychic reality. Similarly, it is possible to honour and deploy the bodily reactions citizens have in response to the political world and the culture's social reality. Just as client and therapist are in it together so, too, do citizen and political problem inhabit – quite literally – the same space.

Citizens could start to function as therapists of the political world, learning to use their bodily and other subjective reactions as organs of political wisdom, helping them to understand the problems of the political more deeply and guiding the course of their actions. It would be another way to speak the political.

The evolution of a kind of political knowledge analogous to the therapeutic encounter would reflect the fact that so many people already possess a therapeutic attitude to the world. Many of us want to participate in nothing less than the resacralisation of our culture by becoming therapists of the world. But it is hard to see how to go about it.

I certainly didn't invent the notion that citizens have bodily and other subjective reactions to the political – we all know of that from our own experience of our own bodies and our own subjectivities in the political world. But it may be a novel contribution to suggest, as I do, that the political, with its problems, its pain, its one-sidedness, may actually be trying to communicate with us, its therapists. Does the political really want therapy? Will it come to its first session? Will the unconscious of the political and the several unconsciousnesses of us, its therapists, get into good enough communication?

So I am trying to do something with what is already known about citizens and the political – but not, as yet, much theorised over. I don't think I am the only one working in this area by any means. I see this 'therapeutic' way of speaking and doing politics, not as something regrettable, an over-personal, hysterical approach to politics; rather, I see it as one path left open to us in our flattened, controlled, cruel and dying world. What official politics rejects as shadow – and what can undoubtedly still function as shadow – turns out to have value. Is that not a typical pattern of discovery in therapy anyway?

Putting the citizen in the therapist's seat is itself a dramatic and radical move. For in many psychoanalytic approaches to politics, the citizen is put firmly in the patient's seat, or on the couch: citizen as infant. Then the citizen has to be regarded as having only an infantile transference to politics! It is not as empowering as having a counter-transference and it is the therapist's right to speak – the therapist's power – that I want to spread around.

The personal is political

This strategy for empowerment is a psychological extension of the feminist insight that the personal realm reflects the political realm, that what we experience in the subjective world can be the basis of progressive action and change in the political world.

I am trying to explore these ideas at public workshops. At a workshop in New York, shortly after the LA riots, I asked a largely non-professional audience to imagine themselves as 'therapists' of a 'client' called 'the LA riots' and to record their physical, bodily and fantasy responses to their client (ie to track the 'counter-transference'). Unexpectedly, just doing the exercise itself created a cathartic effect. Participants eagerly reported how they had often reacted somatically or in other markedly subjective forms to political events. But they feared these responses would not pass muster in everyday political discourse. Their conception of politics was conditioned by the notions of 'objectivity' that I mentioned earlier; they had bought the con trick of the powerful.

A whole range of novel, imaginative and practical ideas about urban and ethnic problems came out of the group process of this audience. Moreover, 'the political' was redefined, reframed, revisioned. Most of those present did not believe that there were avenues available in official political culture for what often gets stigmatised as an irrational approach. I think their assessment is right. Utilising a perspective derived from one hundred years of the practice of therapy, in which so-called irrational responses are honoured and heeded, is a small beginning in creating a new, more psychological approach to the problems of power and politics.

Lest it be thought that only an American audience could manage to do the exercise described just now, let me say that I have found similar reactions in Brazil, working with people in liberation theology, and in Leningrad (as it then was) working with young Russian therapists hungry to marry their inner worlds with what was going on around them.

I feel that this kind of politics, this other way of speaking the political, favours participation by those who are presently on the margins of power: women, gay men and lesbians, members of ethnic minorities, those in transgressive families, the physically challenged, the economically disadvantaged. These are the people with whom psychologists and therapists should stand shoulder to shoulder – in the same ethos of unknowing and humility and respect for the wisdom of the other that characterises all good clinical work.

Those diverse groupings should not be regarded as Marx's hopeless lumpen proletariat; rather, they are the last untapped sources of new energies and ideas in the political and social realms. Disempowered people certainly do need the kind of economic and financial transfusions that only politics of the official kind can presently broker. But they also need validation from the profession that makes its living and derives its authority – its power – out of working with the feelings, fantasies, behaviours and embodiments that are banned and marginalised in life in the late modern world. There is potential in everyone to be a therapist of the world. Throughout our lives, all of us have had private responses to politics. We need to raise to the level of cultural consciousness the kind of politics that people have carried within themselves secretly for so long.

Andrew Samuels is a practising analyst and author.

Note
1 Taken from A ndrew Samuels, *The Political Psyche: Subjectivity and Politics*, Routledge (London), 1993, p38.

ANDREAS EMPIRIKOS
IN THE STREET OF THE PHILHELLENES

One day as I was walking down the Street of the Philhellenes, the asphalt softening under my feet, I could hear, from the trees that line Constitution Square, crickets chirping in the very heart of Athens, in the heart of the summer.

Notwithstanding the high temperature, the traffic was brisk. Suddenly a funeral carriage rolled by, followed by five or six cars filled with women dressed in black, and as my ears caught smothered bursts of lamentation, for a moment the traffic was halted. Then a few among us (unknown to one another in the crowd), looked into each other's eyes in anguish, trying to guess each other's thoughts. But all at once, like a charge of dense waves, the traffic continued.

It was July. In the street, buses were lumbering past, crammed with sweating humanity: with people of all sorts – lean adolescents, stocky moustached males, fat or scrawny housewives, and many young ladies and schoolgirls on whose tight buttocks and palpitating breasts many in the jostling crowd, as was natural (all flaming, all as bolt upright as the club-carrying Heracles), were attempting, with mouths half-open and eyes dream-taken, to make those contacts usual in such places, so profound in meaning and in ritual; all pretending that simply by chance, because of the dense crowding and the pressures of the crowd, these frictions, these pressures, these gropings were all simply happening on the spherical attractions of receptive schoolgirls and ladies; these intentional and ecstatic contacts in the vehicles, these pressures, these frictions, these rubbings.

Yes, it was July, and not only the Street of the Philhellenes but the Fortifications of Mesolonghi, Marathon, and the marble phalluses of Delos were all throbbing, vibrating in the light like the upright cactuses of the desert in Mexico's parched expanses, or the mysterious silence that surrounds the pyramids of the Aztecs.

The thermometer had been rising constantly. It was not only warm but unbearably hot – the heat born of the vertical shafts of the sun. And yet, notwithstanding the burning heat and the rapid, gasping breath of all passengers, or the procession of funeral cars a short while before, not a single passer-by felt oppressed; nor did I, although the street was blazing. Something, like a lively cricket in my soul, compelled me to advance with a light step of high frequency. Everything around me was made manifest, tangible even to the sight, and yet, at the same time, everything was almost immaterialised in that great heat – both men and buildings – and to such a degree that even the sorrow of some of the bereaved seemed to evaporate almost completely in the equal light.

Then, with my heart fiercely beating, I stopped for a moment, motionless amid the crowd, like a man who receives a sudden revelation or sees a miracle taking place before his eyes, and I cried out, bathed in sweat: 'Oh God! This searing heat is necessary to produce such light. This light is necessary so that one day it may become a common glory, a universal glory, the glory of the Hellenes, who were the first in this world, I think, to make out of the fear of death an erotic urge for life.'

Andreas Empirikos (1901-1975) was a Greek poet and a practising psychoanalyst, and closely involved with the Parisian surrealists.

Guest-editor: *'Urban Fantasy', spatial multitude by Anamorphosis Architects, attempts to highlight the spatial problematic in Samuels and Empirikos' texts. What activates a spatial statement is the assertive, affirmative positioning of the subject 'before' and as a mirror of the symbolic ordering of space. Its politics lies in acknowledging this real positioning as a propositional tool capable of guiding design. This puts in operation an extended urban site beyond 'natural' and visual figurations of space, cutting across domestic-public, inside-outside close-distant polarisations, thus re-employing the objectal world away from discursive enclosures.*

Real positioning specifies a spatial-subjective commitment rather than a mere placement of subjectivity in space; it is not motivated by identificatory and transferential needs, but proceeds from positions of customisation and alreadyness as poles of resistance and politics. Morphological propositions are not applications of ideas but overlocalisations of them; function is the leading discourse of such overstatements and can be recognised as such. The sense of the unreal here is an effect of the overrealisation of symbolic reason rather than an expression of irrationality or sublime imagination. In a 'spatial statement' space is not the background to a human scenario but actually foregrounded through personal real positioning. The latter is not an accidental juxtaposition of image-profiles but proceeds through spatial associations proposing unreasoning syntheses.

From the transferential individual's point of view real positioning appears as fantasy-imagination; but from the locus of the social countertransferential subject it is a fantasy-reality – a procedural imaginary. The difference between flâneuring and citizenship comes into play again: the former as space-consuming, applying symbolic scenarios, the latter as space-proposing, organising spatial possibilities. The first idealises and disables space (as fragmented and unaccomplished); the second registers with the accomplishedness of positions (as marks of fulfilled desire) shaping the socio-political role of subject-as-person. In this context we could refer to Adorno's critique of Heidegger's dwelling (Minima Moralia, Verso, p38). The social uncanny (failure of dasein) must not be confused with the spatial uncanny. Individuality leads to homelessness metaphorically and literally; nevertheless, real homelessness knows more about spatiality. Un-dwelling is not only a cultural reminder of the economically repressed classes but also the spatial means by which personal/social politics can be articulated against private-life ideology.

The spatial dialecticisation of countertransference enables certain links between psychology and psychoanalysis; while it offers an analytic dimension (of fantasy) at the level of sociality, it also introduces the 'social' on the couch as analysand. The crucial debate is also reopened between individual and person, between a linguistic-transferential and spatial-countertransferential process; between the West European logico-spatial modelling of totality as a catholic application to the local, and the East/Greek European spatio-logical concept of totality as revelation of the local. NG

PAVEL BÜCHLER
A SHADOW OF THE CROWD

On the one hand, it is still possible to speak of the *presence* of sculpture in the contemporary city in the 'objective' terms of time and space; on the other, any discussion on the *role and function* of such material manifestations of creative or artistic interventions in the physical environment must, sooner or later, turn towards the question of the conceptual, technological and logistical conditions which determine their perception. Central to this will be the question of collective public interaction for which public sculpture, in a historical sense, provided both a possible focal point and a means of regulation (as an expression of legislative power or authority, as well as part of an overall spatial or environmental scheme).

It could be argued that with the advent of modern communication media, particularly photographic and digital image technologies, and the consequent necessary changes in the demarcation and self-perception of the 'public domain', the primary role of public sculpture may have become substitutive rather than communicative (it *stands for,* rather than *says,* something). Instead of being a physical 'marker' of collective interaction, it has become the last symbolic reminder of the absence of 'the crowd' from the conceptual 'space' of the contemporary metropolis.

The crowd is both a product and an active agent of the urban milieu. The notion of the crowd is virtually synonymous with the dynamics of the modern city which facilitate circumstantial concentrations of collective activity and which are, in turn, affected by the constant necessity to regulate and absorb such activity. Yet, it is possible that in the contemporary Western city the crowd can no longer be perceived as a distinct formation – that it is no longer distinguishable from the forces it is ruled by – and that it has been diffused or dispersed throughout the demographic and social structures of the city.

The disappearance of the crowd, its dissolution, is a result of changes in communication and perception which parallel the shifts in technology and economy by which the post-industrial urban society sustains itself; from sequential modes of communication and exchange to the mode of instantaneous contamination – or, seen from the perspective of the crowd, from a participation in a process to a random exposure to effects and products. Both the historical and the geographical coordinates of the crowd (its 'time' and its 'space') have been radically affected.

The early modern city was steeped in an indirect conception of time, where time could only be derived from the experience of succession and simultaneity of phenomena in space. The contemporary metropolis, however, informed as it is by the irradiative model of instantaneous contamination of entire regions or populations, embodies a dramatic alteration in the conditions of perception. Space is now suddenly condensed, and time, rather than passing, exposes itself.[1]

The effect of these changes on the state of the crowd can best be seen if the crowd is considered not as a social configuration, governed by general socio-economical laws, but as a conductive field of interrelationships among individuals – a *medium of communication* – particular to the conditions of the temporal and spatial relationships which occur in the contemporary city.

The most visible feature of the crowd understood as a medium of communication is the ripple effect caused by the spreading of information from individual to individual through direct contact (like a rumour or virus).

The crowd is, undoubtedly, a symptom of activity: a shape of an event. It is formed and held together by a response to external stimuli. Our everyday anthropomorphic vocabulary unites such a response into a single 'body' and one 'voice'. But the seemingly immediate reflexes of this 'body' only trigger off further complex reactions involving large numbers of individual relative operations. A round of applause is a typical example: it erupts (almost) instantaneously as a direct 'corporate' reply to an outside impulse but it develops, breaks up, and eventually comes to an end through mutual interaction among the people in the crowd.

Information spreading throughout the crowd is, as in any system, subject to friction, entropy and absorption. But because it spreads through active contacts among *individuals*, through constant re-coding and re-formulation in a continuum of social exchange, the inevitable modulations and mutations of the initial impulse facilitate an awareness of collective interdependence as they affect the very social bond on which the transmission depends: the flow of information is conditioned by a *mediation of immediacy*.

Thus the internal cohesion of the crowd and its existence as an active agent are determined by the individuals' experience of their participation in a collective transformation of information into knowledge. 'Being there', in a place and at a time, means sharing in the power to transmit; that is to say, the power to *transform*.

The crowd has no centre. There are no firm points (and no fixed hierarchy) in the crowd, only an external shifting focus which becomes internalised and ultimately dissolved in a process of continuous mutation.[2] Information travels throughout the crowd from a more-or-less random point of entry in all directions at once, generating a wave of response and affecting gradually the overall state of the crowd.

However, a mode of transmission which can neither be regulated from a centre (because such a point cannot be isolated within the 'system') nor coordinated externally (because any external focus is always created only by the gaze of the crowd itself) is inevitably unpredictable and uncontrollable – and potentially disruptive to the 'normal' functioning of social mechanisms.

As a controlling measure modern society has therefore introduced a whole array of technologies and standards aimed at systematising, synchronising and simplifying the functioning of the basic components of the 'system', the relationships among individuals: from legal provisions governing the rights and social obligations of the individual, through health and safety systems, to the system of education and professional qualifications, urban planning and coordinated design, standardisation of working hours and leisure time etc. While these measures do not eliminate the transformative powers of the crowd, they do nevertheless enable external agencies to control the spreading of information, its radius and its influence more efficiently by allowing them to predict and locate with some accuracy the moments and points at which the process of transmission can be interjected, polarised or disrupted. Indeed, these measures can effectively be used to turn the power of the crowd to transmit and to transform into the means of self-control.

Yet controlling the 'system' through selective regulation of the social contact among individuals is not only too slow but, importantly, it requires individual interpersonal links to be maintained. To be effective, regulatory principles must be integrated into the process of transmission itself in such a way that, for example, criteria of interpretation precede information, or ready-made 'facts' strategically coincide with 'common knowledge'.

It is only when an external agency can reach every individual simultaneously, that the active social interrelationships become redundant. The modern mass-communication media provide the necessary conditions: a contraction of distance through ultra-rapid transmission, a massive scale of operations, and the anonymity of de-humanised technology.

A key role in harnessing (and utilising) the transformative power of the crowd is played by the camera technologies, from photography and film to television and video. In particular, the transition from symbolic representation to mechanical recording and to image processing, storage and manipulation (in both analogue and numerical formats) has, since the beginning of the 20th century, produced a new order of information which, being neither true nor false, denies participation, resists transformation and generates instant polarisation of positions. The photographic or photo-based image is not merely an inert trace but an implosion of a 'photographic event'. As with a black hole, metaphorically speaking, nothing can escape from the image. Nothing can therefore be transformed in the process of communication. Instead, communication itself seems to be absorbed by/into the image.

This, however, is not to suggest that these images, moving or still, are in any way immutable. On the contrary, subsequent manipulation with the recorded image is in many respects intrinsic to photo-based media. (Its use dates back to the beginnings of photographic time and is not only standard practice in all movie making, advertising, propaganda, editorial illustration, architectural design and, of course, art, but it is also a necessary condition of the image technology.) The manipulation of the image presents itself as an effect of (technological) reality which cannot be re-absorbed into the immediate reality of direct social contacts. It seems to be precisely technology's power to manipulate time and space, to collapse it into the image, that lays claim to individual perceptions, consciousness and memory while it demobilises the collective powers of the crowd.

It abolishes the connections between space, time and experience by seamlessly fusing the present moment with the past in a perpetual appearance and disappearance of images, which follows its own chronology of broadcast and publication schedules and overthrows the order of geography by uniting all locations into one, on the same 'dimensionless' picture plane or screen.

The confusion that this creates is best illustrated by the example of the everyday diet of the news. In an older model in which the dissemination of information still involves human interaction (and the necessity of active participation), such as the purchase of the newspaper from a street vendor, a certain awareness of a chronology of events is maintained: we know that even the 'latest' news is already old news; or that, metaphorically speaking, there is no such thing as 'today's paper'. With the more technologically advanced media, such as television, which combines 'live' elements with recorded and reconstructed information, it becomes very difficult to maintain a sense of correspondence between space, time and experience.

We are 'bombarded with images', as the old cliché goes, in a kind of perpetual 'precision bombing' campaign (a notion which emerged at the time of the first 'television war', the American intervention in North Vietnam in the mid-60s). The same technology which assists a 'pin-point accuracy' in disseminating death also creates a deadly isolation of each individual when it is aimed at the crowd.[3]

In the near future, the miniaturisation of equipment, electronic super-highways, interactive television etc, will probably shatter even the last remains of collective public interaction by vastly multiplying image-realities and competing for the 'public domain' from a myriad individual and corporate centres of influence.

In the same way as the projected collides with the reflected and 'architecture becomes the paradox of the show' in an open-air cinema at night,[4] the contemporary city is a continuously reorganised image-space. Its walls and boundaries are not merely shifting, contracting and expanding with a flow of images – they are, in fact, only perceptible as 'after-images' (retinal residue) always in the process of disappearing. The street, the agora, the forum, or piazza, have all dissolved in the limitless periphery of global satellite TV transmissions and mail-order shopping. The only space still reserved for 'public gatherings' is the self-defining space of closed-circuit television – a space not of transformation but of passive transit.

Pavel Büchler is Research Professor in Art and Design at Manchester Metropolitan University.

Notes

1 Michael Feher and Sanford Kwinter, Foreword, *Zone* 1/2 (New York), 1987, referring to the article 'The Overexposed City' by Paul Virilio in the same publication.

2 Literary expressions such as 'at the centre of the crowd' or 'leading the crowd' really signify outside positions: 'surrounded by', 'followed by' etc.

3 Indeed, one could almost speak of the effects of these technologies in terms of organised violence, even media torture, in so far as torture and organised violence can be defined as 'an assault on the links and connections between people and the patterns of relationships through which [. . .] the individual develops further patterns of interaction and communication'; RD Blackwell, *The Disruption and Reconstitution of Family, Network and Community Systems Following Torture, Organised Violence and Exile*, Medical Foundation for the Care of Victims of Torture (London), 1989.

4 For an illuminating discussion of the (con)fusion of urban and cinematic space see Nikos Georgiadis, 'Open Air Cinemas: The Imaginary by Night', *Architectural Design*, vol 64, no 11/12 (London), 1994.

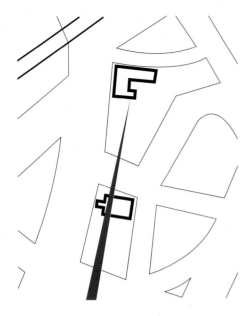

Pavel Büchler, Red Flag – *proposal for a public art project staged in Manchester, 1-7 November 1997, commissioned by Book Works, London. The work is an outcome of research into the circumstances of Karl Marx's frequent visits to the city from 1845 to 1880, drawing on the minimal 'traces of Manchester' scattered through Marx's correspondence.*

FROM ABOVE: Site plan; Reading Room, Chetham's Library; OPPOSITE: St George's flag on the spire of Manchester Cathedral, illuminated at night by a red searchlight from the Reading Room window where Marx and Engels worked in 1845

JEAN-FRANÇOIS LYOTARD
DISCOURSE, FIGURE: DIGRESSION ON THE LACK OF REALITY

Here the reader will feel that we need to make a distinction that has not yet been attempted. We need to distinguish between the real and the imaginary. The position of discourse is different when designating the one or the other. Frege emphasises that the proper aesthetic position is precisely that of the discourse which is indifferent to the existence of its object; as Freud puts it: discourse which does not question its own reality, avoids the test of reality. But what does this test consist in? Words and acts. How can we know that the object about which we are speaking exists? By giving it a name that allows us to recognise it (persistence of perceptions) and by carrying out operations on it that allow us to transform it (gratification of needs). These criteria refer us to problematics different from our own, even though they easily link up with it: the problematics of the praxis which is communication with others and the transformation of the outside world; the problematics of knowledge, which is the constituting of reality and of a coherent discourse. I need only point out that reality is constituted from a starting point in the imaginary. That which is given at the outset is the fantasy object. The formation of a 'real' object is an ordeal that corresponds to the formation in the subject of the reality-ego. Reality is never anything more than a sector of the imaginary field which we have agreed to relinquish and which we have agreed to cease investing with our fantasies of desire. This area is bordered on all sides by the imaginary field, in which wish-fulfilment fantasies go on perpetually.

And this evacuated sector itself bears the trace of the struggle for occupation between the pleasure and reality principles. Reality is not fullness of being standing against the emptiness of the imaginary; it retains lack within it, and the lack is so important that it is precisely within this lack, in the flaw of non-existence borne by existence, that the work of art takes place. The work of art is real, it can be treated as an object of acts of denomination and of manipulation before witnesses to assure them that there is indeed a painting or a statue here and now. And yet it is not real: the expanse of the *Waterlilies* is not placed in the same space as the gallery of the Orangerie; Rodin's statue of Balzac at the Raspail-Montparnasse crossroads is not planted in the same ground as the trees along the boulevards.[1] And reality is so fragile before the powerful consistency of the image, that in the struggle between the work of art and the world in which it is placed, it is the work of art that charms and attracts the world towards it – the basement of the Orangerie allowing itself to be drawn through its own walls into the luminous mist that floats on the painted ponds, and the boulevard Raspail acquiring a certain perspective from Rodin's backward-leaning statue that pulls the street downwards towards Saint Germain.

Not only does the presence of works of art make evident the absence of the object and the lack of reality in the world, but also, the absence that is 'realised' within works of art draws towards it the alleged existence of the given, revealing its very lack. The world is engulfed in works because it has an emptiness within itself and because the artist's critical expression lends a body to our desires

questing objects. What matters to us here is that, at the end of the axis of designation, there is an image. We have been supposing that the image cannot be grasped. In that regard, it is not certain that the image differs from the 'real' object: the 'grasp' itself can do no more than give images, and is probably no less fantasmatic than sight, imbued as it is with vision. Only the slightest difference between being *in* the moon [trans: 'being in a daydream', or 'mad'] and being *on* the moon.

The dividing line that is pertinent to our problem does not run between the imaginary and the real, but between the recognisable and the unrecognisable. This introduces a consideration of the third space, as different from the space of language as from that of the world. The difference is literally the unconscious. By penetrating the space of the signifier or the signified, this difference transgresses the system of regulated oppositions; it eclipses the message; it blocks communication; it treats phonemes, letters and words as things; it forbids the eye and the ear to understand the text or speech, to 'hear' it. And when it takes possession of the space of designation, of sight, it undermines the outline that revealed the object and permitted us to recognise it, and undermines the good form which made the multiplicity of given sculptural elements hold together in the field of visibility. That difference leads us to another world – a world without any recognisable face or form. This non-recognition of the respective orders of discourse and the world, which in turn renders the units of the one and the objects of the other unrecognisable, is the sign that desire pursues its accomplishment by taking hold of givens that are organised according to rules which are not its own, in order to subject them to its own law. The figures it gives rise to, as much in language as in the field of vision, have the essential attribute of being able to confound recognition. At most, as we will see, they allow us to recognise them *as* unrecognisable.[2]

Translated by Vivian Constantinopoulos

Notes

1 'The artist is originally a man who turns away from reality because he cannot come to terms with the renunciation of instinctual satisfaction which it at first demands, and who allows his erotic and ambitious wishes full play in the life of fantasy. He finds the way back to reality, however, from this world of fantasy by making use of special gifts to mould his fantasies into truths of a new kind, which are valued by men as precious reflections of reality. Thus in a certain fashion he actually becomes the hero, the king, the creator, or the favourite he desired to be, without following the long roundabout path of making real alterations in the external world. But he can only achieve this because other men feel the same dissatisfaction as he does with the renunciation demanded by reality, and because that *dissatisfaction*, which results from the displacement of the pleasure principle by the reality principle, *is itself a part of reality.*' Freud, 'Formulations on the Two Principles of Mental Functioning', (1911); my italics.

2 Translator's note: Lyotard's term 'lack of reality'/'le peu de réalité' is evocative of André Breton's exploration of what constitutes 'surréalité'. This piece is an extract from the book *Discours, figure* (published by Klincksieck, Paris, 1971), a philosophical work on aesthetic experience which makes full use of psychoanalytical theories of artistic works, mostly those found in the writings of Freud. The artistic work in the psychoanalytic topography seems to be the pre-conscious. Lyotard has much to say about the importance of unconscious processes and their irreconcilability with conscious processes. The interface of the unconscious and conscious and its crucial importance for aesthetic experience is for Lyotard the place of 'figure'.

Guest-editor: *Lyotard's text is introduced here as an attempt to break with visuality and reveal the spatiality of* figure. *Although* Discours, figure *reveals a series of spatial insights, these seem to be abandoned in Lyotard's later writing, having strong affiliations with the positivisation of the Freudian/Lacanian 'symptom' and desire, also seen in Foucault, Deleuze and Guattari's work. Various readings have reduced the spatial rigour of* Discours, figure *to the contextual frame of the visual arts, and in many ways it has served to analyse visual/countervisual philosophy and the aesthetics of visual realism. This presentation, however, aims to highlight its spatial principle on one hand, and on the other to show the problematic metaphorisation of such spatial principles in the visual arts.*

Perhaps Lyotard's text should be read in a symptomatic way. Although the text he elaborates is profoundly spatial, what is manifestly missing in this analysis is the spatial paradigm (architectural experience knows very well what is like working 'at the same place', and how built work operates with the specifics of location). But these concepts are symptomatic of Lyotard's work in general, especially in that his reference to architecture in his later The Postmodern Condition *(1979) lacks any spatial conceptualisation and rigour, and treats architecture mainly at the level of symbolic meaning.*

In Lyotard's text the work of art could have a radically spatial meaning. Certainly, Rodin's statue of Balzac in the street and the painting Waterlilies *in the basement signify the absence of the real object. But more importantly, their very allocation process introduces a radical distance between the original symbolic discourse and the spatiality (and objectiveness) in which they operate. The artworks are not in the same 'place' but, equally, the place in which they really are discloses a so-far repressed condition of sameness or, again, sameness takes over as a discourse independent of the original symbolic bind.*

In relation to Rodin, and furthermore, in opposition to Rosalind Krauss' discussion on his work and on Lessing's understanding of Laocoön (see Krauss' introduction in her Passages in Modern Sculpture, *1977), it seems that the question to address is not that of the static, synchronic mapping of the 'decentering' or 'dismembering' of the body (according to its temporality) in space; instead it is the embedding of the characteristics of the surroundings, as a full irreducible experience (functional spatiality), in the course of the synspatiality of the allocation process itself. What seems to be characteristic in the Laocoön statue and in Rodin's concept of sculpture (in contrast to works by Serra for example) is that in both cases it is the environmental condition which is morphologically inscribed in the artwork, rather than the artwork being expressive of some sort of body-realism (whether temporal, visual, or symbolic) in a 'neutral' space. The dialectics of opacity is not a matter of an intrabody or a bodies-in-space affair but of an awareness of the real opacity of spatial experience which can be found in abundance in urban space.*

To that extent it could be argued that the snake in Laocoön is the advent of the environment as constraint sent by the gods (in the Trojan myth) to punish Laocoön and his sons for their disloyalty to the gods; the snake therefore is a mark not of any unconscious recurring 'scary' real, but of the mortals' inattentive but customised struggle-cast manifold reality. One could also pursue the hypothesis that the nudity of the statue (or in Rodin's case Balzac's heavy coat) is not expressive of any blind desire, but that desire comes as an operation of registration with the visible/spatial, both in retaining its passionate figuration as an accomplished event and in 'addressing it to the open' – a gesture of morphological incorporation of the open as uncertainty and as (familiarly) unknown. After all, direct registration with the exhibited artwork is a discourse in itself operating in the relation between the art object and the direct spatio-functional environment; and in today's visual arts, more than ever, it seems to operate at a very low level.

The question is how, in the artwork, the real returns to itself revolving into this sameness as a spatial repetition rather than a similarity or symbolic repetition. That sameness extends the 'physical' limits of space, both inwards and outwards, introducing the dialectics of the static object rather than of 'drifting'.

If we miss the anticipatory power of real space, we end up with the 'gallerisation' of urban space and the concomitant singularisation or anti-singularisation of the artwork, as well as an entropic understanding of urban experience. The issue here is not what art does to 'space' but what customised (ie habitual) space – ranging from the actual facial or physical characteristics of a man (Balzac) to the actual flowers and daylight luminosity (Waterlilies) – does to the artwork when it encounters (in an art form) that portion of spatial experience which artistic gesture has borrowed, as in its initial symbolic intentions.

Lyotard's imaginary certainly has a rather propositional and operational form. What seems to matter in such a contextualisation is the fulfilment of desire as accomplishedness; and further, that the encounter with lack (of truth) is processed, paradoxically, via spatial plenitude – after all, the deprivation of function in the visual arts and its concomitant divorce from architectural experience is already a sign of a visual discourse based on unfulfilment and unaccomplishment. Function, then, seems to convey a discourse of objectal accomplishedness (not to be confused with finiteness) and re-encountering (ie the sign of fulfilment), which also points to fields of feminine desire, spatial discourse, domesticity etc.

In pursuing the point further, one can argue that architecture meets the plastic arts in the proceedings of the 'static object' in the un-expressionist and over-impressionist operations of what is termed nature/environment/object/form etc: a state of lost expression *(lost logic/truth) and* false impression *(agitated homogeneity rather than unification or fragmentation) – a false consciousness invigorated in a fully operational form. NG*

DOREEN MASSEY
SPACE-TIME AND THE POLITICS OF LOCATION

The social spaces through which we live do not only consist of physical things; they consist also of those less tangible spaces we construct out of social interaction: the intimate social relations of the kitchen and the interactions from there to the backyard and the living room; the relations with neighbours. These local spaces are set within, and actively link into, the wider networks of social relations which make up the neighbourhood, the borough, the city. Social space is not an empty arena within which we conduct our lives; rather, it is something we construct and which others construct about us. It is this incredible complexity of social interactions and meanings which we constantly build, tear down and negotiate. And it is always mobile, always changing, always open to revision and potentially fragile. We are always creating, in other words, not just a space, a geography of our lives, but a *time*-space for our lives.[1]

Sitting there so solidly, so silently, so implacably, in Grove Road, so physically in just the place it always was, and yet so clearly out of place, House worked as a disruption of such social time-spaces. It jumped into and threw awry the 'normal' time-spaces, and the ideas of time-spaces, which we construct in order to live our lives.

It worked this disruption, first and most obviously, in a predominantly temporal sense. It set a familiar past in the space-time of today; it made present something which was absent; it was the space of a house no longer there. Secondly, however, it worked spatially: it turned the space inside out. The private was opened to public view. The intimate was made monumental and yet retained its intimacy. And this effect of our prying into intimacies was reinforced by the tearing down of the rest of the terrace. For neighbouring houses provide protection, enable you to put on only your best face. With them gone we could see what lay behind that solid public frontage. We could see the back-spaces as they fell away in size and somehow in significance, through back bedroom, back extension, scullery, lean-to shed. From public solidity and the front room to the more precarious, personal and informal spaces where most of daily life was lived. Now we could see all of this too.

Thirdly, House disrupted our accustomed sense of time-space by apparently solidifying the volume that had once been the interior of the house: the living space, the space of life. Its openness had been filled in. All that was air was turned into solid. In House, social time-space was deadened, muted. The movement, the noise, the interchange; these things through which we create the time-spaces of our lives were gone. House was emptied of all that, and such a way of asserting what social time-space really is – precisely by so brilliantly emphasising its absence, its current impossibility – is one of the most provocative things about this work. Through its very negation it brought home the true meaning of social space.

Given all of this, what is crucial to any assessment of House on these dimensions is the way in which the three aspects of space-time disruption work together. Much must turn on the way in which these disruptions functioned in the responses to and interpretations of House, perhaps especially by local people – people in the East End of London.

Nostalgia

Let us begin this inquiry with the fact of reference to the past – or, better, reference to 'a past', since the point is precisely that there are many versions of this history. Much comment on House has focused on memory, on the first – temporal – disruption of space-time which it works, with much reference to nostalgia and to nostalgia for a specific place and time.

Now, that kind of nostalgia has been interpreted by many as being a symptomatic, defining, element of the postmodern condition. This, in turn, has been variously explained. On the one hand commentators such as David Harvey see in a nostalgia for place merely a defensive response to the new burst of the globalisation of capital, the new and accelerated phase of time-space compression.[2] For them, such a response is a negative evasion of 'the real issues', and nostalgia for place is likely to end up in political 'reaction'. Yet there is another way of understanding this nostalgia which again would see it as a product of the present era but would not condemn it out of hand. Thus Angelika Bammer and Wendy Wheeler interpret it as a symptom emerging from the deprivations of modernity, a response to the too-long-maintained repression of affective desire by Modernism in its various forms. Postmodern nostalgia is the return of Modernism repressed.[3]

How then is it to be interpreted? Wendy Wheeler, who links this aspect of affect precisely to notions of the uncanny, stresses the element of sharedness which it entails. Postmodern nostalgia she defines as 'the desire for communal identifications'. 'Nostalgia . . . turns us towards the idea of the individual as non-alienated, as knowing and being known by others in the commonality of the community which is identified as "home".'[4] It is not necessary to accept that this is the only form of postmodern nostalgia in order to agree that it is an important component. Angelika Bammer, too, addressing the specific issue of 'home', writes of 'fictional constructs, mythic narratives, stories the telling of which have the power to create the "we" who are engaged in telling them. This power to create not only an identity for ourselves as members of a community . . . but also the discursive right to a space (a country, a neighbourhood, a place to live) that is due us, is – we then claim, in the name of the we-ness we have just constructed – at the heart of what Anderson describes as "the profound emotional legitimacy" of such concepts as "nation" or "home".'[5]

But if this interpretation, in contrast to that of Harvey, accepts – as it is surely correct to do – the 'emotional legitimacy' of nostalgia for place and home (even if only on grounds of recognising its inevitability) it is nonetheless the case that such nostalgia can be problematical; for memory and the desire for communal identifications can cut both ways. They can be an aid to reactionary claims for a return (to something which of course never quite was, or which at least is open to dispute). They can erase other memories and other identifications. They can exclude some groups from membership in 'the commonality of the community which is identified as "home"', or they can be a basis for the mobilisation of emancipatory political change. Particular evocations of nostalgia must, for that reason, be evaluated individually, in their specificity. Jeffrey Peck, for instance, concludes that in certain times and places (he is writing of Germany at the end of the 20th century), the particular concept of 'home' is so unavoidably full of references to exclusion, blood and territory that it is virtually unusable for other, more disruptive emancipatory purposes.[6] Another approach, maybe in other contexts, might be to argue the pressing need for its reformulation. The question is how, in any particular circumstance, a specific form of evocation of memories functions? What effects does it produce? What solidarities (what we-nesses) does it conjure in the imagination? Are its workings those of exclusion or of openness?

House clearly aroused memories and provoked thoughts about nostalgia. Moreover it did so, and quite deliberately, at a specific moment in space-time: a late 19th-century house in a once-settled, now partly demolished residential street in the heart of London's East End. How, then, in relation to this question of nostalgia, did House work its effects?

The question can be posed at two spatial scales. First, it can be posed at the scale of house and home. Feminists, for instance, have long argued that the resonances once so usually associated with 'home' must be disrupted: that home is not necessarily a place of rest or of repose, that it can be also a place of work, a place of conflict, a place of entrapment. Bammer suggests that 'home, in a sense, has always been *unheimlich*, unhomely; not just the utopian place of safety and shelter for which we supposedly yearn, but also the place of dark secrets, of fear and danger, that we can sometimes only inhabit furtively'.[7]

Secondly, the question of House's affect/effect can be raised at a broader geographical scale: that of the local area in which it was made. Here what needs to be investigated is its relation to a politics of location. For the sculpture was set in the East End of London and, more specifically, in the borough of Tower Hamlets. And memory and nostalgia are difficult and dangerous things in that area these days. On the one hand is the enormous freight of meaning – and of different meanings – the very words 'the East End of London' bring with them. On the other hand is the wrenching disruption of this space in the recent past. The docks have closed, their use and meaning is being quite consciously re-worked; to the south Canary Wharf rises on the obliteration of a past which is drawn on only to add a touch of local colour to the new, global developments. And in September 1993, at the very time when House was being constructed, the British National Party won a seat on the local borough council.

In this local area, memory and nostalgia are active forces precisely in the constitution of communal identifications and political subjectivities. They are crucial axes around which political constituencies are articulated and individuals interpellated into wider constellations of attitudes. So House is an irruption of a past time-space into a present where references to 'the past', and interpretations of the nature of that past and of the relationship between past and present, are key political stakes.

The issue, therefore, is not to attempt to eradicate memory and nostalgia. It is, on the contrary, to ask: how do those other two aspects of the potentially uncanny spatiality of House work to subvert what *could* be, given its placing in this time and space, an all-too-*comfortable* nostalgia of home and locality.

House and 'home'

What effects, then, do the turning of the space inside out and the solidification of space have when considered at the level of the domestic: at the spatial scale of the home? One thing to say first is that, of course, this sculpture was not called Home; it was called House. Naming immediately distances us, it uses a word somehow from the public sphere to designate a work which is so evidently redolent of what we customarily think of as private, and a word, too, which refers more to the physicality of the walls and roof, which have been removed, which now no longer are, than to the space of social interaction which, in contrast, has now so physically been both exposed and filled in. The very naming, then, gives clues to the spatial disruptions House effected.

The first of these two spatial reversions – the turning of the space 'inside out' – works particularly powerfully at this scale of the individual house/home. It is immediately shocking and disruptive. It exposes the private sphere to public view and thereby to questioning. Most importantly, it defamiliarises house and home. And in achieving that, it challenges us to put our own meanings on them. It exposes the normal, comfortable mythologising of 'home'. Bammer, following up her argument for the intrinsic double nature of home, suggests that 'Perhaps, in this light, the best we can do about home at this point in time is to bring it, in all its complexity, out into the open'.[8] This, surely, House achieves. It is not merely physical space which it turns inside out but the whole burden of meaning and metaphor which this space has so often had to carry (the actual bearing of the burden usually predominantly being done by the women who lived in those spaces). Potentially at least it exposes the complexity of the meaning of 'home'. House emphasises the fact that its meaning always has to be interpreted; that there was never any simple 'authenticity'; that the meaning(s) of home are always open to contestation.

Postmodern nostalgia, it has already been pointed out, has been argued to be the return of the repressed of Modernity. More specifically, it is the return of the repressed in the form of the 'other' sides of all those dualisms which are made to provide the (ultimately oh-so-precarious) foundation for Modernity's assertion of the dominance of unsullied Reason.[9] Among the core set of this bastion of dualisms is that between the famous pair, the private and the public. For Hannah Arendt the distinction between the two is 'between things that should be hidden and things that should be shown'.[10] In House the things which should be shown are removed, leaving only their defining shape; while the things which should be hidden are (almost, potentially, in outline) exposed to view. It is a reversal which, certainly, could bear 'the name for everything that ought to have remained... secret and hidden but has come to light'. Moreover, to take a final step along this particular line of thought, Homi Bhabha, drawing on Carole Pateman's work in *The Disorder of Women*, argues that 'By making visible the forgetting of the "unhomely" moment in civil society, feminism specifies the patriarchal, gendered nature of civil society and disturbs the symmetry of private and public which is now shadowed, or uncannily doubled, by the difference of genders which does not neatly map on to the private and the public, but becomes disturbingly supplementary to them'.[11]

The second spatial reversal worked by House, the solidifying of the once-open space both further complicates this questioning of the public/private divide and produces other, different effects. For the 'private' sphere is of course *not* in fact exposed to view. What used to be a space-time created out of living social relations is by this second reversal made mute and blind and inanimate. On the one hand this forces us, again, to interpret. By defamiliarising, silencing the private world now exposed to public view it compels us to do our own work. Mute it stood there, asking us to remember, to think, to question. On the other hand, by evoking so profoundly the absence of that previous life, those now-stilled social relations, by the fact that the house has gone and that the potential for the reconstruction of that social space has been so finally ended by both aspects of this spatial reversal, House insists on the impossibility of the recovery of that past. This is crucial; it is potentially, and productively, disturbing. It is a positive, dislocating, evocation of memories. It makes clear that, however you interpret the past, you can't have it back.

There does seem to be here a glaring – and fascinating – contrast with the way in which the classic 'heritage site' performs its work. In many heritage sites not only are the buildings retained, but within them and around them a version of the social relations of the chosen moment of the past is acted out. A particular reading (sometimes more than one) of those social relations which constituted that particular space-time is preserved, and re-presented. There is frequently a commentary, maybe a written guide explaining things. Such sites, too, can be provocative of nostalgia. As Wheeler says, 'That these are commodified images in no way lessens their effect'.[12] But the effect of this nostalgia is likely to be different from that of House. While House is a prompt and a disturbance to the memory, the classic heritage site fills in those spaces and restricts the room for interpretation and imagination. Instead of questioning memory and pre-given understandings of the past, the classic heritage site will provide them ready-made. Instead of defamiliarising the supposedly familiar, it is meant as an aid to further familiarisation. It is, by design, an understandable rather than an unsettling space, a comfortable rapprochement with another space-time.

The use of such sites in particular localities can also sometimes have the effect of presenting history as continuity, as tradition in its conventional sense. On this reading, 'tradition' is something which we inevitably lose, as it fades into the past. Such notions of tradition can so easily be congealed into a static essence, as the *real* character of the place: what do we mean when we say 'this is the *real* East End'? And what contexts would provoke us to say it?

It has recently been argued by many writers that white British culture and society are undergoing serious anxiety about the nature of tradition and their relationship to it. Kevin Robins has argued that the burgeoning industry of 'heritage culture' has been in part about attempts to construct, or to respond to the felt need for, 'protective illusions' in the midst of all this anxiety.[13] In one way House clearly disallows such protective illusions; the very vulnerability of its inside-outness, for instance, prevents such easy recourse to tradition in this sense. But there is another aspect to the critique of this concept of local tradition which raises broader issues. In this critique what is called for is a rejection of the all-too-frequently 'internalist', inward-looking, character of tradition and a recognition of the past – and the present – as always having been hybrid and open.[14]

The politics of location

House was conceived and made in the context of the East End of London. And the East End is an area which oozes meaning as a place, both locally and in the national psyche. It is a locality in which notions of community and of constructing that 'we' of which Angelika Bammer writes, and the communal identifications named by Wendy Wheeler, are at the very heart of politics and of daily life. A reference to 'tradition' in the East End can bring to mind radicalism and ethnic diversity or racism and community closure. In such a context it becomes particularly important to ask how the evocation of memory is working and what effects – social and political – it is producing.

The debates which took place over House complicated these issues still further, sometimes productively, at other times troublingly. So-called 'traditionalism' in art crossed swords at times with forms of traditionalism of the locality. The predictable debate as to whether or not this was 'art', although a sterile confrontation in its own terms, threw into relief some other, less expected, alignments. On the one hand, as people from inside and outside the area, indeed from all over the world, flocked to see it, there was an appreciation of the work which was at times undoubtedly elitist.[15] Some highly dubious lines of counterposition were thereby drawn up, between experts and ordinary folk, between I-know-what-I-like traditionalists and an avant-garde which was actually now the establishment, between worthy locals (and local worthies) and elitist outsiders. Thus, one aspect of House's provocation of constituencies looked, at first sight, pretty dismal.

Yet in an interesting way it was also contradictory. Thus in one, and only one sense, it was something of a relief that it was, in this public debate, the traditionalists and those who claimed to speak for 'ordinary local people' who so often disliked the work. Had these defenders of all that was so great in those days really loved House, it might have been necessary to question the manner in which it was evoking memory. Had House stimulated a positive evocation of the East End for these groups it would probably have fitted into images of good old England and cuddly (white and patriarchal) working-class communities. It says a lot for House that it does not seem to have been interpreted in this way directly; that it did not play to that kind of nostalgia, did not stimulate the reinforcement of a backward-looking, reactionary, communal identity. But neither was it rejected by these detractors because it *problematised* that kind of a nostalgia of place. The issue was simply not raised. What these commentators disliked was House's nature as (not) Art, not its representation of the East End.

Matters were equally confusing on the other side of these self-built fences. Although the work was proudly defended by some as modern in artistic terms, some of the evocations of its meaning by the self-consciously artistically adventurous were alarmingly traditional *socially*.

Take the issue of housing, and what it represents socially. John McEwen in *The Daily Telegraph* paraded the classic contrasts: 'grim 1960s high-rises' and 'tarted-up 1980s ones' and 'the twenty-first century megastructure of Canary Wharf'. And, having let us know what he doesn't like, he gives us the alternative: 'the snug 1880s terraced family homes of which House is an example'.[16] McEwen's response to House did not place him within a 'traditionalist' camp. But when it comes to family-values, domestic bliss and housing, what he appreciates is snug families. Non-traditionalism in art combined with an utterly traditional nostalgia about home. Not only does such a response fail to take on board the potential critique of such forms of domestic organisation, but it harks back uncritically to an age which itself has come to have many dubious and debatable political meanings – the Victorian era.

But housing in this area raises other issues too. The iconography of house and home performs a crucial role in the various imagined pasts of this part of London. The far-right election victory in September 1993 was largely orchestrated around battles over housing (of which there is a grotesque shortage), and over the right of 'the locals' to local housing over the rights of others. Housing was at the centre of the battle over who was, and who was not, part of the local community. It was a crucial organising issue for the increasingly vocal racisms. The British National Party in the East End uses a mythic version of the past of the place as white, as pure English. It refers to a non-existent past 'before immigration'. And Bow, where House stood, is, and is seen as, a relatively white enclave within that East End. It was one of the first places where the housing strategy 'for locals' was tried. The fact of the work being a house, and in this precise location, was therefore potentially highly symbolic. What House did not do, maybe at the wider spatial scale it could not do, was challenge that kind of construction of home as once pure and now corrupted; that notion of tradition, of traditions of place now lost. While it said that no past is recoverable it didn't problematise, *at the level of the locality*, the memory of what that past was. Although its location was important, House did not say much about the East End as a wider area or about Bow within it: as a place of cohabitation of radicalism and racism, as a meeting-place of immigrants from all over the world and over centuries, as a repository of a bit of English identity, as a site of contradiction between a persistent localism and the context of having been for two centuries and more at the hub of a global Empire. It is often argued, as we have seen, that the current intensified phase of globalisation has hybridised all our homes. In fact this is by no means a new phenomenon. Quintessential Englishness is utterly founded and dependent upon relations with elsewhere. And in few places is this clearer than the East End, with its constant flow of new communities and its centuries of contact with the trade routes of the world. The hybridity of a place called home is not new. Could House have set in motion forces towards the construction, the reinforcement or the subversion of communal identifications in this place? And what 'discursive right to a space' (Bammer) does that allow such a community to claim? These issues are central to the politics of location in this area. Might the work provoke longings for an imagined past 'pre-immigration'? Or could it help in the construction of a 'we' which is inclusive, and neither defensive nor essentialist? To me, it seemed that House did not broach these issues substantively.

This is not to suggest that the work could have addressed these issues directly, and certainly not that it need have answered questions rather than merely raising them. For this is the point. At the level of the internal-domestic, House clearly problematised issues. One could not look at it without asking questions. At this level, House worked all three disruptions to time-space. It brought back a previous time-space, but it also inverted and apparently solidified it. It thoroughly de-familiarised it. It is less clear at the level of the locality, however, that House really posed questions, really *unsettled* in any way the terms of the accepted debate. Could it have de-familiarised the locality too? And while, certainly, it was mute, it was not without content. In its specific location and its evocation of house and home, it might have courted the danger of provoking a nostalgia for a white East End.

And yet it seems not to have had that effect, or not among the reactions which found a wider public. The alignments faced the other way. The British National Party, by all accounts, were utterly offended by the work. Maybe, ironically, what was active here was House's glorious combination of the evocation of tradition precisely in a non-traditional form of 'art'. If this meant that the history of the locality was not problematised, at least it meant that the work did not become the focus for the celebration of a mythical white past. Indeed, the first graffiti sprayed on House read: 'HOMES FOR ALL BLACK + WHITE'.

Doreen Massey is Professor of Geography at the Open University and joint editor of the journal Soundings.

Notes

1 For a more detailed discussion, see Doreen Massey, *Space, Place and Gender*, Polity (Cambridge), 1994.

2 David Harvey, *The Condition of Postmodernity*, Basil Blackwell (Oxford), 1989.

3 Wendy Wheeler, 'Nostalgia Isn't Nasty – the Postmodernising of Parliamentary Democracy' in Mark Perryman (ed), *Altered States: Postmodernism, Politics, Culture*, Lawrence and Wishart (London), 1994.

4 Ibid, p99.

5 Angelika Bammer, 'Editorial: The Question of "Home"', *New Formations* (London), no17, pxi, 1992.

6 Jeffrey M Peck, 'Rac(e)ing the Nation: Is There a German "Home"', *New Formations*, no17, pp75–84, UK, 1992.

7 Bammer, op cit, pxi.

8 Bammer, op cit.

9 Wheeler, op cit.

10 Hannah Arendt, 1958, *The Human Condition*, Chicago University Press (Chicago), p72, in Homi Bhabha, *The Location of Culture*, Routledge (London), p10, 1994.

11 Homi Bhabha, op cit.

12 Wheeler, op cit, p98.

13 Kevin Robins, 'Tradition and Translation: National Culture in its Global Context', in Corner, J and Harvey, S (eds), *Enterprise and Heritage*, pp21–44, Routledge (London), 1991.

14 See also Homi Bhabha, 'Beyond Fundamentalism and Liberalism', *New Statesman and Society* (London), 3 March 1989; Robins, op cit; Hanif Kureishi, 'England, your England', *New Statesman and Society*, 21 July (London), 1989.

15 See for example, Andrew Graham-Dixon, 'I don't know much about art, but I know what I hate . . .', *The Independent* (London), 24 November, 1993; Deyan Sudjic, 'Art attack', *The Guardian* (London), November 25, 1993; *The Independent* (London), January 14, 1994.

16 John McEwen, 'The House that Rachel Unbuilt', *Sunday Telegraph* (London), 24 October, 1993.

Guest-editor: By reading Massey's reading of Whiteread's House we can pursue an Other dimension of the sculptural: a condition of disappointment of the sculptural (positive or negative) in the course of spatial propositions of function; a condition which stops any further expelling of the utilised by the sculptural and any concomitant conversion of the former to an essentially 'cold', 'entropic' and opaque real that invests in the individual's private 'psychoanalytic' uncanny world – a comfortable womb-alternative fostering yet another foreclosure of space.[1]

Perceived in these terms, a crucial point that House can make can be seen not in the negativisation of the visible or the banalisation of the usable, but in the radical distinction between the visible and the usable, which occurs at the level of domestic/urban/historic reclaiming.

Massey's House is not a deadly (non-articulable) opaque or imploded antiform – a singular object 'gallerising' public space, 'exciting' and dragging us into short-circuit interpretative operations, taking for granted and neutralising spatial givens. A spatial (as opposed to visual) understanding can introduce the specific artwork not at the level of an (a-political) 'elsewhere' or 'everywhere' or 'inexchangeable real', but as a contextualisation of a radical political no-where – that is, a 'place' whose very presence puts in question its 'yes/no' symbolic convictions. The differences between opaque or cast entropic visuality and dialectical opacity; between a general asymbolic condition and specifically unsymbolic conditioning; between the real as a metaphor for death and the real as a problematic of the specific – all of these converge on the difference between negated space and procedural spatiality.

The problematic of nostalgic space is not concerned with a memory-bound condition but is instead a spatial engagement that seeks to activate repressed subjectivities such as the feminine, sociality, tradition. At a technical level, however, the political recurrence of spatiality seems to operate as a re-encountering of place as we – spatially deprived as we are – gradually become immigrants ourselves within our own 'homely' urban environment. At a spatial level the immigrant returns not as guest or traveller but as pure citizenship, as an Other domesticity – a spatial awareness crossing all 'natural' (ie communicational) distances, involving a total and unlimited reference to space, from domestic utensils to the city itself, to a 'new' country.

'Homes for all black + white' can be read as a spatial hypothesis. Massey's House seeks the spatial precision which would objectify the symbolic at the level of desire – rendering the symbolic articulable rather than merely polarised and ruling. So a politics of location urges a practice of radical de-idealisation and, in turn, a binding of the symbolic. This is perhaps the most important point here: that the supposed entropic condition of the inverted building can actually become focused. From a spatial non-point of view, beyond the visual or sculptural, the graffiti's well-known symbolic polarisation can now be reallocated in a gesture that takes on board the local socio-spatial culture as a critique of any asymbolic (apolitical) interpretation which the artwork as a mere sculpture 'in space' would entail. Of course the graffiti does not demand homes for blacks and whites separately (two different types of dwellings for two distinct categories of people). What it advocates is a spatial (rather than worldly) bind of the two racist categories – the making of a living space out of one undiscriminating solid spatial quality, which would synthesise and potentially erase symbolic differences (as the latter have always been effects of relations of opposition and mutual idealisation).

We cannot help but remember the famous Lacanian anecdote of a boy and girl sitting at opposite seats in a train arriving at a station who start arguing about the ladies' and gentlemen's toilets. From the spatial non-point of view (and contrary to many symbolic interpretations of the Lacanian concept) the issue here is not to see that the opposite 'signifieds' slide or polarise over (caught up in an endless intertransferential discourse) an untouchable and randomly moving 'signifier', in an act of symbolic appropriation or misappropriation; instead the point is to acknowledge the urgency of a practice of affluence of the referent/space and its binding countertransferential allocating principle which can defuse symbolic polarisations. Countertransference is particularly important here, because merely celebrating relations of 'otherness' between the two symbolic poles does not seem adequate. What does seem to be necessary is the collocation and spatial exchange of the actual, 'different', referential conditions at issue. So it seems that 'we' people should know how to dwell in 'two' collocated places: 'one' as blacks or ladies and 'one' as whites or gentlemen. NG

Note

1   For an elaboration of the 'entropic' and 'uncanny' in relation to House, see, respectively, Rosalind Krauss, 'X Marks the Spot', in *Rachel Whiteread: Shedding Life*, exhibition catalogue, Tate Gallery, Liverpool, 1996 , pp 74-81, and Anthony Vidler, 'A Dark Space', in *House: Rachel Whiteread*, Phaidon Press Limited (London), 1995, pp 62-72.

Rachel Whiteread, House, Grove Road, London (October 1993-January 1994)

ROGER CONNAH

UNINFLECTION AND STUBBORN ARCHITECTURE
The Work of ARRAK Architects

The shots have nothing to do with each other. They are not a record of what the protagonist did. They are not a record of how the deer reacted to the bird. They're basically uninflected images. But they give the viewer the idea of 'alertness to danger' when they are juxtaposed. That's good filmmaking. David Mamet

Contextualising uninflection and the obtuse

It may be good architecture too! Much formalism and mannerism abounds in recent contemporary architecture, especially architecture visually exuberant enough to appear endlessly in international magazines. We have seen, in the 1990s, the desire to play up to a neo-modern style. Expressive, somewhat restrained architecture is perpetuated by a shifted, sometimes emptied, deconstructive play. A neo-avant-garde opts for the semiotic spectacle of form and material whilst hopefully hooking on to an authenticity of material and tectonic logic. Very often this reinforces the nostalgia of a supposed brave and coherent radical past that belongs to an earlier part of this century. Domain and identity-giving structures are commonly associated with this stylised, image-made architecture.

Such strict aesthetic classification within contemporary architecture leaves *other* architecture, more obtuse work in whatever form it takes, less able to be promoted and less open to critical analysis. It is then but a short step to see this other work dismissed by loose, pejorative, often misplaced terms, like organic, regional, vernacular, subjective, romantic, idiosyncratic, instinctive, intuitive. At the same time, however, it would be a mistake to reduce all this other architecture to the competent, discrete work of a critical tectonic but ultimately blunt regionalism. Architecture such as this often remains uninflected, outlasting the im*media*cy of architecture as represented through magazines and journals. This is an architecture that is doubtless contemporary yet can appear ageless. It is an architecture that is styleless yet can conform to identifiable signatures. It is an architecture that can be stubbornly cultural and isolated, uninflected, yet must borrow symbolic investment from a variety of traces. It is an architecture that can appear undeveloped in relation to more visual current trends but gains by a slow, even shrewd, juxtapositional grounding in site, material and culture.

The key here is uninflection, and as an initial contextualising clue to such 'procedural' architecture, I propose to take off from David Mamet's notion of juxtaposition in filmmaking. Juxtaposition can be said to aim for – if not necessarily achieve – an *alertness to architecture*. This alertness is neither contained only in the immediate informational level *projected* by the architecture, nor is it merely registered at the second *symbolic* level that an architect may hope will be conveyed by the work. Such alertness in architecture always invites a further level. There is a third, experiential level that so often avoids immediate grasp and timing in architecture. Combined with the previous two levels it can, even, exceed the phenomenological. Through the notion of juxtaposition, as that confluence where *function* and *environment* in architectural experience converge, we might propose a third effect in architecture.

The third effect

This third effect, in architectural terms, is a form of found and lost montage. Created by a critical and experiential architectural montage, a careful refusal to opt for immediate accessible style-defined solutions, this is not a third meaning, the obtuse meaning (Barthes on Eisenstein). It is a stubborn inventive practicality and responsibility, arising only in and out of the architectural process. We can call it an *obtuse architecture* if we consider such work uninflected: uninflected in the sense that the architecture is slow to reveal its subtlety or its totality; uninflected in the sense of an architecture less than immediate and all that that implies in a media age; an architecture that by so lacking the visual props and semiotics of more exuberant work demands more subtle and less accessible symbolic grounding. *Uninflection* is, necessarily, shy of the visually immediate. In architecture any visual instancy invites an increased, even accelerated, expressive grasp.

It is therefore not surprising that in a society like Finland, which is so driven by national signatures, historical anxiety and the need to script coherence of culture through architecture, uninflection struggles to gain critical recognition. Indeed, it must baulk at such access. The more classificatory, visual examples often associated with Finnish architecture, those stylishly polished works that conform to a *semiotic* narrative of identity and culture, invite and ensure continuing promotion. Architecture that might consider the alertness to critical response and cultural innovation to be elsewhere, an architecture undemonstratively exploring the site, the climate and the building techniques of a region using innovative ecological materials, an architecture exploring the third effect, demands a quieter discipline. As in Arctic planning, there is, in such architecture, a slow and gradual logical progression towards an ordered state, however disordered and scattered the departure and initial drama may be. Architecture such as this may only come to rest long after the settlement has been built, long after more immediate function and semantics have been served. Architecture so uninflected, to differentiate it from the more generalised vernacular 'modernism', expresses a commitment first to building, second to culture and third, effectively over time, to stubborn revelation.

Uninflection and stubbornness

To make relevant our idea of uninflection and the third effect, and to locate its links to a stubbornness in architecture, it is worth a brief digression. Finnish architecture is often confused by its promoted 'collective' notion. It is a notion trimmed to a visual style and polish that struggles to avoid including its variants. An ethical trace is seen to be 'read' aesthetically; discipline and detail are equated with style and polish. Not particularly inter-

The Samis as Sheep Herders, *Andreas Alariesto (1900-89)*

Valintatalo Supermarket, Matinkylä

ested in self-promotion, there is a number of small practices in Finland that have, since the late 70s, produced a consistent body of work – uninflected work we are suggesting – which cannot easily be classified as regionalist or vernacular. Sharing responsibility for the architecture achieved, these are collaborative practices where one or other of the partners assumes the lead, guiding and steering the project through the brief, the various stages of the project, confirming and testing at all steps a series of carefully scrutinised guiding principles.

There are clearly risks in such commitment. Often possessing a stubborn stylelessness, this is, in its pace and detail, an architecture that can and must stand detached from more inflected sensuality and poetics. A practice with an apparent lack of a clear 'style', undeveloped or then uneven, is perceived to be inconsistent in terms of conventional critical analysis. Committed smaller practices, such as the Finnish architects ARRAK, suggest that the stubbornness of this architectural variance deserves deeper exploration. ARRAK is an acronym using the first two letters from the Finnish words for architecture (ARkitehtuuri) and the first three letters from the word for building (RAKennus). Held within this is a contract and commitment with architectural responsibility itself. Like a director thinking of the next step, their buildings evolve from a clear *indistinct* sense, a slowness even, if not from stubbornness.

'Get into the scene late, get out of the scene early, tell the story in the cut.' Mamet offers sound advice and avoids easy seduction. Implying a range of careful, at first possibly indistinct departures; from the ecological use of timber, from locations (just as a film might), from regional myth or realism, from tradition and culture, ARRAK proceeds through a dialectics of building methods and architectural expectations. The practice can speak of a styleless architecture grounded in a layered, even local symbolism. Meanings, when they come from their work, are additive and not always secondary, and clearly the results are not always recognisably 'ARRAKIAN' because such departure, such design methodology and cultural symbolism does not predispose consistently identifiable aesthetics. There is, in their layering of the work, in the tectonics and symbolism of the building methods and use, no envisaged 'semiotic' or formal consequence to their work when it begins. This is the obtuseness of their approach; as if there is a hidden hand, as if slowness knows when to accelerate the architectural process and read significance in the insignificant.

The significance of insignificance

The 1980s was a period in which architecture was wedded to a public symbolism. No coherent notion of Finnish architecture survived the treacherous levelling of the 1970s. Postmodernism arrived and confused just about everyone as architecture was tempted by its semantic potential. Suspicious contractors conspired with clients to demand the simplest commercial boxes with or without optionally applied reference. One of ARRAK's first buildings, the Valintatalo Supermarket – a monument to the last suburban 'empire' of Matinkylä – is a decorated shed: metal box frame and timber elements with a Venturian echo. Any slight organic touches, ecological concerns and ironic use of time were lost on the client, however, and drowned in inexperience. Yet, at the same time, the practice's ideas on uninflection were manifested in the two most significant projects of their early work: Espoo Bridge (1982) and the Aleksis Kivi Cottage (1982). Uninflection and a stubbornness to the visual immediacy of the decade needed to take form; applying references to buildings was not the only way to make remarkable the apparently insignificant.

The Espoo Bridge is accretional: the tectonics obey a strict logic of structure and agglutinisation. No inflected structural image or sensuality guides the bridge's form, no grand sweep or expressive sketch, no cultural input familiarises us. No symbolic lift is offered; no sensation or sentimentality sought. The resulting robustness merely – not insignificantly – resonates. ARRAK was clearly confronting a serious problematic in architecture; the inevitable significance of apparent insignificance in architecture. Even clumsiness had to be confronted.

The cottage where the Finnish National Poet Aleksis Kivi died is not a remarkable work in any sense. Over the years, along with Kivi's reputation and existence, the cottage settlement has been ignored, mutilated and altered beyond recognition. In 1952 it was renovated to a former condition by Errki Helamaa (supervised by Lars Pettersson, from the Art History department of Helsinki). In 1982, again after repeated decay, the modest architectural exercise for ARRAK was one of mere subtraction; to strip down even further to the obvious. The obvious in this case was the rather insignificant little cabin. Basic building techniques were used and had to suffice. It would have amounted to an upholsterer's job if not for the research necessary to attain this insignificant character. No trimming, no stylistic emphasis or fidgeting could make the cabin what it was not. No further cultural pointing-up or fakery was felt necessary or attempted. There could be nothing more

Aleksis Kivi Cottage

The Arctic Centre, Rovaniemi, exterior views

site-specific and source-orientated than Aleksis Kivi's dying place; nothing more obtuse, more stubbornly architectural than this unremarkable cottage!

Forced to deal with the apparently insignificant, a disparate, even unprovocative, cultural environment schooled the practice in the obvious. It also contextualised for them a series of guiding principles which we identify as uninflection. Source, trace, points of departure for the work had to be grafted from the modest, the unremarkable, the unnoticed and even the insignificant. Uninflection and detail are inherent in this schooling. Rather than relying on recognised visual forms, a desire to make architecture from such a modest commission demands a methodology and a commitment to serve the client in more innovative ways, even those more waywardly cultural and mythological. There could be no predisposed image for the architecture they wished to build. For this reason, their Arctic Centre (1983-85) has become such an important and pioneering project within Finnish architecture.

Discontinuous planning

The Arctic Centre in Rovaniemi is a series of buildings designed mainly for the purposes of tourism and representation. Progressively 'built up', the series results from an additive approach. The scattered incompleteness of Arctic spacing produces the dynamic and the separate 'settlements' that house the various functions of the Centre. Alluding to but departing from the naive style of the painter Andreas Alariesto, and to flatness and slowness, migrancy and unrest, ARRAK's methodology arises from and responds to the materiality, privacy and grouping of the traditional arctic settlement. Alertness to architecture here is, in filmic terms, 'in the cut', juxtapositional; between landscape and nature, between material and the built form made from it.

(In)significant function, alongside timber detailing and careful tectonics, renders the building a styleless feel which is difficult to date. Clearly the buildings are not old, yet they do not conform to associations that are recognisably *modernist* or identifiably *regionalist*. Initially, the materials of a finished building can possess a robust almost undeveloped look. The uninflected remains uninflected, discontinuous. Over time, the building alters. Using a dispersed but not disconnected spatial structure, we get something akin to those song-lines explored by Bruce Chatwin. We might speak of trace-lines; site and space lines guided by low sun angles, the deep, soft contours of the surrounding environment, mythology, the orientation of dwelling and shelter,

material availability and 'buildability'. Such remoteness also necessitates an ecological sensibility. Uninflected individual lines and sites are traces and only actualised by locating the architecture where it is within the forest. It can appear random only to assume significance long after the architects have departed. Timber details can suggest forest mythology, small narratives known only to the few, or then freely associate with more general Arctic morphology. Roofs cascade to take away the heavy falls of snow, wood details are robust, stout and solid. Alertness in the uninflected, eventually an extended form, is created over time as the stubbornness of the architecture comes to rest and a settlement takes shape.

In different environments, and for a variety of functions, this apparent slowness, this apparent desire not to accelerate architectural grasp and symbolic meaning, is what gives ARRAK's work its operational significance and guiding principles. Though we can often return to the Arctic Centre for the *modus operandi* of this procedural approach to architecture, we should not confine ARRAK's work to such formal principles. The success of the Arctic Centre in fact hijacked their own practice. Visitors, so often encouraged to seek the visual in Finnish Architecture, were indirectly responsible for the practice's promotion as the ecological timber-and-organic outfit, with the expectation of similar buildings. Modesty and the lack of serious critical writing rebounded on ARRAK. The steering principles of its uninflected work were lost. Like many victims of the unfortunate cultural industry in Finland during the 1980s, ARRAK could not obtain larger commissions. By the end of the 80s, during the recession, the practice was forced to apply its innovative skills – not insignificantly – to renovations and extensions, the most significant of which has been the Klondyke Development in Kerava (1988-91).

In the cut

Get into the scene late, get out of the scene early, tell the story in the cut. David Mamet

If architecture can depend on the cut and 'in the cut', the uninflected depends on where the architects wish to take their operational significance for each project. The risks are obvious. This can lead to an apparent unevenness and is nowhere more evident than in the material eclecticism and the wilder tectonic logic of two interior projects by ARRAK for Gramex (1987 and 1994). Procedural necessity and a grounded symbolic package might be too grand to define the Gramex projects of ARRAK, yet

ABOVE AND BELOW RIGHT: Customs and Border Station, Vaalimaa – the Finnish side; BELOW LEFT: Gramex 2

the demands for the Music Recording Copyright Offices were more predisposed to a loose, Hawaii-rock Bahama effect than Arctic survival.

The site lines are gossip and hipness. Materials for the first office in 1987, in the form of an innovative rough aesthetic (a rare use of the 'disposable' in such a tightly controlled architectural culture), give way, by 1994, to the cool business interior of the second office; just as business itself took over the music world and mobile phones were no longer considered pretentious but essential devices. To talk of humanising gossip in these palm-beach interiors is a touch rich, but then the rock musicians who visit are.

However, a visual unevenness can also be carefully balanced by the continued desire to explore and convey insignificance in architecture and by the building of sharply regional, uninflected detailing. The uninflected in one part of a project can be complemented and invite totality by inflection with another. This defeats somewhat usual ways of assessing architectural practices. Uninflection can also work intra-culturally where a State brief demands more visually signalled work. Coincidences abound.

For the Customs and Border Station in Vaalimaa (1996), the State clients demanded an instantly classifiable building; one that was instantly aligned to a recognised Finnish modernism. Insignificance takes on ironic echoes. This necessitated a utilitarian if not disposable innovation to meet stringent budget requirements. As the first building to be seen when entering Finland from Russia, the building had to communicate a distinct, national quality. It does so by conforming to the profession's expected and familiar image of modernism. Kiiskilä, as the architect in charge, turned the utilitarian on its side. Discontinuous materials gain their sensuality from detail and siting. White laminated boarding is among the variety of building techniques that suggest innovation from wood technology used in steel. The ambiguity and robustness of timber is transformed by the use of steel, yet the principles remain the same. This is a heterogeneous building, dissolving timber and steel detailing.

One might have imagined the necessary State image of Finland to be associated with wood. On first glimpse however, the formal pragmatic had to purvey 'Finlandia', architecture as a promotable 'semiotic'. The irony here is an accident of culture and promotion. The cool aesthetic suggested by the lightness of steel obviously 'inflects' on the border. To Finns, it is a reminder of an order they might not discover when they leave. To Russians, it is the reminder of an order they rarely experience anyway. Juxtaposing architectural scenes that are discontinuous produces the third idea, that third effect. Cool steel is not merely cool steel; nor is cool or clumsy timber!

Uninflection and cultural unevenness

ARRAK's architecture does not conform with desired images or a predisposed semiotic, nor can it quite be defined as a carrier of national excellence and identity (in the same way as the recognisable work of Juha Leiviskä or the Heikkinen and Komonen practice). Although their architecture clearly does possess a national excellence, something else, something more obtuse, is at work in their commitment. Another enquiry is necessary to chart how critical attention often fails in response to the uninflected.

We know that culture itself can be deflected by its own visual unevenness. ARRAK is not alone as a committed architectural practice that has gone 'against the grain' of the visually expressive. But this should not allow us to be deflected by its use of timber or the 'natural innocence' this recalls. Here there is no literal attempt to apply the metaphors of nature and culture to a free-form rational dialogue. This approach does not evolve from a committed radical stance or a polemical position but a series of careful principles, inevitably styleless because it is close to realism. A consistent, informable but careful consideration of building technology, function and environment can produce a subtle and sometimes memorable morphological density. Uninflected plasticity and sensuality are harder to achieve.

Not all procedures will result in an Arctic Centre, buildings not subject to time, and any resultant sensuality is less contrived as a theoretical dimension. Yet we need not characterise ARRAK's work as essentially intuitive nor as architectural sensation avoided at the expense of structural and louder semiotic concerns. Theirs is a craft applied to the scale of architecture and building, a dimension achieved in their material poetics that – culturally informed – produces an alertness to architecture. As we stated at the outset, this alertness can lose out to more fashionable theories of phenomenological trace and the archetypal response some architects use to 'talk up' the relative and relevant sensuality of their work.

Alertness to architecture

The narrative of ARRAK's development of trace from the late 70s to the present is not really as neat and identifiable as I have described. It probably has even more stubbornness and possibly more subtlety on closer inspection. The obtuseness of such architecture however gains unjust critical ignorance. ARRAK was, for a period, unfairly marginalised by this uninflection, by this stubborn alertness to architecture; that is, until their stubbornness began to *look modern*. Yet the uninflected has no common morphological strain, nor does it refer necessarily to previous project semiotics. And it has a very real effect on the architectural culture, for uninflection in architecture can clearly dissolve the boundaries between the historic and the modern. It can upset the usual frames associated with regional and vernacular tendencies. Not subjected to accepted time frames it can also upset notions of the urban and pastoral, the suburban and the rural. Moreover, it clearly dissolves the myth of the signatorial; the death of the author-architect! In this way, we can speak of uninflection producing this alertness.

Although ARRAK's architecture may not possess familiar totalities and is uneven in a positive sense, it does suggest less objectified work where a stubbornness to the visual invites a spatial, functional and experiential drift. Over time this can be seen to complete their work. If there is a stubborn coincidence in conforming somewhat to the recognisable semiotic, a neo-modernist echo in Vaalimaa, there is also the pull of the more unpredictable, (in)significant architecture of the uninflected in the Arctic Centre. We are, by this, no nearer to knowing what the next ARRAK building will look like, which is a good thing. We do know, however, the principles of uninflection – a third effect – that will be applied, a stubborn thoroughness that can make us alert to a strangely styleless, even timeless architecture.

Roger Connah is a freelance writer and architectural historian currently living in Stockholm.

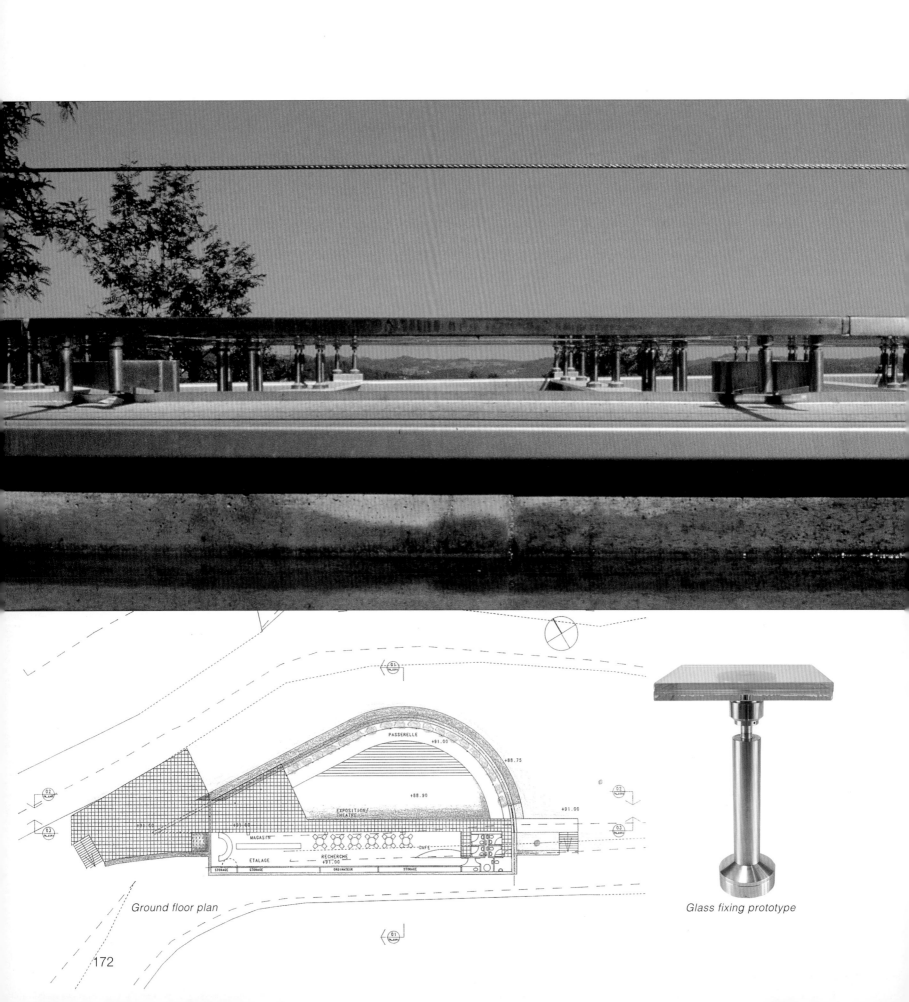

Ground floor plan

Glass fixing prototype

IAN RITCHIE ARCHITECTS

THE GREENHOUSE FRAGMENT

Terrasson Lavilledieu, Dordogne, France

In 1996 a five-hectare park known as Imaginary Continents was conceived by Paysage Land/Kathryn Gustafson and interpreted in collaboration with Ian Ritchie Architects. The design evolved from historical, landscape and social research of the different intellectual, cultural and spiritual landscape expressions found in selected sites throughout the world.

The Greenhouse Fragment comprises a reference library and research centre on plants, as well as a public space for exhibitions, seminars, film shows and other municipal events.

The structure is set into the hillside on a steep north-facing slope. With its glass-roof surface at ground level on the upper side, it appears as a lake – relating to features elsewhere in the landscape and reflecting the changing sky and foliage of the surrounding trees.

The glass roof consists of two layers of 8-millimetre toughened glass, bonded with a 3-millimetre polyvinylbutyral interlayer. The thickness of the interlayer

enables a flange to be accommodated on the head of point fixings, which penetrate the inner layer of glass only, leaving a sheer and unbroken reflective surface to the exterior. The fixing head is articulated on a spherical bearing, close to the plane of the glass. This allows the fixing to rotate with any relative deflections between glass and supporting steelwork, and minimises the transfer of any additional local bending stresses. The method evolves from the 'phantom fixing' developed by the practice in 1987 for the spherical-glass Pearl of the Gulf project in Dubai.

The low-gradient glass roof represents the entire roof to the building, together with a long *bassin d'eau* which forms a safety barrier to the public path at the upper ground level on the south side. The walls are constructed of large local stones held in steel mesh 'cages' (gabions), thus allowing the building to 'breathe' naturally.

The internal space is treated as a tempered external environment, with permanent ventilation around the

perimeter of the roof. During the winter, spring and autumn months, the sun will raise the internal temperature, shining on to the gabion stone wall to the north side, which functions as a thermal store. In the summer, provision is made for solar shading between the roof beams to control the temperature, supplemented by evaporative cooling, using the mass of the gabion stone wall to the north. Orange trees planted against the south-facing wall benefit from water which is sprayed on to the stone wall as part of the irrigation system.

In a landscape which otherwise emphasises the open, outward-looking prospect, the greenhouse is a calm, intro-spective space, illuminated by natural zenithal light.

Project team: landscape architect – Paysage-Land/Kathryn Gustafson; architects – Ian Ritchie Architects: Simon Conolly, Edmund Wan; engineers – Ove Arup and Partners: John Thornton; site engineers – ARC Ingénerie, Brive

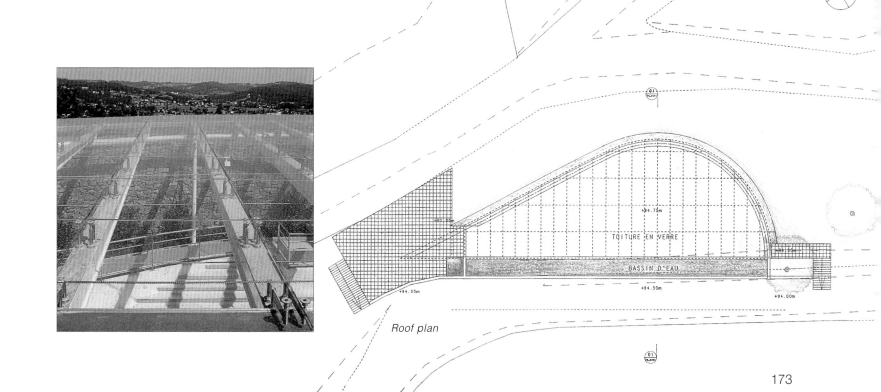

Roof plan

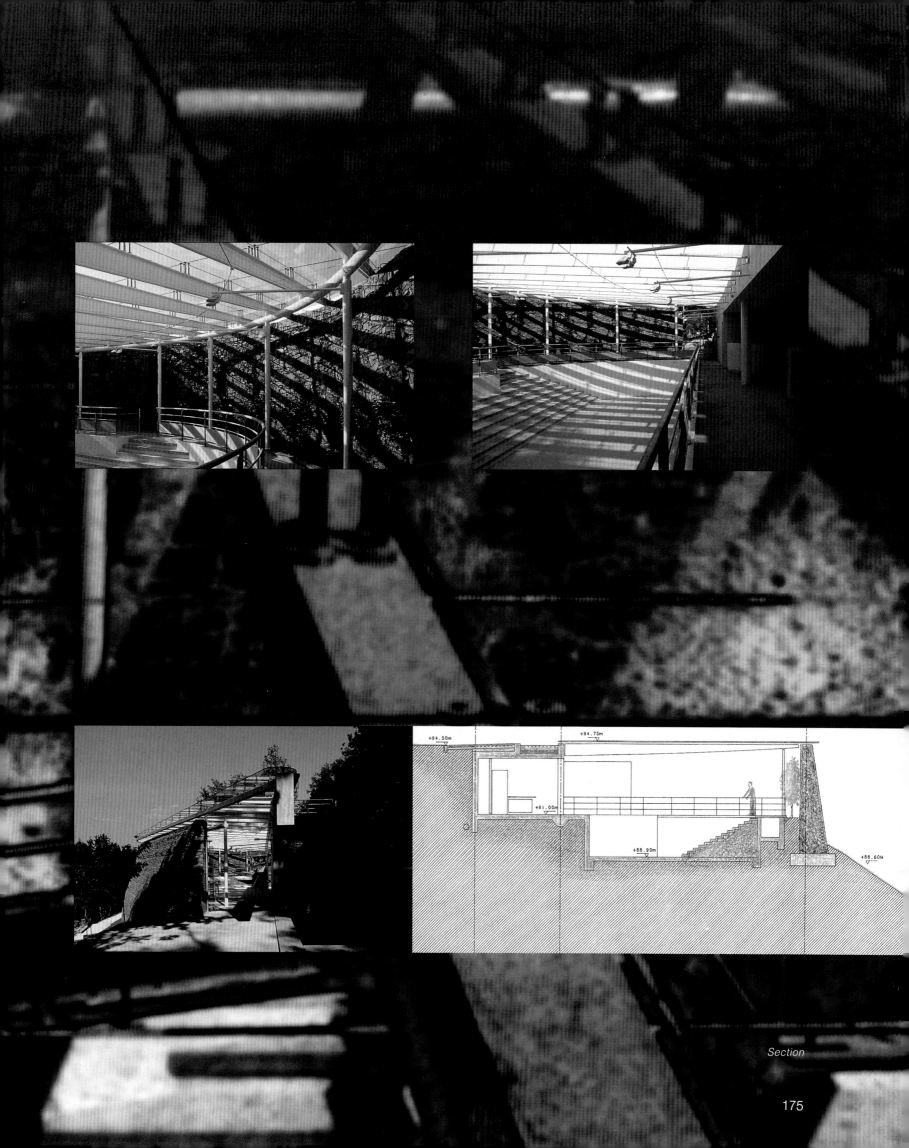

Section

FRANÇOIS ROCHE

VILLA MALRAUX ARTISTS' RESIDENCES AND STUDIOS
Maïdo Road, Reunion Island

Introduction

Sites and territories nurture identities, preconditions and affects that architecture and urbanism have continuously restrained and eradicated. The architectural object, having claimed authority for four centuries,[1] has the power of unparalleled destruction of modernity to maturity. But in so doing it signals its own limits and end.

The numerous 'aesthetic orthodoxies' born in the antechamber of reason and the wastedumps of ideology have now not only become unworkable but are also criminal in their discrepancy with society.

Judging each operation on the validity of hypotheses within an enormous assortment of ever-increasing facts and artefacts is not an easy task. Signs and referents are not pre-given, like a symbolic reference, but have to be discovered in real time, on the 'real site'.

If architecture did not know or could not substitute for the modern culture of breaking-in a culture of place (more attentive to what it was bulldozing), it is because it was already contaminated – a genetic error, in short . . . The horizons of the world of perception, of corporeality and of place have only too rarely been the mediums of production.

Territorialising architecture does not mean cloaking it in the rags of a new fashion or style.[2] Rather, in order that the place gains a social, cultural and aesthetic link,[3] it means inserting it back into what it might have been on the verge of destroying, and extracting the substance of the construction from the landscape (urban or otherwise), whether a physical, corporeal substance within it, or climates, materials, perceptions and affects.

This is not historical regression, nor modern projection, but an attitude that affirms itself by what it doesn't belong to, outlined against a razor's edge, in permanent equilibrium. It is a process that is renewed at each new place, allowing for an *in situ* attitude rather than just another aesthetic code. From that a radical displacement of our function can be born.

176

To identify that which characterises a place is already to interpret it and to put forward a way of operating on it. But linking a being to its ecosystem can only save linking the body to the body of architecture. This process of reactive mimesis is not a simulation of the 'exquisite corpse' game, a visual avatar, disappearing and camouflaging itself with an ecological alibi. Its ability to take hold of a territory without subjugating it depends on the unclear identity that develops within it, on the transformation it operates, on the gap of its implementation, on the ambiguity of the network of extraction/ transformation that the materials have come from: from a gabion of loose stones to maple foliage, rusted metal to uncut plywood, quarried stone to false wood PVC, apple espaliers to walls of lichen.

This antidote to the separate,[4] autonomous body, this 'live' production process could not operate were it not nourished by these active materials: 'there are the images of materials . . . sight names them and the hand knows them'.[5] In order that these 'barren' propositions do not add, subtract but rather extract, and in order that the object of architecture can spur on the real, like a contorted alterity of the territory in abeyance, we should, perhaps, shift the origins of architectural referents into a precondition that states, 'there is'.

Villa Malraux Artists' Residences, Maïdo Road, Reunion Island

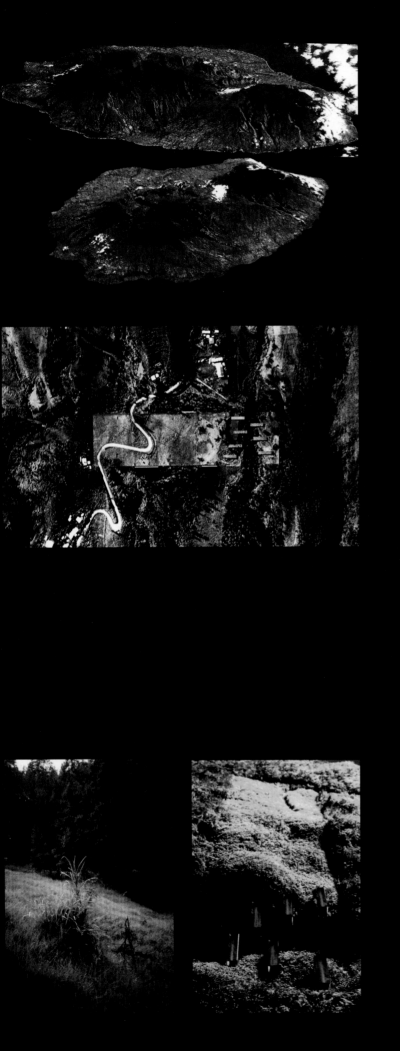

The Maïdo road, from the sea to the peak of the 2,200-metre high Mafate mountain passes an extraordinary sequence of terraces of tropical vegetation: from open dry grassland at 100 metres, sugar cane fields at 300 metres, bamboo ravines at 500 metres, forests of Eucalyptus, cryptomeria plantations, fallow fields of acacia mimosas at 1,000 metres, geraniums and reeds at 1,200 metres, tamarind woods at 1,500 metres, and broom at its peak.

The road offers a perspective of the land, yet at the same time is the agent of its destruction. Halfway up Mafate, at 1,200 metres, lies a clearing. The building is this empty space intensified: an enclosure open to the sky, bordered by cryptomerias, acacia mimosas, the edge of the clearing and a ravine.

The exhibition spaces and public places are developed randomly around the trees, with the clearing's edge bordering them at one side. A large, reflecting clear-plastic wall indicates the building. The cryptomeria trunks perforate the construction, so as not to interrupt the clearing's vegetation. The artists' residences and studios are constructed on stilts, embedded into the trees, their facades of plastic shutters reflecting the tops of the acacias.

The Ti-Jean Garden (landscaped by Gilles Clément) is located at an altitude of 1,500 metres. The entrance is accompanied by micro-facilities on a ravine (eg, cash dispenser services). The design is an extension of the layout of the Villa Malraux.

MUSEUM AND MEMORIAL
Soweto, South Africa

Soweto Road is more than simply an axis
running through the township. It was the
scene of the children's march of 1976,
and the scene of the tragic death of one
of the children, Hector Peterson, who is
buried here on the site of the memorial.

To avoid fossilising history on the site
and maintain a live quality, the ANC
archives have been reintegrated into the
building programme, rather than being
kept in Johannesburg University. This
allows for research to take place on site,
which seemed to be the first locational
necessity. Equally as important was to
offer the ground and underground area to
the mining population of Soweto, who
was previously only responsible for
mining gold.

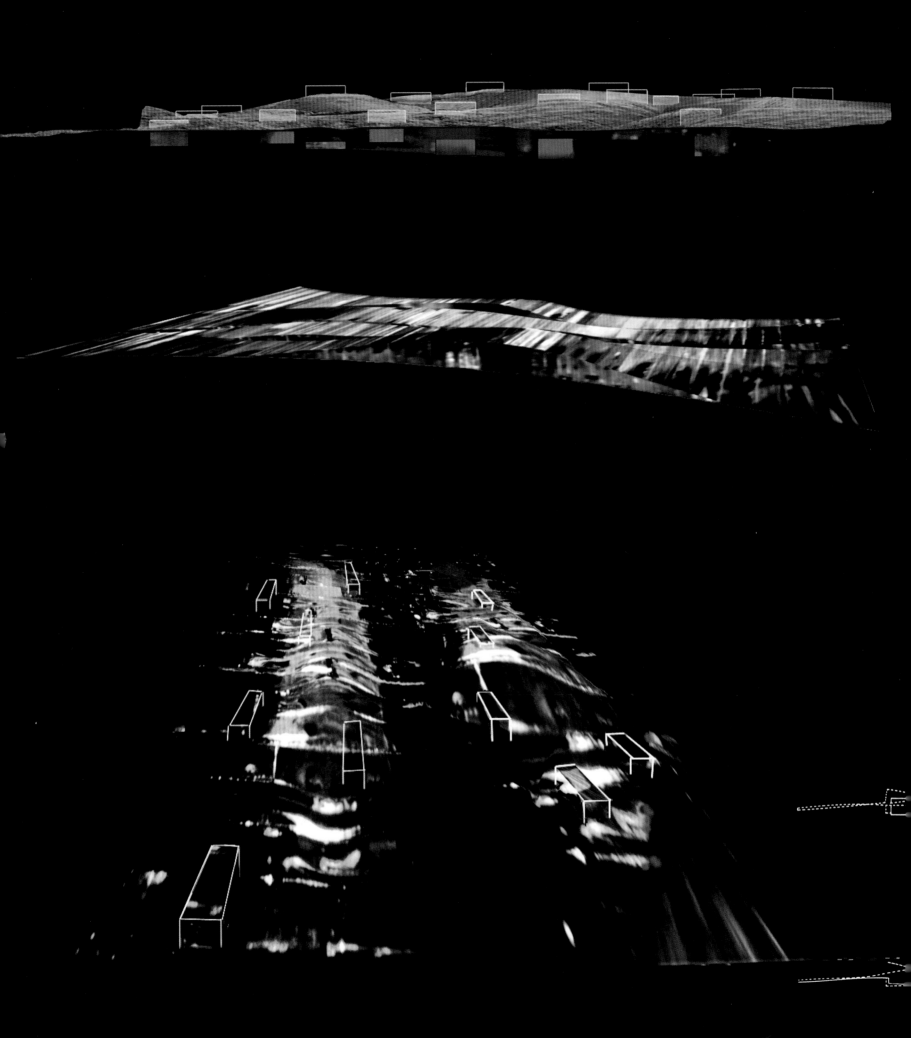

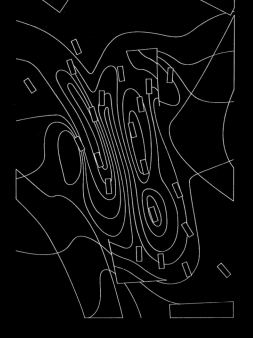

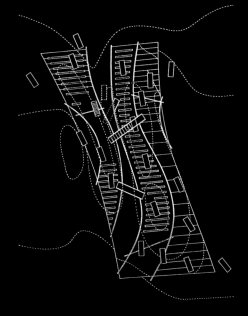

The surface of the project is made of savannah grasses, or 'bush', preserving the bareness of the site in the face of the tombstone, and taking advantage of the site's natural vegetation. Transparent glass volumes, the size of containers, emerge from this layer.

The interior layers of glass manipulate the folding ground to protect the archives and the exhibition and conference spaces on one level. In contrast to the orange-red surface, the depths of the buildings are perforated by 'tubes' of light and glass. The dysfunction between what is indicated (that this is simply a fragment of open grassland) and what is actually perceived (fleeting light), is inevitably ambiguous – itself a reflection of the complex, interwoven, hybrid relationship of the place; both north and south at the same time.

Notes

1 Brunelleschi's perspectival geometry is responsible for this, in the rationalisation of instruments of production and the domination of architecture on the site. The rule of visual representation is thus substituted for corporeal perceptions.
2 See the notion developed by Félix Guattari in his *Schizophrénie Analytique* on ecosophy, that architecture has 'imploded' and is condemned to being pulled and torn in every direction.
3 In a sense attributed to it by M Maffésoli, *Du Temps des tribus*, 1988, 'History can promote a moral doctrine (a politics), in regard to which space will favour an aesthetic and exude an ethics'.
4 See Augustin Berque's *La Théorie du paysage en France*.
5 Gaston Bachelard, *L'Eau et les rêves*, 1942.

Project team: Roche, DSV & Sie.P – François Roche, Gilles Desévèdavy, Stéphanie Lavaux, François Perrin

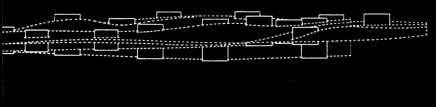

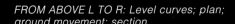

FROM ABOVE L TO R: Level curves; plan; ground movement; section

Ground floor plan

JANEK BIELSKI
HOUSING PROPOSAL
Palmdale, California

Being Between

The last remaining vast open spaces surrounding the Los Angeles area are in the desert terrains, where housing tracts and commercial strips, which characterise much of the area's current development, continue to spread. This proposal suggests a synthesis between natural and built conditions for residential blocks located between an existing commercial strip and tract housing.

Los Angeles' growth is limited on its north-eastern extremities by the natural boundary of the San Gabriel mountains. On the other side of the mountains is the threshold of the Mojave Desert. The perilous San Andreas (earthquake) fault lies at the seam between the desert and the mountains, closely paralleled by the California aqueduct which supplies water to the desert communities.

The city of Palmdale is located at the intersection of these features, which extend far beyond its city limits. The existing desert community represents a typical exurban city (a perimeter condition on the edge of a metropolitan area). Though sited in a precarious and elaborate natural context, the constructed interface between natural and built conditions exists largely in its engineered infrastructure and building preparations; for example, storm drains, flood control and the construction of building pads. Its streets and avenues are surveyed according to the 1785 National Land Ordinance, which established a uniform matrix transcending all landscape or climatic fluctuations. The severity and complexity of the desert is disguised within this mesh with imported buildings and landscape designs.

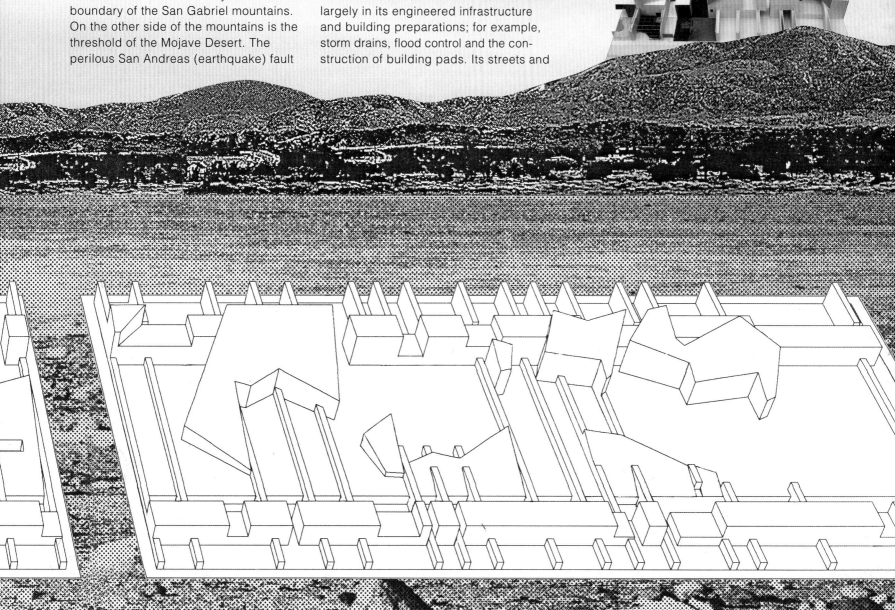

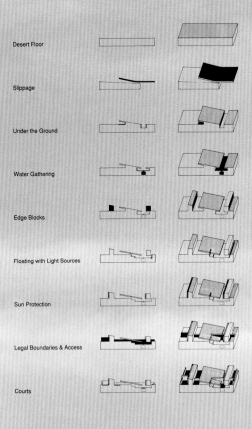

Desert Floor

Slippage

Under the Ground

Water Gathering

Edge Blocks

Floating with Light Sources

Sun Protection

Legal Boundaries & Access

Courts

The city was built almost entirely through private speculation with minimal planned oversight. The typological significance of its discrete parts becomes mute, being overshadowed by the generic planning regulations of density restrictions, lot lines, setbacks, and zoning ordinances. These 'limited' guidelines shape and sustain a low-density fabric with frequent accidental adjacencies among buildings, infrastructure and landscape.

The Palmdale housing project was conceived following observations of these conditions, with the intention of integrating their actual and potential utilitarian, perceptual and ecological qualities.

The separation of these issues characterises contemporary exurban development: engineered swales maintain water control; imported Mediterranean or New England images create the iconography of 'home', and ecological areas are largely confined to individual private or public lots. This is typical of most exurban developments in Southern California.

In the process of developing the project, these isolated circumstances were reconfigured and overlapped, blurring their separateness. The resultant hybrid landscape-building reveals, or masks, selected qualities of the context, creating unexpected linkages and associations.

The project is structured as a series of independent operations, each of which derives from or responds to a particular existing condition (built or unbuilt):

Land – Palmdale is located at the seam of the Mojave Desert and the foothills of the San Gabriel mountains. The metaphorical lifted plane simulates the geological shearing of the ground plane which originally gave rise to the mountains. By that means, the existing natural conditions inform a critical component of the project, automatically creating a series of conditions conducive to various interior and exterior spatial types.

Water – During rainfall, this flows naturally down the San Gabriel Mountains on to the desert floor. The aqueduct bisects this natural course, supplying water to the desert communities. The lifted plane collects rainwater and diverts it to subterranean courts, beneath which cisterns are located for collecting and recycling. In these sunken courts, a narrow water channel cools and animates the spaces, simulating the aqueduct in the foothills beyond.

Allotment – Lot lines allocate properties for freestanding houses and commercial buildings. The lot line has been rendered

as a three-dimensional physical presence. These 'thick wall-fences' bridge across the 300-feet-wide block, connecting rooms and open spaces, creating deep garden edges and providing overhead skylight zones as they penetrate interior spaces. Each view between these walls becomes a unique freeze-frame of the project and the context beyond.

House – The 'individual' tract house becomes lost in its repetitive pattern of siting. Two continuous bars, one on either side of the block, challenge the existing *faux* image of tract house individuality, while maintaining their height and set-back. They establish an edge to the street and maintain an individual or shared private realm.

By overlapping these four operations, a range of unit types emerges from various combinations between the lifted plane, subterranean spaces, walls and bar. Community activity spaces are located at strategic points with connections to the commercial strip. The existing commercial buildings and their signs are virtually masked by the lifted plane, which sustains grafted 'hyper-nature' images from the immediate desert or foreign landscapes. Subterranean units, water harvesting/recycling, and denser housing contribute to the ecological

issues of resource conservation.

Palmdale epitomises the widespread practices of current exurban development in a location which belies its apparent ordinariness. Formidable natural conditions are at work here, which are easily detected upon the most cursory of investigations. The current interaction between an insidiously benign built fabric and an elaborate natural condition is fertile ground for speculation on the potential workings between the pragmatic and the lyrical.

To ameliorate a condition which characterises the popular Californian disrepute for higher density, compensatory housing qualities are necessary. Maximising choice of unit size and type is perhaps the simplest persuasive tool. Subtler reasons reside in an economy of means, where disparate issues are folded over in the making of a building-landscape component.

A morphology gradually emerges that is simultaneously of the land, of the senses, of pragmatic requirements and of their aggregate experience. In this way, the project is conceived as a place between the built and unbuilt, as well as between stages of ex/urban development.

Assistance: Jeff Miller, Jennifer Ruth Siegal, Carolee Toon, Paul Lee, Mark Bielski

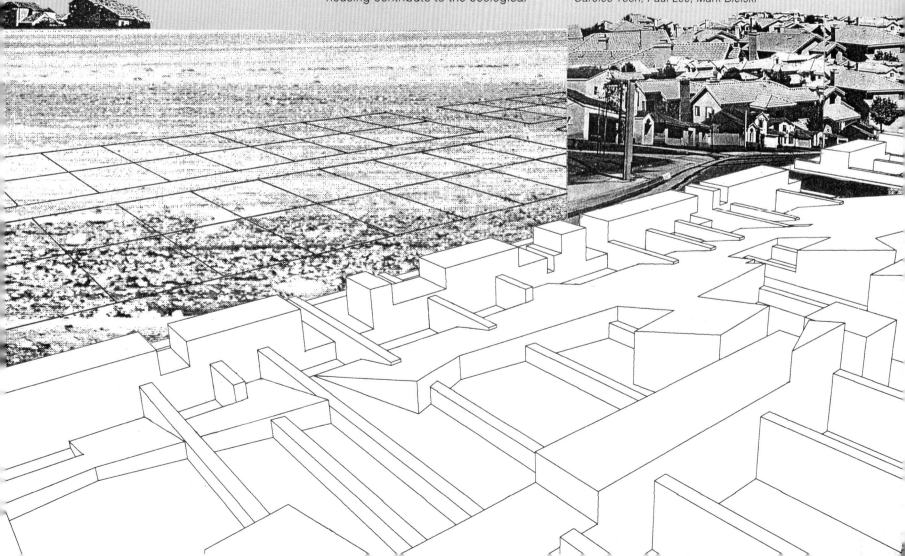

LIVADY ARCHITECTS

URBANITE LIGHT
Helsinki

The 'Good Night' lighting plan was an entry in an invited competition organised by the city of Helsinki. The brief was extended to include the entire public space with a lighting plan that was conceived as a sphere of information, knowledge and interpretation: individual light effects act as the interfaces, or actualisations, of this strata of ideas and complex reality.

A creative leap

Change in urban space is an open process that involves several actors. Actions implemented on the environment, whether planned or unplanned, generate unexpected series of events. Positive intervention in urban life requires a sense of orientation. It makes no sense to provide an open process with a plan which has a definite, final situation; implementation is a creative leap enriching urban life.

Helsinki light

Changing light conditions are an integral part of life in Helsinki, which breathes light. In the dead of winter there is less than eight hours of light, and artificial light is required even in daytime. In midsummer there is plenty of natural light around the clock; it is not dark even during the few hours between sunset and sunrise. The role of public lighting changes in accordance with the seasons. What is an essential prerequisite for everyday life in winter is a stage decoration in the festive summer season in the public city.

In order to accentuate the characteristics of the centre with light, the objective was to create a thorough, extensive analysis of the spaces of central Helsinki. The nature, atmosphere and meaning of these spaces have been charted through various means. The lighting idea for the space evolves from these features. In order to illustrate the various spatial ideas, some places have been provided with a lighting example – a proposition for an actualisation.

Light as a means

Light can be used for directing attention and creating emphases. Lighting is an act of selection: the city by night is a variation on the city by day. The lighting plan was devised as part of the night-time urban landscape and as part of the residents' experience of their city. As a consequence, analysis and design have a special relationship: the existing lighting can be read as a mirror of the residents' relationship with the city. On the other hand, light can be used for catalysing urban interaction.

Instead of norm-dictated general lighting, a light scheme was created that would: react to places, spaces, and situations – pedestrian and traffic areas, business, romance and monumental spaces; emphasise the characteristic features of the urban landscape and reveal the form of the material environment, perhaps in a way which interestingly differs from the daytime landscape; utilise light tones systematically for different lighting purposes; avoid glare and unnecessarily diffuse light; utilise the dynamic potential of light and dark – lighting and living in the dark are equal means of differentiation.

Sequences as pieces of the urban texture

A city can be interpreted as consisting of somewhat independent (alternative or mutually synchronised) systems. A single place in a city does not fulfil all the requirements of urbanism; it is comple-mented by the adjacent sets of blocks. The convergence of substructures – sequences of spaces, functions, atmospheres, memories – gives a city its special character.

Time has made sequences unique and autonomous: they are not mere physical sets of spaces ('space series' in architec-tural jargon); rather, they indicate the gradual transformation of the city and meanings attached to the buildings over the course of time. One sequence reveals a small seaside town run over by an administrative centre, another a whirlwind of surplus goods, time and energy.

ABOVE: Maps of the peninsula and the city centre of Helskinki

Project team: Mikko Bonsdorff, Marko Huttunen, Pekka Lehtinen, Panu Lehtovuori, Mikko Mälkki, Lauri Saarinen

186

Three urban sequences – the meanings of urban space

The three main streets of the centre of Helsinki (Aleksanterinkatu Street, the Esplanade, and Mannerheimintie Road) seem to attract three sequences which form the central cityscape.

The market place/esplanade system is like Hellas, the archaic Golden Age: lucid and spacious, a democratic arena of individuals. It trusts people, rather than confines them in a blocked order. Aleksanterinkatu street, a direct descendant of the aforementioned, is reminiscent of Imperial Rome: it is a rapidly degenerating stage of conflicting interests and utilisation. Each square inch is strictly controlled, yet is rich in form despite the orderliness.

The Mannerheimintie sequence freely and inconsistently draws from both these sources, in addition to everything else the surroundings provide. It can be compared with pluralist euroculture.

The sequences develop according to their own logic, but not without interaction. The spacious promenade environment of the esplanade and the unrelenting business bazaar of Aleksanterinkatu communicate through numerous small streets and alleys.

Moving from one sequence to another is always surprising. Mannerheimintie is like a jungle of people, cars and meanings, into which everything flows and again moves forward. Around the Stockmann department store and the city business block, the themes and energy of the three sequences unite; what emerges is the liveliest, most urban circle of Helsinki.

Dostoyevskian Helsinki

The commercial centre of Helsinki has moved to the west during the last century. Kluuvinlahti Bay, which used to demarcate the border of the town, was filled in the 1840s and replaced by a new commercial centre. Unioninkatu Street, which once was the main street, became more like a museum, a borderline separating the centre of historical monuments and the commercial centre.

FROM ABOVE: A 110KV cable being installed in Senate Square, 1963; the Esplanade; 'starry-eyed excitement' – lighting design for the Glass Palace

Aleksanterinkatu

Perpendicular to Unioninkatu Street, Aleksanterinkatu Street cuts into the sediment of this development. The eastern end of the street has fallen into a 100-year sleep, which is more Dostoyevskian than fairy-tale in nature; the western end houses Western commercial powers. One experiences a gradual transition from one world to another when walking along Aleksanterinkatu.

The spaces of Dostoyevskian Helsinki, the symbolic centre of the city (Senate Square and Ritaripuisto Park), are clear and uniform. The stone landscape maintains the authority of the social institutions. Institutional ownership also enables uniform lighting solutions.

The western end of the street has an abyss-like character – a verticality. The street wall is a permanent display window. It is built-in completely, but the continuing change of the stage-settings of market economy makes the details – company names, the forest of neon lights and streamers, the windows and the street surface – burst forth in such a way that any change goes unnoticed. The walls abound in messages, but the street between them is a spartan, gloomy, empty space, lacking even cars.

The idea of lighting

The light scheme has taken into consideration the development of Aleksanterinkatu at its various stages. Plentiful lighting that accentuates detail works best with business signs.

The lighting fixtures will be installed on the facade. Possible objects of lighting include window recesses, pilasters, balconies, sculptures and decorations. Only part of the surface should be lighted, and in order to decrease the amount of diffused light the street lamps should be lowered, which would make the pedestrian space more dense.

Towards the east, the lighting decreases. It is lower and employs simpler means. No facade lights will be installed to the east of Senate Square because the diffused light of the occasional street lamp is sufficient for the quiet neighbourhood at night.

The interior and exterior of the city: the relationship between facade and space

Although Helsinki has no city wall, the borderlines of the solid urban structure are very clear in some places. At certain spots one can also perceive the gate-like corridors guiding the visitor inside; through these, the exterior of the city penetrates the interior with its tentacles.

SOUTH

STOCKMANN

Mannerheimintie Road

Mannerheimintie Road is one such corridor. Both its facades are fronts, edges of the city. In this light, Mannerheimintie itself is exterior although it is located in the heart of the city. The neigbourhoods have grouped themselves in a row behind the facades of the road. The facades are like display windows of the cities behind them – a promise of what lies ahead.

Around Mannerheimintie, the structure consists of forms of electronic communication and motorised traffic. A modern geography of visibility functions. Its space is advertising space in earnest; the facades are directed out of the city, into the universal, nocturnal blackness.

Mannerheimintie is like a huge mouth, presenting the urban system to the visitor entering the city from the north: car traffic, tram traffic, sidewalks, department stores with their display windows. Towards the south, Mannerheimintie disappears into the cool, stony lap of the metropolis. In the north there is nature: Töölönlahti Bay, Central Park, and the mythical connection to Lapland through snow-white Finland.

The idea of lighting

The buildings which border Mannerheimintie seem to be isolated, grouped like islands in an archipelago. Thus it makes no sense to provide a lighting scheme that is aimed at uniformity. Instead, the objective is diversity – different facades represent the alternative cities behind them.

Both sides of the street are like shores. The wide sidewalks will be transformed into independent macro-elements of the streetscape. Paved with light colours and amply lighted, they view each other across the troubled waters. The roadway lights will be made more dense, thus decreasing their dominating position.

The Glass Palace

The Glass Palace is in its original 1930s state; its neon lights are like a manifesto of contemporary Mannerheimintie. The 100-metre neon lines and bright display windows, decorated with luxury products, used to declare a new century of motoring, electronic communication, international trade and progress to the people of the old, agrarian Finland. Despite the passing of time, the starry-eyed excitement of the Glass Palace is still appealing.

ABOVE: Aleksanterinkatu Street, a gradual transition from one world to another; OPPOSITE: Aleksanterinkatu Street, the complex and quiet ends; RIGHT: Mannerheimintie Road, winter view and advertisements – the geography of visibility; BELOW: Mannerheimintie Road, penetrated by the tentacles of the city exterior

THE GLASS PALACE

NORTH

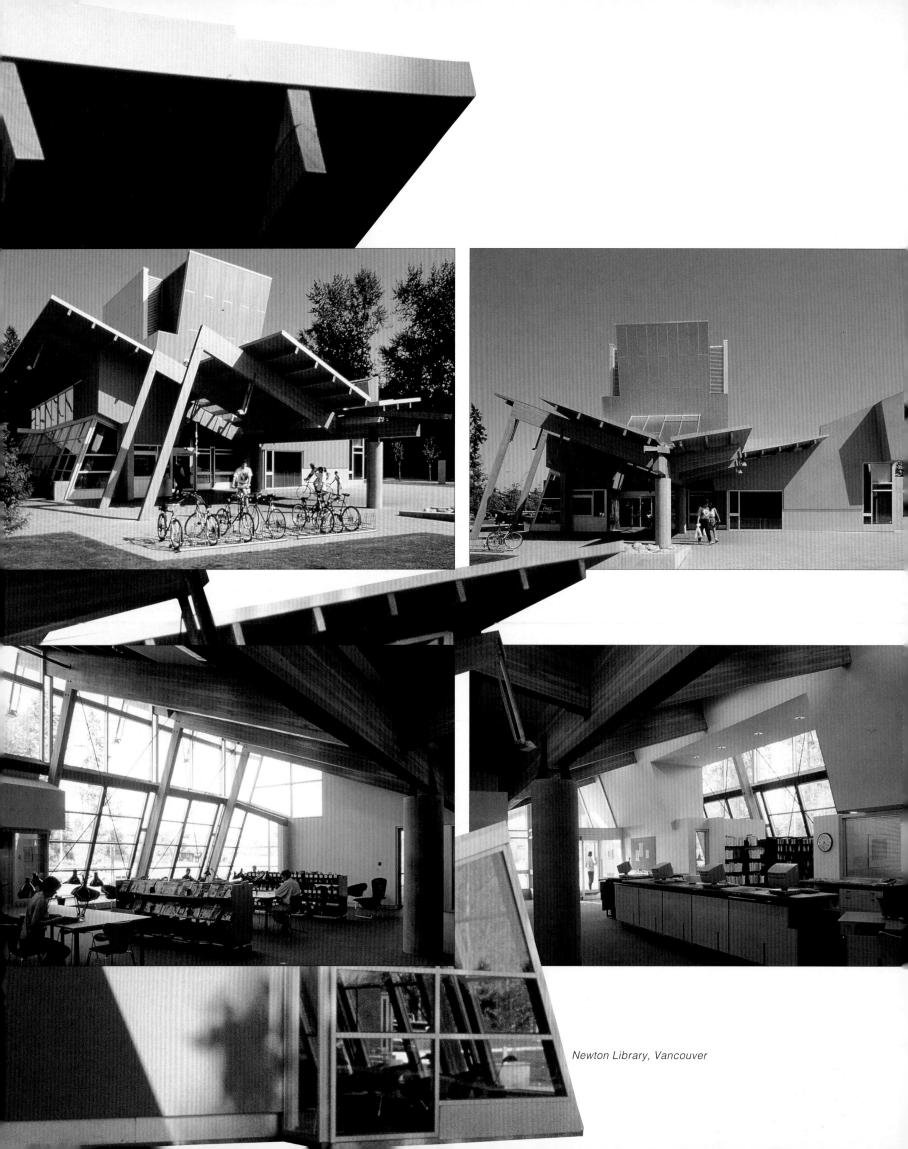

Newton Library, Vancouver

PATKAU ARCHITECTS
JIM TAGGART

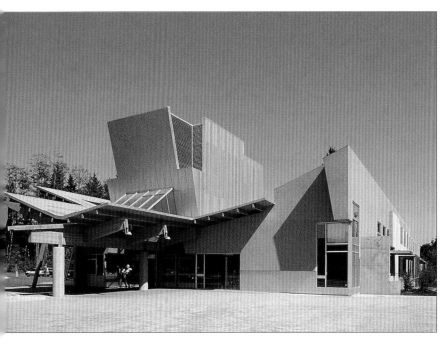

A chronology of the work of Patkau Architects is characterised by an increasing complexity and richness. Explorations begun in past work are carried forward and intertwined with new investigations in a process John Patkau refers to as 'reflective practice'. Consistent throughout the work is the dialectic between the general and the particular; between the aspects of a culture or place which are shared with others, and those which are unique. In urban and suburban settings this dialectic has been made manifest in a series of highly particularised buildings in opposition to the banality and uniformity of their surroundings.

While many subtexts remain in Patkaus' work, one line of investigation has become more clearly legible in recent projects. In the late 20th century, man's dominance over his environment – symbolically represented in the formal abstraction of the Modern and Classical traditions – is increasingly being challenged as both inappropriate and irrelevant.

Emerging in Patkaus' work is an overtly expressed interest in the vernacular tradition, in which the choice of form, materials, envelope design and orientation are influenced primarily by environmental and micro-climatic considerations.

The first project in which these pragmatic concerns were clearly manifested was the Newton Library (1992), located in suburban Vancouver. To give this modest, single-storey building a presence befitting its public purpose, the north and south walls are exaggerated in height. The north wall is a striking, sloped curtain of glass; the south wall, facing the sun, is more solid with punched openings. The roof planes descend from these edges to a valley, which serves to make the entrance, at the west end, more intimate in scale. It also defines the central circulation spine, around which the library and its service spaces are arranged. Large projecting scuppers drain water from the roof to rock ponds at the east and west ends of the building.

The tectonic expression of the building draws upon and develops themes from previous work. The structure is heavy timber and concrete, symbolic of the naturally occurring sticks and stones of the site, and is exposed around the building in the form of plinths and canopies. These materials are also exposed, where possible, within the library. However, their low reflectance means that where light must penetrate deep into the space, the structure is clad with plasterboard or stucco. The juxtaposition of the clad and unclad, the fine delineation of function, creates a dialectic which enlivens and enriches the building.

The Strawberry Vale Elementary School in Victoria, British Columbia, completed in 1996, is Patkau Architects' latest built work. It occupies an elongated, undulating and partially wooded site, within an outwardly conservative, and homogeneous residential community.

The organisation of the school is similar to that of the earlier Seabird Island School, with a central spine flanked on one side by a classroom, and on the other by administrative, resource and other special areas. Strawberry Vale is more informal in plan, and

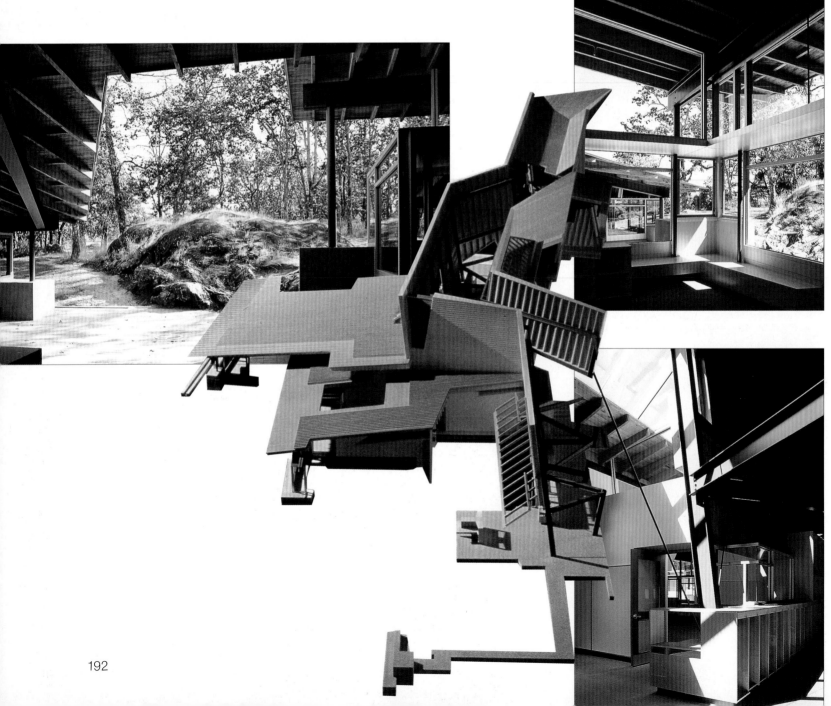

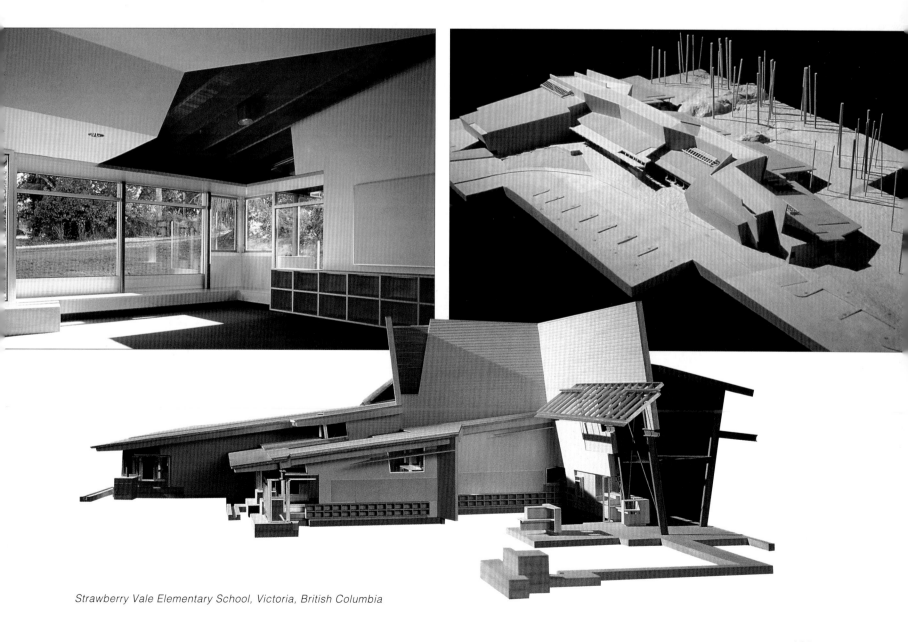

Strawberry Vale Elementary School, Victoria, British Columbia

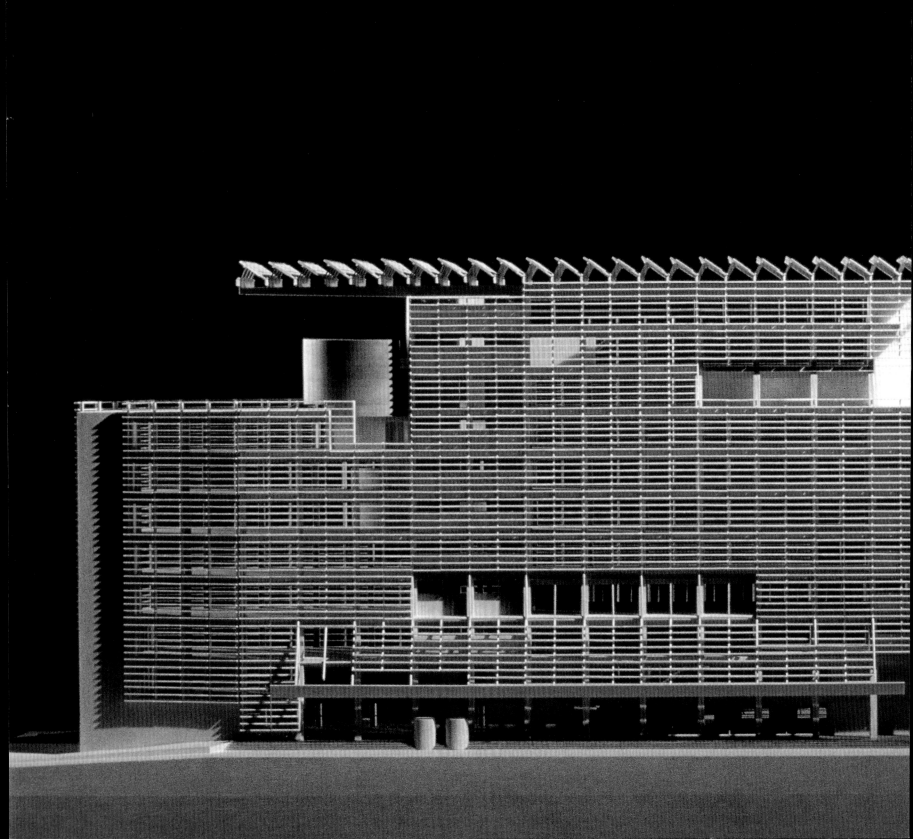

its geometry more finely articulated. The meandering spine is a figurative extension of the forest paths outside, an image reinforced by the double-height volume of the space, its outwardly flaring structure, and the clerestory windows which connect it to the sky.

Strawberry Vale School is, in many respects, a reinterpretation of the vernacular tradition. Whereas the existing community around the school imposes a Cartesian order on the natural world, creating a place which is 'other'; the school illuminates new possibilities by distilling the essence of place, and the particularity of circumstance – its materials, topography, climate, programme and culture – and encapsulates them.

The School of Nursing at the University of Texas, Houston is currently being designed. Unlike earlier projects, which had clearly defined and finite programmes, this has a 100-year life expectancy, with much of its long term programme indeterminate. Moreover, the building is many times larger than any of Patkaus' previous projects.

Earlier projects engaged in a dialogue between their own particularity, and the generality of their surroundings. In contrast, the Nursing School, which contains both particular, permanent programme elements and generalised flexible spaces, introduces that dialogue within the building. On each of the 12 floors the permanent programme areas, including such functions as library and cafeteria, form a cluster, allowing maximum long-term flexibility in the organisation of the remaining space.

These permanent programme areas are grouped above and below one another into vertically-linked, and in some cases exterior, 'porches'. These create areas for interaction, which are essential in academic life, serving the same purpose as the quadrangles of historic universities. The porches are highly particularised and sculptural in expression.

The building mitigates the effects of the hot and humid Houston climate through a grid of operable exterior louvres on the east and west elevations, and photovoltaic 'parasols' on the roof. In addition to collecting energy, these shade a roof garden. A collection pond – another feature of the rooftop garden – moderates discharge to the storm-water system.

This new application of technology, as a mitigator of environmental influences rather than a barrier against them, has expressive possibilities which are clearly exploited in this building. Despite the sophistication of the technologies, such expression is firmly rooted in the vernacular tradition. Choice of materials and envelope design are the result of the same environmental and regional imperatives that have operated for centuries in vernacular architecture.

However, in the same way as all of Patkaus' projects, the School of Nursing goes beyond the scale of the region to express the particularities of programme and the specifics of site. It represents a further, significant step along a path initiated by the Newton Library and elaborated on at Strawberry Vale. The dialectic of differentiation, with its vernacular subtext, opens a new chapter in the work of Patkaus Architects. One which might be entitled 'Particular Pragmatism'.

Jim Taggart is a Vancouver architect.

LEFT: School of Nursing, University of Texas, Houston, second, third and tenth floor plans and model

JONES PARTNERS

HIGH SIERRAS CABINS
Hope Valley, California

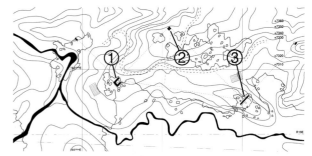

Site plan: 1 Meadow's Edge cabin; 2 Guest cabin; 3 Coyote Rock cabin

On 360 acres of high Sierra forest and meadow in Hope Valley, California, two Stanford professors will build cabins, outbuildings and assorted guest quarters for themselves, colleagues and students. The site is zoned for two dwellings and accessory structures.

The property includes portions of the largest high Sierra meadow remaining in private hands and is bordered on all sides by federal land that is not able to be developed, either designated National Wilderness or National Forest. The area is bisected by a low ridge running north and south, which divides the meadow on the west from a shallow wooded valley on the east. Across the meadow and beyond another ridge, US88 ascends to Luther Pass, where it can be seen only from the highest point.

Access to the site is from a spur road off US88, several miles to the north. This runs down 'behind' the eastern edge of the property on its way to Blue Lakes, a popular backpacking destination located 12 miles further south. Off this spur runs a barely recognisable dirt track, which only the hardiest four-wheel-drive vehicles

can negotiate. The site is thus splendidly isolated and in pristine condition, partly because it is surrounded by much more famous recreational areas that have attracted the backpacking legions away.

The two building sites are located primarily in relation to the meadow, which is the property's most dramatic feature, but they are not visible to each other. They reflect the professors' different attitudes about the wilderness.

The northern site is situated on the broad, gently sloping flank of the ridge, just inside the tree line. Although its primary orientation is toward the meadow to the south, which can be seen through a screen of pines, it enjoys a sense of security within its forest setting. A magnificent view of the surrounding hills would be afforded from a high enough vantage point on the building. In contrast, the southern site exploits a rock promontory that caps the ridge line, exposing the meadow on one side and forest on the other.

Upon visiting the property there is a strong sense that the first site is where something should be built, and the second is where something really wants

to be built. This sums up the difference in the professors' attitudes, and the reason why it is important that the two sites are not visible to each other.

The outbuildings include a well structure and a building to house the generator, located back in the woods, roughly between the two sites. Some preliminary work has been done: each site already has its own leach field and a well has been dug. Buried connections will link the well and generator to the sites. Single-room guest huts will be placed elsewhere on the property, three initially, to take advantage of other interesting features. They will be skid-mounted and fitted with self-contained water and waste systems in order that they can be moved around in response to seasonal or other demands. To preserve the property's isolation, no additional roads or parking facilities will be provided. It is expected that guests will park at the spur road and then hike the rest of the way. The professors will drive in if required by supply or maintenance needs.

The buildings are designed to respect the isolated situation and are intended to

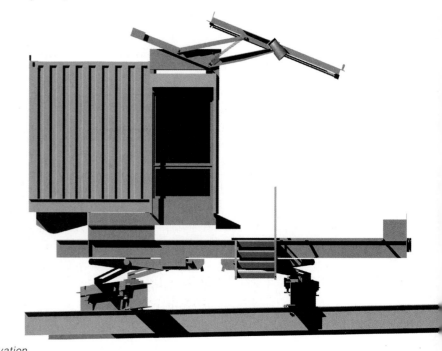

Guest cabin – posterior view; elevation

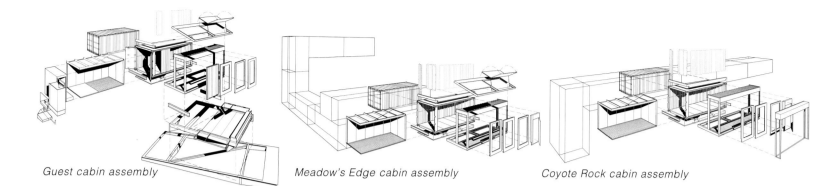

Guest cabin assembly *Meadow's Edge cabin assembly* *Coyote Rock cabin assembly*

embody the professors' attitudes in relation to the differences between the two sites. They will be constructed from 20-foot shipping containers, which in industry are used as a basis for temporary shelters all over the world, in addition to the shipping purposes for which they were originally designed.

The containers are extremely hardy, inexpensive, and eminently transportable, which recommends their use for this project. Due to the remoteness and difficult topography of the proposed building sites, they will be delivered to the property by truck and then air-lifted into place by Sky Crane helicopter.

The inexpensiveness of the containers allows the architects to propose extensive modifications, within a general modular approach. Their durability also provides for a measure of security, weather and fire resistance that is not common in vacation homes but is important because of the lack of a constant ownership presence. Moreover, the mobility of the containers allows the construction standards for the units to be raised considerably, since the entire assembly

can be shop fabricated. Much of the design effort has, in fact, been spent ensuring the road- and air-worthiness of the module units.

The specific designs for the two cabins evolve from the way in which the construction technology responds to the unique characteristics of each building site and the personality of the particular client. In each case, the essential linearity of the original container module has been maintained (departing from the typical industrial configuration in which the containers are arranged side by side in an attempt to overcome the perceived limitations of their narrowness).

On the northern site the containers are arranged like wagons into an outward facing circle that is not closed in either plan or section. This provides the more retiring client with a discreet sense of security, while acknowledging the different views and places that might be created on the forest's edge.

On the north side of this configuration two containers have been stacked vertically end-to-end, braced by an additional external structure, to create a

tower. A library runs alongside the stairs, with desks on the landings. Above the tower, spanning the site at the level of the thinning upper branches of the surrounding trees, is a study/observatory with extensive views and an operable roof that permits stargazing.

On the rock promontory, the more assertive client has dictated an alternative configuration. Here the containers have struck a bold, horizontal line across the rock plateau with commanding views out across the meadow and back into the woods. To the rear, a protected area has been captured between the cabins and the few wind-blasted trees which have managed to prosper up here. However, the face of the cabins is relentlessly exposed to the merciless sun, wind and views. A combination of a sunshade, windscreen, security closure and active solar device has been designed to mitigate these forces without compromising the confidence or openness of the figure.

Their provenance in transportation technology ensures that the container-cabins sit lightly on the land. They demonstrate no desire to burrow in to the

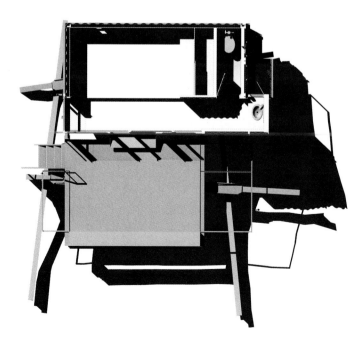

Guest cabin –plan; anterior view

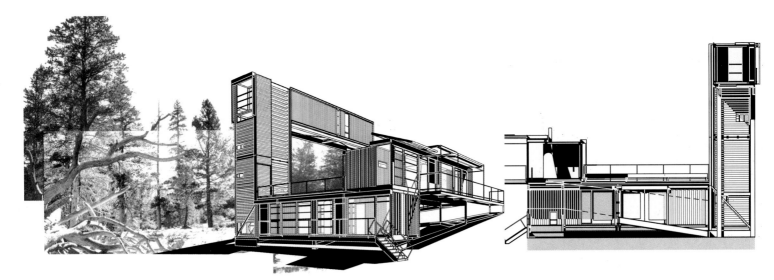

landscape or mimic 'natural' forms, nor do they adopt traditional, picturesque vernacular forms. The structures adapt to the existing conditions according to their own requirements, in the same way as the trees and rocks. Secure in their own internal motive force, the cabins make no absurd claims of ownership or dominion over these rocks and trees.

Since everyone, including the owners, is a visitor to the cabin, each of these communities starts out as an outpost. The metaphor of the home is not appropriate; beyond raising the question of whose home, or the assertion of an undesirable sense of dominion over the land (as property), the idea of domesticity seems out of place in the dramatic context of the site. Viewing the community as an outpost casts all the visitors as adventurers, explorers, or at least guests, in this territory; even the owners feel this each time they visit.

The seeds in this project are humble, they have no intention of organising anything beyond their immediate charge. Yet, the responsibility to constitute a civilisation at this outpost bestows upon these humble pieces an exaggerated importance. With limited means at their disposal, the corrugated steel, structural shapes, plywood, glass and paint can accept this attention only by reasserting the traditional vernacular's unconscious goal of suitability. Where efficiency dictates humility, there is no room for flourish or indulgence. There is no ownership here to be flaunted. This humble equipment serves all the visitors equally.

FROM ABOVE, L TO R: Meadow's Edge cabins – view from west; section looking north-west; view from north-east; plans

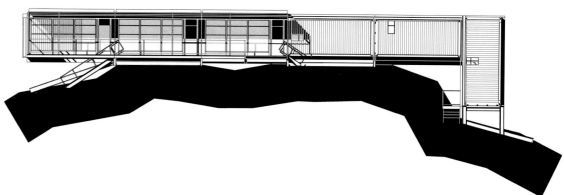

FROM ABOVE L TO R: Coyote Rock cabins –
view from west; south elevation;
view from south; plan

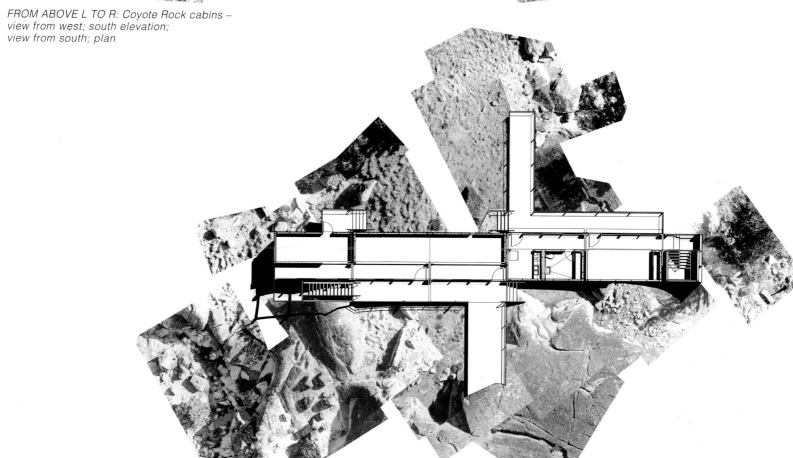

JONES PARTNERS

ZIMMER STAIR

University of Cincinnati, Ohio

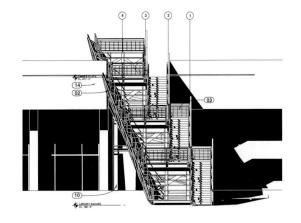

The creation of a new plaza in the midst of an eclectic collection of campus buildings from every period of the University's history provided the opportunity to create a space-defining sculptural object. This stair folly connects the two principal levels of the plaza, conferring a dynamic orientation and focal point to the otherwise amorphous, flowing spaces of the plaza.

Located opposite the engineering school, the stair provides an oversized celebration of structural steel; its wide-flange vent mainframe, trussed tubular subframe, and stick-built angle-and-channel-stringer assembly make legible the classic division of labour between servant and served elements in the design and relates them to the scale of service they provide. Efficiency is not a goal in this; expression is. The sheer visceral appeal of a WF33 can be touched – it's right there!

In order to emphasise the capabilities of such a handsome piece of steel, the nose of the structure cantilevers from the elbow of the bent – about 20 feet; its broad-sweeping snout hovers inches above the plaza without touching down. The structure also cantilevers at the opposite, upper end, where it bursts through the parapet guardrail of Zimmer Plaza, enunciating the presence of the stair to visitors approaching from above.

The northern edge of the stair is defined along its entire length by a solid plate guardrail. Along the southern, bleacher edge the guardrail is glass. This reinforces the structure's sense of orientation to the plaza and the sun, providing a solid edge to the space on the north side and an open condition to that on the south.

The stair's traditional role as a gathering place is acknowledged by the inclusion of bleachers along its entire length. These also add bulk to the structure, providing it with a scale that is more appropriate to the space it commands, and broaden the structure to correspond more with its length.

The stair was designed to be erected in three major assemblies, facilitating shop fabrication and transportation. Apart from the WF33 subframe, the entire 80-foot structure was fabricated in California and shipped to the site nested onto a single flatbed semi-trailer.

ABOVE: East elevation; BELOW, L TO R: View from north-west; detail looking up

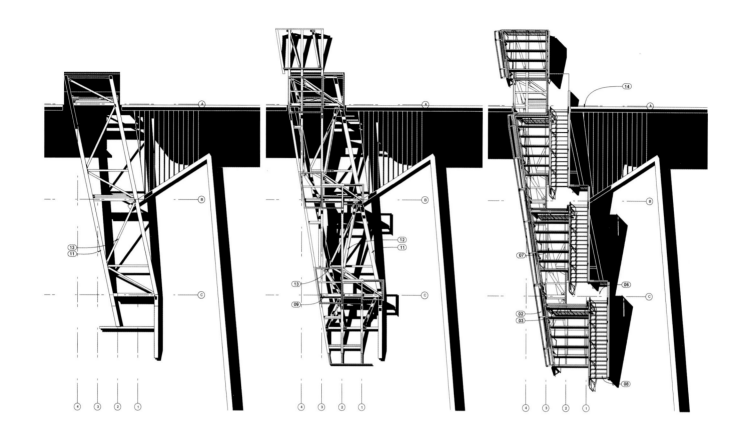

ABOVE: Plans; BELOW, L TO R: View from north-west; detail view from south-west

LAPEÑA–TORRES TUR

CASTLE WALKWAYS
Castelldefels, Barcelona

As the first stage of the development and landscaping of the hill surrounding the castle at Castelldefels, a pedestrian walkway was built to give access to the castle from the city centre. To overcome the difference in levels between the city and the castle, the ramps zig-zag up the hill with supporting walls for the levelled areas.

The walls are made of reinforced concrete and Corten steel formwork. They are held in place using inclined struts. The top ends of the steel formwork are extended to form handrails for the walkways.

The project was designed to provide a way of access from the city to the castle, making use of one type of material and method of construction. Its appearance – halfway between 'iron papiroflexia' and urban development – evolves from the uniform nature of the design, the way in which the wall is sectioned, and the fact that the walkways form a continuous unit more than a kilometre long.

Project team: José Antonio Martínez Lapeña, Elías Torres Tur, Miguel Usandizaga Calparsoro

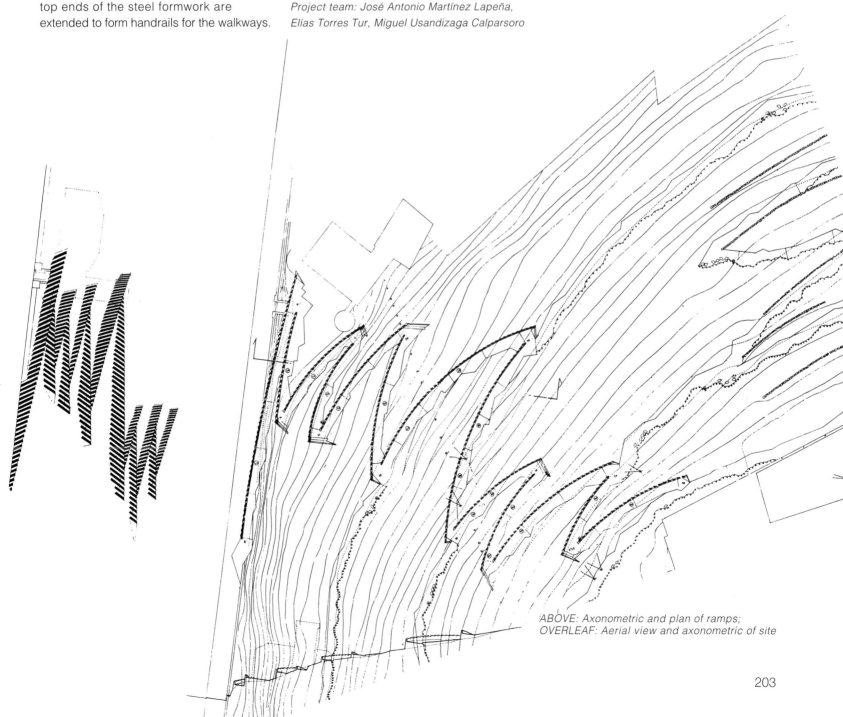

ABOVE: Axonometric and plan of ramps;
OVERLEAF: Aerial view and axonometric of site

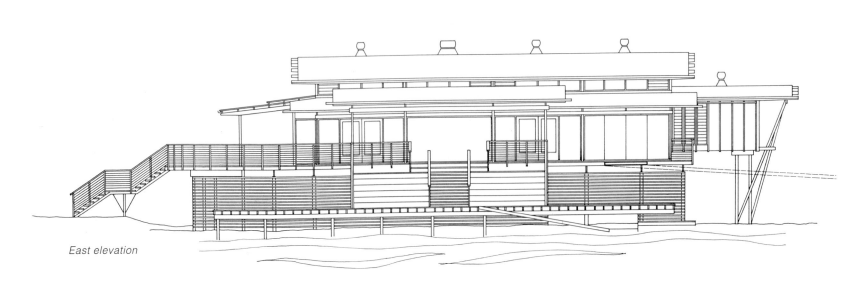

East elevation

CLARE DESIGN

SKI + SKURF CABLE SKI KIOSK
Bli Bli, Australia

Even a remarkably beautiful region such as the Sunshine Coast can be reduced to placelessness and kitsch at the hands of the tourist industry. Many members of the community sense the loss of authenticity that pervades not only tourist attractions but the shopping centres, public places, streets and housing within our region.

The Ski + Skurf tourist park caters for the young 'surfie' set of the Sunshine Coast. Waterskiing can be experienced without the need of a boat. The building serves the surf culture and is enriched rather than reduced by its acknowledgement of water, sun, breeze, youth and sport.

Only five kilometres from the ocean 'as the crow flies' and located close to a slow bend in the Maroochy River, the ski complex relates closely to its low-lying caneland environs. It is hoped that the tourist who visits this complex gains more than a ride on a ski. Instead of the typically superficial or partial experiences of theme parks, the visitor is met with a genuine building that expresses both new content and excitement without losing relation to its place.

The original building was razed by fire in August 1994. A new kiosk/pavilion needed to be fully designed, documented, approved by council and built within 16 weeks to be ready for the Christmas tourist season. The excitement and energy of such a tight programme is reflected in the end product.

The building has been described by others as a culture house – a casual, vibrant and very flexible series of spaces accommodated beneath gentle, undulating roof forms. Many of the groups who frequent the building arrive for breakfast, spend the day and also take advantage of the night skiing and a restaurant and bar that operates in the summer months.

The building is placed on a narrow spit of land between two lakes and was built upon the original timber piles that survived the fire. These ready foundations set the site and building position. Because the new building bears no resemblance to the original kiosk designed by others, some interesting spans and cantilevers can be discovered from below.

For flexibility of use and speed of construction, the building was designed as a simple portal-frame shed structure with surrounding ancillary amenities and verandah spaces. It was required that the administrative office be placed in such a position that would enable the entire complex to be overseen from both within and without. Such a position of surveillance allows the park to operate smoothly in peak tourist times and also to be operated by one person during the off-season period.

Timber posts were bolted on to existing piles, creating a platform over which the main structures were placed. Materials such as plywood, fibre cement, zincalume, custom orb and 'Suntuf' polycarbonate were chosen for their qualities of lightness, durability and cost effectiveness.

The combination of simple planning and structural expression, robust finishes, lightness, openness and colour creates an appropriate festive coastal mood for the visitors, users and employees.

Project team: Lindsay Clare, Kerry Clare, Jeff Lee, Scott Chaseling, Terry Braddock

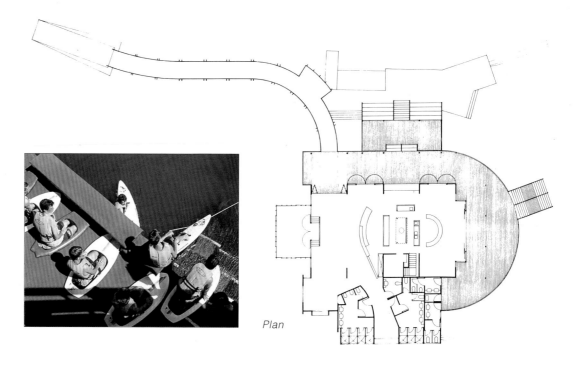

Plan

207

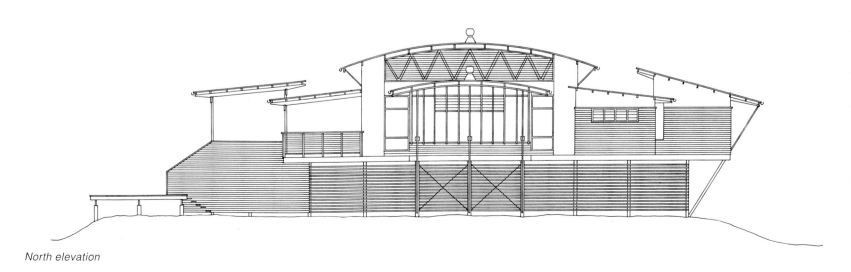

North elevation

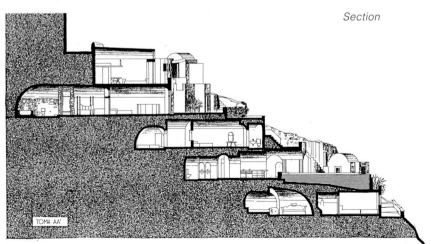

Section

ANTITHESIS ARCHITECTURE

CHROMATA

Apartments and Swimming Pool, Imerovigli, Santorini

This complex of 17 holiday apartments, with guest facilities and a swimming pool, was created amongst the existing, mostly subterranean houses of the village of Imerovigli, perched on the edge of 280-metre-high cliffs overlooking the volcanic landscape. Old cave dwellings and some remnants of existing buildings were restored and converted to apartments.

The form of the complex evolves from a rational approach to the guests' needs, in conjunction with maximum use of the existing context and the addition of new, external buildings. Distinguished by the use of colour, the new structures follow the organisation of the existing buildings.

The complex develops organically from the study and analysis of the local, traditional structures and the recomposition of their elements, while simultaneously reworking some fundamental modern principles.

The peculiarities of the environment, the needs of the guests, and modern technology were essential factors of the design. Especially important in achieving the end result was the participation of local, expert builders, thereby combining tradition with technology and modern materials.

The structure is spread over six levels that vary in height and overlap in many places. The second level accommodates the reception area, swimming pool, bar, dining and sitting areas, while the remaining levels are used for the apartments.

Entrance to the complex from the street is above level six, where a central staircase provides access to the four upper levels. This staircase then splinters to serve the pool/reception area and the apartments on the lower levels. Consideration was given to the movement of guests between the spaces to ensure the privacy of each apartment.

In the shaping and arrangement of spaces, solutions were found which respected the lighting, the view and the privacy of all the apartments in the complex, in addition to those of the neighbouring buildings. Bright colours

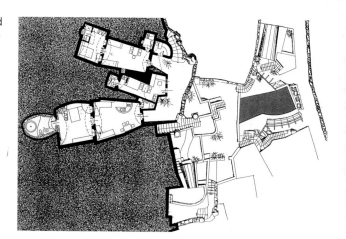

are used for the complex which correspond with the surroundings: earth, sea and sky are represented by ochre and brown, turquoise and azure, white and silver respectively. This gives the buildings a dynamic and harmonious presence in the characteristically harsh landscape.

The selected materials are also in keeping with those used previously for the site: the wooden doors and windows follow the same lines as those of the existing houses. The sections were reinforced wherever needed so that double-glazing could be fitted and openings enlarged where necessary.

External floors are made of rough cement render. Different textures were used to differentiate and clearly mark the edge of the pool. All visible timber is Swedish pine, employing a simple scaffold-like construction. Simple lines and light volumes maintain the coherent quality of the architecture.

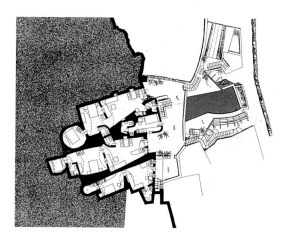

Of special interest is the roof of level six, which consists of two asymmetrical barrel vaults set perpendicular to each other and connected with a tent-like structure. This 'tent', which is lower than the vaults, permits an unobstructed view of the volcano. It highlights the vaults and at the same time provides a dynamic inner roof. Also of interest is the very simple iron bridge which provides access to the middle apartment on level six – preserving the privacy of the first apartment while allowing light to penetrate the lower one.

The pool penetrates the reception area while giving the impression of being suspended: the overflowing water blending visually with the sea below. Three columns support the vaulted ceiling and define the pool. A simple bench at the edge of the pool serves both as a barrier and seating. It is constructed of timber and pine planks and supported by custom-made stainless steel mounts.

The complex is striking in its use of strong shapes and colours yet integrates harmoniously with the surrounding environment.

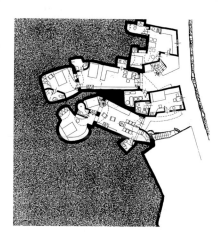

FROM ABOVE: Plans of levels 5, 3 and 1

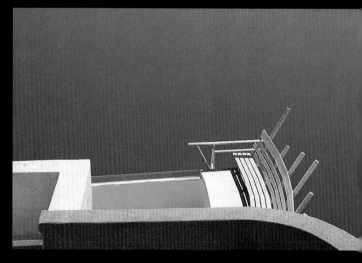

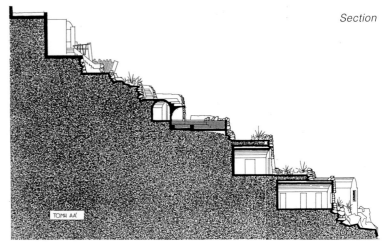

Section

ANTITHESIS ARCHITECTURE

BLACK STONE TERRACES

Apartments, Swimming Pools and Spa, Imerovigli, Santorini

These 14 holiday apartments are also located on the 280-metre-high cliffs of Imerovigli village. The complex is south-facing and benefits from a panoramic view of the island, from the east to the west.

No buildings existed on the site except for some subterranean structures on the upper level. The site was formed in terraces: the typical system used to organise arable land on the steep dry slopes of the Cycladic Islands. Characteristic of the site is the black volcanic stone that is abundant on the island. This is used for the construction of the terraces.

Their carefully studied reformation provided the opportunity to hide almost all the needs of the complex in underground structures. At selected points, however, the stone walls have been shifted to create more internal space, allowing overall breathability and movement. Here, the inner structures emerge as external buildings. The contrast between the black terraces and the dazzling white vaults which break through them emphasises this dynamic rift.

The complex has two pools with a spa. These are integrated organically with the surroundings without being hidden, so that they diffuse and disappear in the composition. The black stone surrounds the water and penetrates it, creating a variety of spaces and sitting areas. Thus, the water's limit is not perceptible. This feeling of continuity is enhanced by the elements that organise the spaces around the pool – through which one is able to move endlessly – and by the water itself, which overflows from one pool to the other. By successively passing through closed and open passages, going in and coming out of the water, and relaxing in covered and open areas, the visitor experiences a space which flows and dissolves the division between earth and water, between inside and outside, and between the location and the sea, 280 metres below.

On the upper level of the site, the building closest to the village was handled differently in order to mark the entrance to the whole complex. It is the epitome of the complex. Here, the antithesis develops – delicately balanced and with a clear spirit of play – which affects the overall composition: the contrast of the old with the new, the conventionally-restored azure building adjacent to the modern freely-structured one, the defiance of the inclined column beside the vertical walls.

All the materials used for the complex can be found here: the black stone, plastered walls and wood.

Free-form wooden structures are made use of throughout the complex as pergolas, parapets, benches, and for the pool bar. Although simple, these structures are dynamic and unobtrusive, but not neutral. They are the product of a free confrontation of functional problems: a basic concept which permeates the practice's architectural solutions.

With this in mind, one can appreciate why the buildings do not adopt the dry principles of clear-cut shapes on such a steep slope; also, that the forms of underground structures are prescribed by the needs of the occupants and the qualities of the earth, rather than mere geometry.

The application of this method of architectural intervention to this particular site thus enabled the architects to resolve all the functional problems and to hide most of the structures.

Project team: architects – K Nikolaidis, C Edwards; structural engineering – G Tsopanakis; construction supervision – K Nikolaidis, G Tsopanakis, C Edwards

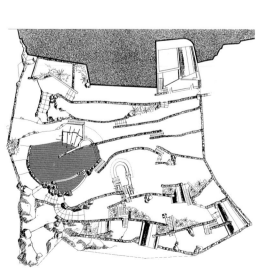
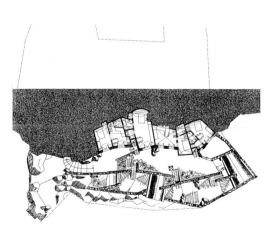
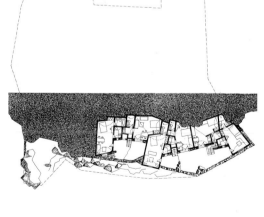

Site plan; plans of levels 2 and 1

THE CITY

THE BUILDING

THE CITY

THE BUILDING

URBAN SPACE:
FROM VISUAL / ENTROPIC REAL TO REAL-SPECIFIC

THE SYMBOLIC AS QUESTED / REVEALED:
FROM THE QUESTION OF THE BUILDING
TO THE QUESTION OF THE CITY

CITY BORDERS
THE BORDER MIDDLE   EXHIBITION   RECEPTION   ARRIVAL / ENTRANCE

NIKOS GEORGIADIS
'AT THE SAME PLACE': THE NEW ACROPOLIS MUSEUM, ATHENS

The ancient Greeks had a ritual that would take place at an altar situated at the top of the Acropolis. The Diipolia, as it was known, involved the ritual slaughter of an ox, as thanks to Zeus and in celebration of the harvest. The participants of the ritual would scatter seeds in the altar and release the sacrificial ox. The ox would approach the seeds, at which point a priest, known as the ox killer, would slaughter the animal with an axe and disappear from the scene. According to the rules of the ceremony, the participants had to turn away from the priest, so as not to witness the slaughter; after his departure, they would begin accusing one another for murdering the ox, and finally take the axe to trial and charge it guilty of the murder. Yet the atmosphere of the ritual was light-hearted and its outcome always the same: the axe would be sentenced to be carried by the participants outside the city walls and thrown into the sea.

One could perhaps recognise the prophetic significance of this ritual in respect of what would occur many centuries later, with the destruction, removal, and 'universalisation' of the Acropolis treasures – an effect of a broader Western attitude which paradoxically seeks an identity in that same ancient civilisation which it has, in many ways, appropriated yet turned its back on. But the ceremony is more useful for its non-metaphoric potential. For through it, the ancients showed that the only way catharsis could arise is through a purely spatial event, a justice advocated *spatially* progressing away from the place of the drama but continually referring to it. The ancient Athenians seemed to be able to operate within the very metaphor and activate its analytic potential, to offer a 'different', more performative solution – transferring the 'place' of sacrifice (of symbolic and visual integration) onto a spatial process heterogeneous to the symbolic dimension of the ritual. Their long journey through the city, far from being merely 'physical', seems to be expressive of location-making as witnessed in urban experience, as the city itself progresses regressively through gradual transformations of *visuality* into *spatiality*, realising its symbolic rituals at real locations.

The participants *turn a blind eye* to the spectacle. In contrast to Oedipus, they do not negate visuality, but introduce aspects of inattention – by turning away and not seeing – and customisation, by carrying around the axe – an object charged with a symbolic cause (*/chose*). Unconvinced by the visual register or its reversals, they seem to take the Zeuxis/Parrhasios story further, questioning visuality as well as individuality and authorship.

The ritual develops as a spatial awareness of the symbolic convention rather than a symbolic awareness of place or object. It is processed simultaneously as a repetition of a lost encounter with 'place' (the symbolic/visual consciousness) and as an intentionalisation of customary space, through the constant ordinarisation of the functional object across the city. This spatial agency is a *trans-placial* process: a 'place by place' movement

progressing in a regressive and anticipatory way – as urban experience ordinarises itself – eventually localising the *transpatiality* of symbolic logic and representation.

The spatial event is not a 'place' (ie an ideal, or non-ideal reference of a given order or discursive signification); it rather actualises a reference both of the ideal (ideal as 'expected', visually integrated), and of the ordinary (practical or functional) aspect of a given signification – in an irreconcilable collocation of the two.

The axe engineers morphological anticipations by lending its physicality to a series of spatial incidents that occur throughout the journey in a spatial manner paradoxical to its original metonymic role as a sacrificial 'tool–agent'. It is not that the axe applies one total symbolic rule to the local level; rather it is engaged with realising as many symbolic completions as possible, at the dimension of the local. Its itinerary is not random but directed by the spatial bind of the city (the 'big' object), and progresses from the symbolic/religious centre (the Acropolis) to the un-symbolic periphery.

If the ox killer incarnates the symbolic cause (*/chose*) of an action, then the axe serves the action as 'good' and 'bad' object, by turns satisfying and disappointing the symbolic/visual ideal, acting as both the reminder of the bad moment and as the means of judging it. The axe's 'distantiation' from the symbolic/visual place (where the ritual acquires its representational value) is a political act of spatial transference of law and reason.

The axe defines the ritual, acquiring the dimension of a self not because it is charged with guilt but because it has the characteristics of an objectal self-referentiality generated around the city. The removal of the axe (as with the Museum) is not symbolic but a real movement, literally a parade of people. Its distantiation from the place of spectacle and symbolic overcharge (the Acropolis) seems to become the one critical position that can stand creatively against and in relation to it. It is the same instrument that integrates visuality and also analyses it by localising it into urban 'pieces'. *Like a museum*, its role in the exhibition process is not denied but, as a tool of procedural space exposing and re-objectifying (rather than reproducing) the symbolic, it is liable to technicalisation and design.

The transference of visual intensity from 'one' place to 'another' defines the critical or *negative* space – a spatio-functional bodily involvement; a technique capable of de-signing and disengaging the subject from its discourses, re-allocating their symbolic values by demonstrating the difference between their real and ideal form. The participants–citizens have already traced an inverted exhibition building by transferring themselves onto the urban process.

Foundness

If we acknowledge that the New Acropolis Museum (NAM) is necessary for the protection of the sculptures, we cannot ignore the fact that their destruction up until today is a result of a general Western attitude which, through the years (centuries,

OPPOSITE: Building-in-process, the three sites

even), has manifested itself in a vulgar way (through theft, destruction, environmental pollution).

It seems that the conflict between the *historical* and the *historic* – history as symbolic and subject to commemoration and history as real – as well as the universal and the local, the sculptural and the spatial (a conflict that invariably works in favour of the former of these pairings) culminates in the case of NAM with the idea of the universalisation of the exhibits' sculptural/aesthetic value (as belonging to everybody) and their concomitant detachment from their original spatio-cultural condition.

The discourse of appreciation (spectacularisation and communicability) of the exhibits' symbolic value seems to be based on a fundamental misunderstanding of the way ancient civilisations constructed their aesthetic environment: in an all-scale design manner which conducted all artistic, architectural and urban expression. However, the Acropolis 'marbles' recur *at the same place*, despite the 'Anglo-Greek debate', and the catholicisation of the treasures (their so-called symbolic universalisation, limited to the territorial confines of the British Museum). *Being at the same place* is not only a gesture that directs its critique against belonging and ownership but is also a dialecticisation of space breaking beyond a series of apolitical, dasein/anti-dasein theses (from applied negativity to entropic space).

The concept of the 'classical' recurs here, as the necessity of detachment from the symbolic and any idea of consensus, and as a question of the symptomatic reappearance of *history* as objectal contemporaneity and permanence (rather than commemoration) of the 'past'; a discourse to be sought not in the visual arts but in the course of architecture as the art of locality.

The NAM competition introduced a twofold problem. First, how to deal with the *symbolic dimension* appearing as: a) spectacularisation of the Acropolis (amplified by its proximity to two of the optional sites) and of the exhibits (of sculptural, non-spatial value – an aesthetic ideal of Western civilisation), both of which are meant to provide symbolic glamour and an abundance of 'referents' furnishing the new museum and its environment; b) as a misunderstanding of the urban structure of Athens as a mere site provider (at the service of the designers), also organised on the basis of visual synchronicity and finiteness (liable to the ideology of finite buildings and monumental centralisations demanding axial or convex visual integrations).

Second, how to operationalise the *spatiality of the Acropolis* as a real but repressed condition that exceeds the discourse of an isolated 'artwork' and operates as: a) a discourse of *archaeological findings* – appearing as a mixture of statues, walls, garments, raw material, jewellery, city patterns, texts etc; b) real discourse (originating in ancient times) fostering a blend of architectural and sculptural artworks concerning a broad field of objectal dialectics under the context of *total aesthetics* – in contrast to any discursive fragmentation of 'artistic' involvement; c) as an *urban experience* involving real localising processes activating a series of spatial anticipations, relations of exposure, etc, extending from the hilltop centre to the city-borders, running parallel to the symbolic development of the city and its rituals.

Lastly, the quality of the museum seems to be a question of making a *popular* building to be used not 'accidentally' by wanderers but purposefully by citizens of the world (natives or tourists), reintroducing polis citizenship as a leading spatial principle of ancient Greek civilisation (as opposed to the legal structure of the Roman state equivalent). It is also a question

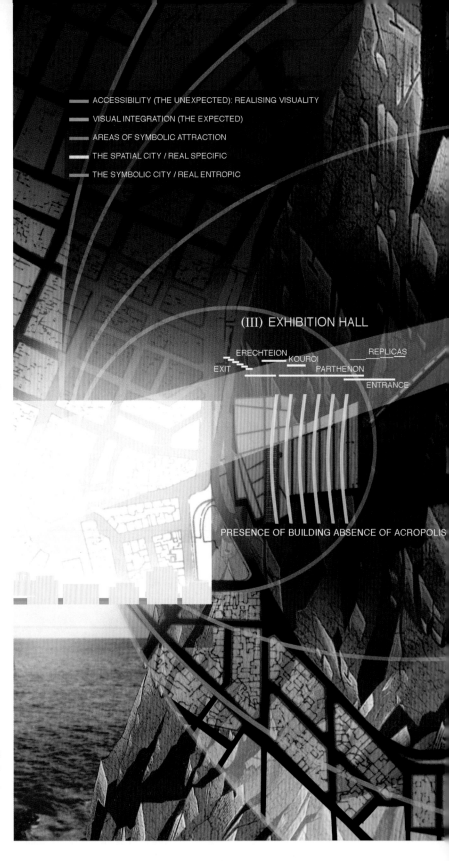

ACCESSIBILITY (THE UNEXPECTED): REALISING VISUALITY

VISUAL INTEGRATION (THE EXPECTED)

AREAS OF SYMBOLIC ATTRACTION

THE SPATIAL CITY / REAL SPECIFIC

THE SYMBOLIC CITY / REAL ENTROPIC

(III) EXHIBITION HALL

ERECHTEION   KOUROI   REPLICAS
EXIT   PARTHENON
                           ENTRANCE

PRESENCE OF BUILDING ABSENCE OF ACROPOLIS

of a *positive* building, not commemorative of any guilt or loss, but reminding us of the 'past' as a discourse of presencing – a cultural overstatement of the real objectal world which now recurs as a historical paradox. *Foundness* – the discourse of the exhibits/ruins, total aesthetics and urban process – is a design principle rather than an amorphous collection of objects, traces of past civilisations, or site availability. Surely there is *no place* available for this museum, nor can there be any, not only because the exhibits should return to their original spatial context, but also because the 'museum' belongs to the all-time classic logic of the urban process, to be lost and aligned with it.

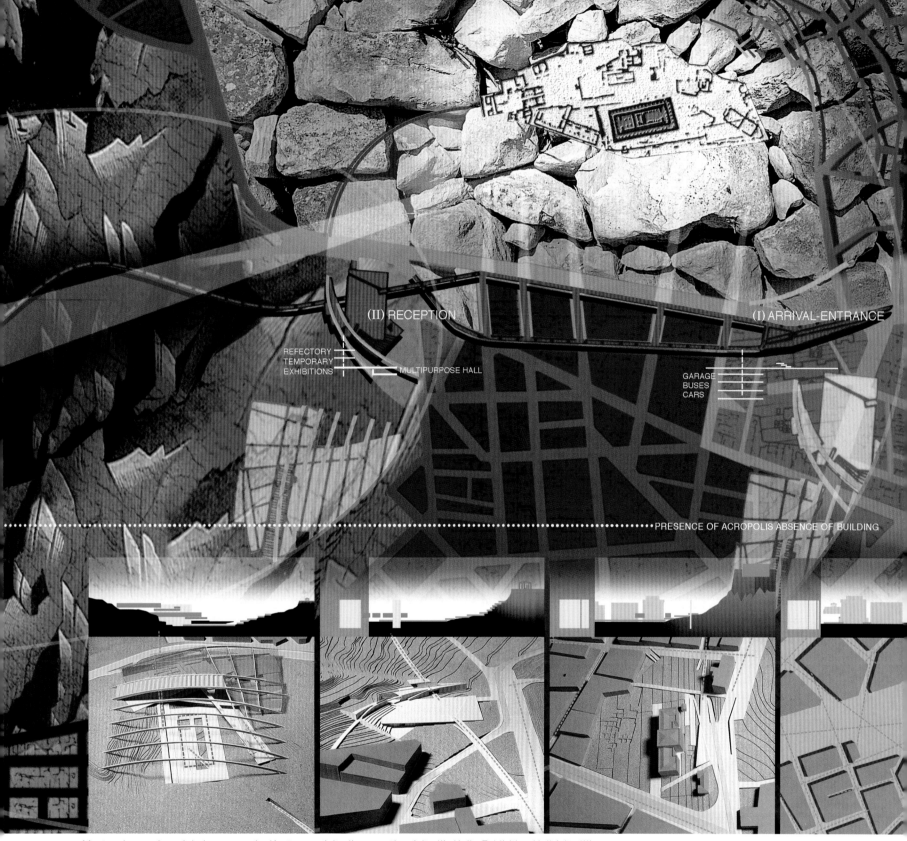

Within the image:

(II) RECEPTION

REFECTORY
TEMPORARY
EXHIBITIONS ———— MULTIPURPOSE HALL

(I) ARRIVAL-ENTRANCE

GARAGE
BUSES
CARS

·········· PRESENCE OF ACROPOLIS ABSENCE OF BUILDING

Masterplan and model views – arrrival/entrance (site I), reception (site II), Koile Exhibition Hall (site III)

Negative space as a design principle

Our proposal introduces the design concept of *negative space*. This is space that negates itself offering a condition of spatial affluence, rather than deprivation or dispersion. It makes no morphological distinctions between small and large scale, building and landscape, part and whole, closeness and distance etc, and reintroduces the hypothesis of *total design* (a concept encountered in ancient times but also in early Modern architecture).

The concept of space negating itself in fact opens up the object to a dialectical condition of *oneness* that operates as a critique of any symbolic finiteness or reduction of space as well as of the catholic application of symbolic reason. At a paradigmatic level, such a condition can be found in abundance on an urban level where spatiality progresses via regressions (rather than as feedback to the imposed symbolic order) in the course of spatial anticipations and repetitions.

Negative space is not the spatial correspondence of a negative brief (ie of negated or entropic rationality – producing dark and unlivable or flâneurish and accidental places). It does not serve or deny a given brief; rather it engineers the condition of its double realisation (or spatial hystericisation). It develops initially as an awareness of the spatial quality that a specific symbolic agency appropriates, as 'its own place'; and then as restoration of such a quality from mere presence to a spatial technique that analyses by

219

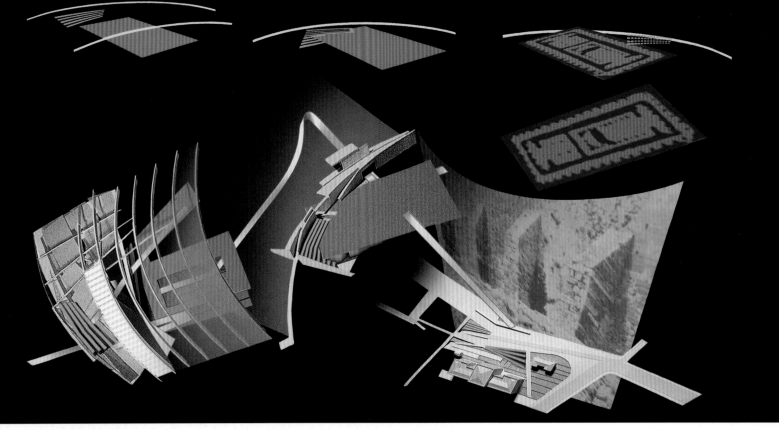

Spatial anticipations

allocating the discursive agencies which it is meant to serve. In the course of continual over-realisations, the original symbolic conduct of the brief ('viewing' in the case of the Acropolis Museum) is converted into a symptom, presented as a 'missed' totality whose very quest sustains and binds the proposed scheme.

Negative space is introduced on three indistinguishable levels which merge together in a procedural building as it is related to the Acropolis, the city of Athens and the exhibits. The building, the city, the exhibited objects are conceived as parts of the same spatial technique which can *realise* three visual/symbolic impositions: a) the idea of the exhibition building as representational of the symbolic/historical centrality of the Acropolis; b) the symbolic ideals of an image-conducted synchronised city, and c) the consideration of the exhibits as visual artworks of universal significance. The space of movement as paradigmatic of real urban experience plays an important role here; movement that progresses via spatial anticipations introduces the building as a continual quest (a lost-and-found signification) rather than as an established place. Furthermore, on a local level it demonstrates how the constant ambiguity of the building's boundaries coincides with the question of the limitation and growth of the city as a regressive intraspatial process.

The proposed scheme is not a finite building (a place) but a *building in process*: realised on all three sites as a complex of three distinct urban steps. As a response to the idea of the embodiment of an autonomous museum building into the greater archaeological area, the complex works as a gradual diffusion of the exhibition/visual activities away from the archaeological site and the Acropolis as urban, symbolic centre. Transition from one place of intensity to another is not a linking space but a critique of the place of visual stagnation (and dispersion); it is the Unconscious of any 'here and now' dasein (and anti-dasein). It is a real procedural space at odds with the placial requirements (and prejudices) of a visitor demanding visual/symbolic inclusivity of the archaeological area (thus taking advantage of the proximity of the Acropolis).

Besides, the real 'givenness' of the three sites (and not their optional or indecisive recommendation by the brief) hints that the design of the museum building is actually a question of urban experience. By using all three sites we introduce the problematic of urban experience into the building itself, setting spatial continuity or accessibility (the unexpected) at odds with visual/symbolic integration or fragmentation (the expected). The museum building progresses gradually in a linear arrangement (Makryianni (I) – Dionysos (II) – Koile (III)) but in reverse to the real presence of the Acropolis and the urban density. In the condition of proximity to the Acropolis (site I), no built volume is proposed and the available open space is returned to the city. As the distance from the monument increases, some modest volumes appear (site II), the wide open space around them partly given to the urban fabric ending in the park, and partly to the museum function. In its detachment from the Acropolis and in its green setting (site III), the main exhibition volume is proposed as a building without a reception or marked entrance, amenities or exterior space, but with a rich and elaborate circulation system. The museum's exterior public space is on site I, its semi-public courtyard space on site II, and its main volume and exit on site III.

In the proposed arrangement of the main exhibition hall (site III) the exhibits acquire significance in terms of their accessibility rather than (visual) availability. The space of the exhibits realises (and is introduced as 'Other' to) the place of the viewer. Accessibility and visuality are collocated in a conflictual state. Long routes, having no exhibits and highlighting accessibility are introduced, often pointing at the exterior space as exhibition-significant.

Building in process – the building 'as split'

Building in process is neither a split building nor a negated one (applying a split or negated programme); it is rather a *multiple building* designed to recur and anticipate itself spatially rather than symbolically; it is a search for a building-place always realisable at the 'next location' as a gesture of affluence of space and presentification rather than a fragmentation or concealment.

The museum brief is realised in three distinct building-site conditions which spatially depend on one another. These are three instances of localisation of the symbolic/visual epitomisation of the museum as an urban-significant building, namely: *arrival/entrance, reception* and *exhibition hall*. These local totalisations of the 'museum' notion can align the building to the urban structure since they refer to building functions related directly to the logic of urban experience and not to any internal brief sub-categorisation; besides, their interdependence is a prerequisite for the operation of a museum building. So here, what is meant to be an automatic transitional non-space connecting 'activities', becomes coincidental with urban space, overlapping the building's spaces of access with the city's equivalent.

In each of the sites an unbindable (un-integrable) couple of two symbolic instances is proposed: one is real (ie the 'arrival/ entrance', 'reception', 'exhibition', urban attributions of the museum), the other imaginary (conveying the idea of the museum as an ideal, whole, autonomous building). Each stage works as a specific localisation of the sign of the museum not in fragments but as a quested and missed 'whole' – articulating a *spatial binding of a missed visual or programmatic completion* – the expected 'place' representing the Acropolis and its sculptures. In all three sites the 'one integrated museum' becomes a missing desired singularity which, on reflection, gives the procedural building a sense of inverted continuity, aligning it with the urban spatial structure. But what mainly contributes to such an operational oneness of the three-site buildings is the activation of a series of *spatial anticipations* – relations of morphological sameness and imperfection, rather than similarity.

At the level of urban experience the three sites introduce three distinct spatio-symbolic processes in terms of the Acropolis' presence and the existing urban fabric. Site I marks a full presence of the 'old' city and 'its Acropolis' as a strong visual and symbolic integration, amplified by the raw appearance of the monument; site II is a distributional space linking the city with the monument, the interface between the 'old' fabric and the non-designed city (the green); site III (in the green) is a hint of a reclaimed, un-visual, un-symbolic, spatial 'new' city. The building appears respectively as quested/approached in the greater dense urban fabric (I), as accessed and addressed at an intermediate surrounding area (II), as entered and local specific reality (III).

The spatial course of the procedural building entails a reconsideration of the symbolic dimension of the city – the quested symbolic is gradually transferred from the context of a total-ideal museum building to that of a total-ideal new city. Here, spatiality and symbolism seem to be reversely analogous to each other. Space shifts from a state of a visual/symbolically conducted entropic real (I) to the dialectical discourse of the real-specific (III); whereas the symbolic totality 'applicable' to neutral space (I) is transferred to a 'missed object' condition, as totality quested in the context of the realising local (III).

So, in the city/building dialectics there is a series of transferential positions progressing from the city as a spatially amorphous receptacle of general symbolic (international etc) strategies (yet

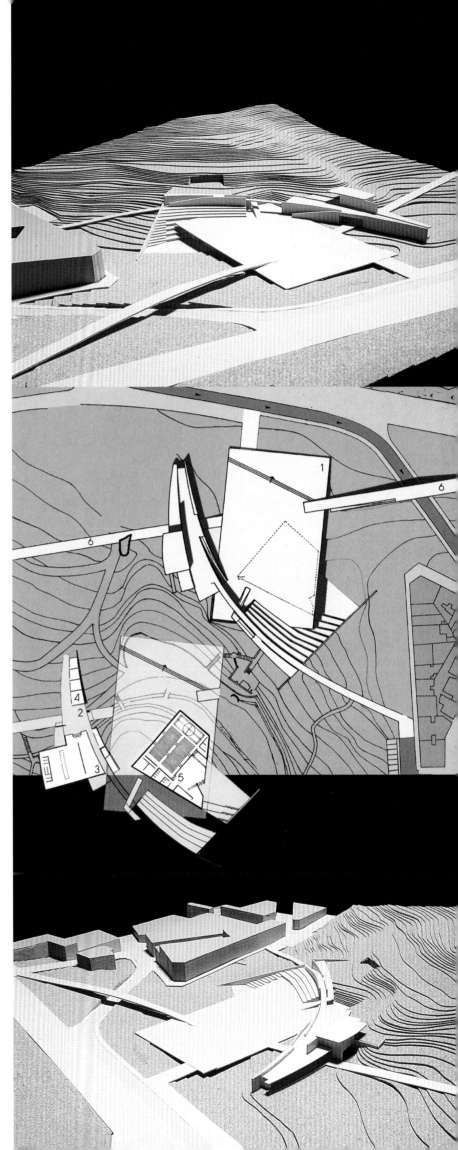

RIGHT: Site II (Dionysos), reception: ground floor plan – 1 the yard, 2 entrance, 3 temporary exhibitions, 4 shops; basement – 5 multipurpose hall, 6 pedestrian path

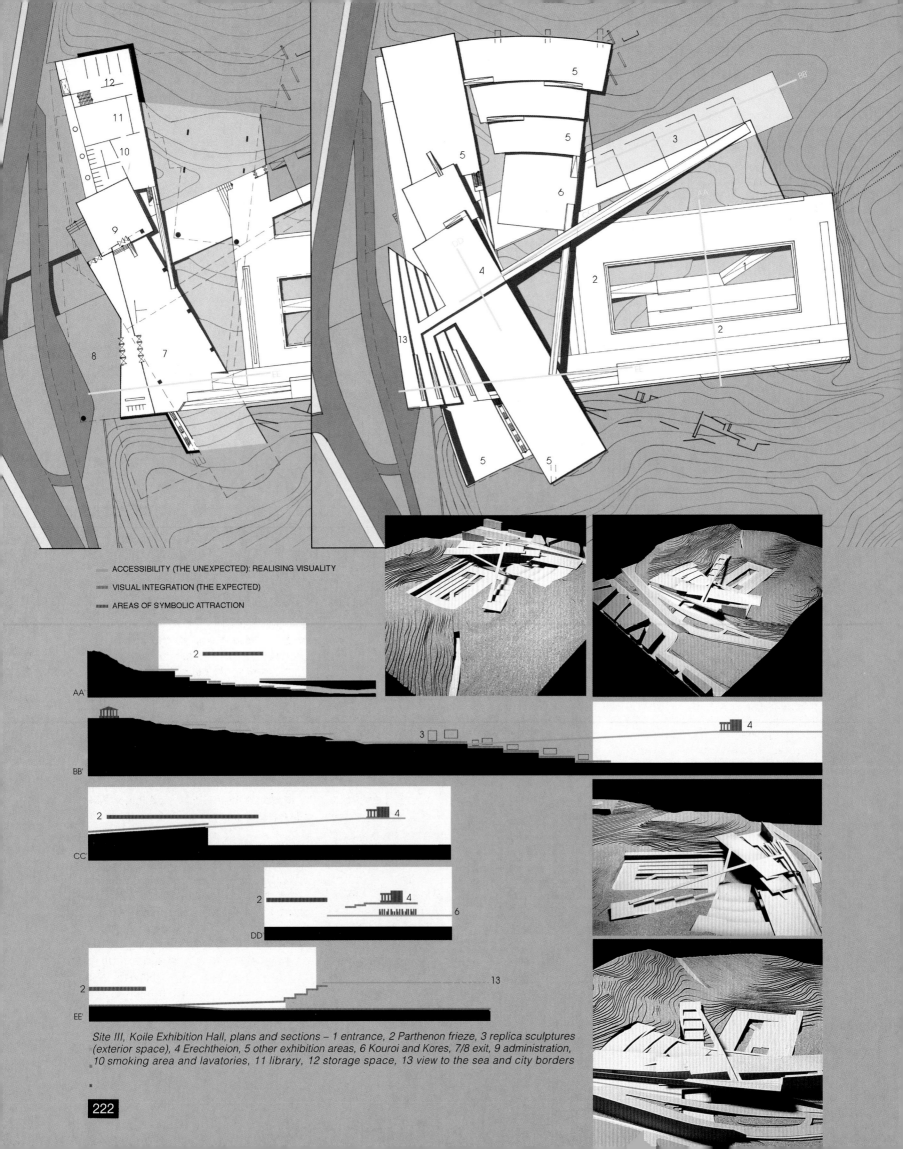

ACCESSIBILITY (THE UNEXPECTED): REALISING VISUALITY

VISUAL INTEGRATION (THE EXPECTED)

AREAS OF SYMBOLIC ATTRACTION

Site III, Koile Exhibition Hall, plans and sections – 1 entrance, 2 Parthenon frieze, 3 replica sculptures (exterior space), 4 Erechtheion, 5 other exhibition areas, 6 Kouroi and Kores, 7/8 exit, 9 administration, 10 smoking area and lavatories, 11 library, 12 storage space, 13 view to the sea and city borders

Site III, Koile Exhibition Hall, model views

bearing in a symptomatic but rich form – the Acropolis – the real tracing process of its own spatial growth) (I), to the city as a possible reworking of spatial distributions (II), to the spatial precision of a function-specific building (III), and further up to the dialectics of the border space; the *local centre at the edge of town; the border middle* (still not 'broken') where the spatiality of the city as simultaneously growing and stopping reveals itself as a dialecticisation of the local specific. Local specific ranges from urban space to architecture to artwork, to garments, to the design power of *the point* – not the point of minimalist or entropic design but the point of richness of space in its regressively realising abilities.

Spatial anticipations – the building 'as one'

The morphological elaboration of the scheme is carried out via the technique of spatial or formal anticipations whereby each building proposes the next, by binding and embedding the form of the previous building in a context of an 'always one more' spatial addition. In each site the same forms are repeated, but serve different purposes. This enables morphologically engineered transferences (of symbolic ideal totalities) rather than transformations of one single symbolic total). Unlike a *folie*, or a *dark space* the morphology of each 'part' of the building does not reflect a variation or negation of an applied formal (Platonic) order but the engagement and activation of the available urban morphology in order to realise, *distinctly* (*un-differently*) in each case, the desire for visual order and reason, as a continually missed encounter. (Such 'available morphology' might even serve as the cast or initial trace of the museum building – and many other buildings – inscribed in the body of the city.) These

distinct parts are fundamentally 'unwandering'; they do not produce individual poles of attraction but spatially conducted locations signifying further destinations.

Accordingly, four major gestures are worked throughout the three different building situations: a) accessibility – bodily movement regressively progressing (versus flâneuring and visual realism), realised as: the (existing) network of access routes (I), the directing and directed route (II), the elaborate self-referring circulation system attributing the exhibition building to both inside and outside (III)); b) concentrated areas (versus visual integration), realised as: the (existing) remote Parthenon temple (I), the empty, open, square space of movement distribution and directed destination (II), the indoor, inverted square of the Parthenon exhibits in the exhibition hall (III); c) sheltering (versus sculptural cast formalism) realised as: the (existing) monumental wall as skin/surface and 'possible trace of the new quested building' (I), the modest curved volume of a (plan-conceived) single-storey building (II), the wide-span steel shelter of the exhibition hall (III); d) the ground as 'functional' self-expression (versus the visual metaphor of the fold) – as *amphitheatric* form realised as a public-welcoming outdoor seating area (I), as a 'seating-the-building' binding interface between the inside-outside, or building-landscape (II), as an unseating area directing the spectacle to its end and exit (III).

In the paradigm of Aristotelian performative mimesis (as opposed to Brechtian realism), what is realised in each of the three stages is not a self-critique of a placial or formal consciousness, but a spatial act of completion, a spatial cast whereby each site performs as a spatial – strictly not visual – mould of the next.

Towards the Koile Exhibition Hall

The desire for the museum appears via detachment and anticipation, gradually shaped and transferred from one location to the next, as the visitor moves away from the Acropolis.

Site I is an open space operating as a general entrance to the museum complex, for visitors arriving by car or on foot. The main underground parking space of the museum is allocated here; administration and sculpture-restoration and maintenance workshops are housed in the existing neoclassical building. After leaving the car the visitor can walk to site II, via two pedestrian paths. While walking through the city fabric (which is eventually left behind) the visitor is 'viewed' by the Acropolis above, either continuously or in glimpses. As the path reaches site II, the visitor has a more complete view of the Acropolis and its entrance.

Here the visitor arrives at an empty orthogonal square which is surrounded by a modest building complex (including a multi-purpose exhibition hall, cafe and amenities) arranged in a curved volume following the morphology of the landscape. The square, detached from the surrounding functions, operates as a space of distribution of routes and destinations, rather than relief or gathering, reminding the visitor that, after a brief stop, his/her task is to go on to the next location. The scheme orientates a view towards the monument, pointing to its main entrance; thus the visitor can look at it for the last time before leaving it behind and taking the path towards the main exhibition building at Koile. Before the path reaches the main building (at site III), it dives into the ground and reappears in the middle of the exhibition hall containing the Parthenon exhibits.

The route has led the visitor from below, straight into a large exhibition space which has the same dimensions as the Parthenon. S/he is 'within the Parthenon', under the hanging frieze exhibited at its real height; the newly-arrived visitor now becomes part of the spectacle – viewed by other visitors standing on the surrounding platforms looking at the frieze and inevitably at him/her.

The exhibition building highlights its circulation and routing system as characteristic spaces of intensity, proposing an elaborate process of transition from one place to the next, whereby route-directing space is often regressive and self-referential. What matters here is not so much the actual placing of the exhibits as visually significant objects, but the way they are reached. It is in this logic that the areas of entrance and exit (the exterior space) often intervene in the progress of the interior journey (the split-building gesture and the allocation of the replicas outside work in a similar way).

The proposed spaces operate as gradual realisations of the visitor's viewing expectations, finally aiming at the diffusion of visual/symbolic intensity. Negative space (spatial figuration) as design technique is a double realisation of the exhibits' discursive significance; it collocates their accessibility and visual integration in a state of conflict to one another, attempting to expose the visitor's need to see (as visually conscious subjects) the exhibits and the other viewers. Exhibits anticipate their view from afar and two fields of vision are introduced: one distant and one close. The proposed spatial significance is often at odds with the visual significance of the object which it is meant to host (eg the replicas section). The attempt here is to achieve a spatial rather than visual continuity. The proposed gestures, far from introducing accidental or disruptive spaces, operate as reminders of the actual principles of urban experience as it is realised through route-alternatives (quick or slow, regressive or linear etc).

Four exhibition focal points are proposed, perceived as *symbolic peaks* which totalise the museum as a whole in four distinct ways. They serve as a condition in relation to which the spatial proposal progresses critically. The symbolic peaks are: a) the Parthenon sculptures – the temple of the city of Athens (emblematic of classical order and purity); b) the Erechtheion – an 'impure' building, combining three different temples, using sculpture as a structural part and facing the public (non-sacred) place of the Agora; c) the statues of Kores and Kouroi – freestanding statue transferences of bodily discourse onto the objectal order, themselves forming a 'crowd' which in ancient times served functional purposes in the open public space, playing a far more complex role than that of simple artwork; d) the replicas of the removed sculptures (by Lord Elgin), which themselves exhibit the real act of universalisation by appropriation, and de-architecturalisation of sculptures, being separated from their original placement on the Parthenon building and now regarded as mere artworks (in an act of gallerisation/collection as it is known in modern times).

There are two routes: the rapid route, allowing for a quick, overall view; and a further route, allowing for a more detailed visit. The first is the Parthenon–Erechtheion–exit route. On the way, the visitor encounters the exterior space where the replica/cast sculptures are exhibited. Axially orientated towards the Acropolis, it is located at the only point of the site from where the Parthenon is visible from afar, and runs beside the main hall of the original Parthenon sculptures.

To reach the upper level, the visitor has to go outside to see the replicas and the Parthenon over the hill of Philopappos, then re-enter and take the ramp to the Erechtheion at the top. On the way the visitor is exposed to the crowd of Kouroi and Kores located on a lower level. From the Erechtheion area, s/he could proceed along the second circulation system (which also allows an opportunity for a second view of the Parthenon frieze) and see the rest of the exhibition. The visitor finally leaves via an empty amphitheatrical space (leading downwards) from which s/he can re-view the interior museum valley before leaving . From this space, looking in the opposite direction, s/he can also see as far as the sea – the natural limits of the city.

Exit

The route began with a search for a building which appeared gradually; it seemed that the city existed without the building. The quest for the building shaped the route (*a spatial experience*). The urgency was the Acropolis itself, as presentation of a drama rather than of an *ideal symbolic*. The route I-II-III (the very structure of the museum-building) transferred all representation far away, first onto the body of the city, then to its borders – there, where the city stops and grows at the same time. The route is irreversible. The 'old' city and its Acropolis gradually disappeared in the light of the 'new' building; yet they remain as a pure tracing process. Now there is a building, but without a city. Before leaving the museum the visitor turns back and views its interior space. Outside, the city is missing; only the sea can be seen far away. The desire for the building now gives rise to the desire for a new city.

Project team (1990): Nikos Georgiadis (principal), Kostis Lambrou, Tota Mamalaki, Anda Damala, Orestis Vingopoulos, Katerina Giouleka; Presentation team (1997): Anamorphosis Architects – Nikos Georgiadis, Kostas Kakoyiannis, Tota Mamalaki, Vaios Zitonoulis